JAL:
EFFICIENCY AND GRACE
A TRADITION OF SERVICE

Highly trained to be efficient while sincerely dedicated to the gracious ways of Japanese service, a Japan Air Lines stewardess transforms your flight into a truly enjoyable experience.

It's the tradition of service.

On JAL.

JAPAN AIR LINES

TOKYO (03)457-1121
OSAKA (06)203-1212
NAGOYA (052)563-4141
FUKUOKA (092)271-4411
SAPPORO (011)231-4411
OKINAWA (0988)62-3311

Travel Guide

JAPAN

*

英文日本案内

TRAVEL GUIDE

JAPAN

First edition 1971
13th edition 1988

The photos in this book, except those taken by the Japan Travel Bureau, Inc., are reproduced through the courtesy of both Mr. Hiroyuki Ishii and The Japan Travel Bureau Photo Library.

Printed in Japan

Photo Composition

by Densan Process Co., Inc.

Printing

by Toppan Printing Co., Ltd.

Daitokuji Temple Hōshun-in : Kyoto

Shinjuku High-rise Center : Tokyo

Tsurugajō Castle : Morioka

Emerald Beach : Okinawa

Mt. Fuji and Shinkansen

Oirase River : Aomori

Engaku-ji Temple : Kamakura

Odaru Spa : Izu

Yosegi-zaiku Wooden Craft : Hakone

Awa Dance Festival : Tokushima

Leading Fashion Bldg. : Tokyo

CONTENTS

Chūsonji Temple in Snow : Iwate

Ryokan Life : Inosawa Spa, Kōchi

Kyoto Style Cuisine

Vegetable Market : Iwate

PREFACE

From afar, Japan conjures up images of Mt. Fuji, geisha, automobiles and electrical appliances. It is all of this and much, much more. This book is intended to help the reader discover the real Japan and it provides comprehensive information, divided into four sections.

"Japan Info" gives general information and suggests model travel courses. "Area Guide" provides practical information on the sights, shopping, dining and entertainment in each of 11 areas starting from Tokyo and its environs, northward to Hokkaido and then from western Japan to southern areas. "Travel Hints" includes tips to help your trip go smoothly and notes on package tours. "Travel Life" provides a handy reference index and phone numbers and addresses.

Japan is a fascinating and complex country, a major economic power, yet one that has preserved its traditional art, culture and lifestyle. It has large bustling cities, yet is still rich in natural beauty and beneath its modern surface, ancient customs and traditions thrive. We hope you enjoy your travels and wish you Bon Voyage!

JAPAN TRAVEL BUREAU, INC

TRAVEL HINTS

TRAVEL LIFE

LETTERING

Japanese words, including personal names are written in italics. Japanese personal names are written using the order used in English of given name, followed by family name. Pronunciation is indicated by a solid line over long vowels, e.g., shogun.

DATA

Prices quoted are charges for adults and do not include tax or service charges. The required traveling times shown in the Area Guide are approximate times and are subject to seasonal changes, traffic and weather conditions, etc. Telephone numbers listed include the area code (the first 2 or more digits up to the first hyphen). Please omit the area code when making a local call. All data in this book is correct as of June, 1988.

LEGEND

JR Line		🚉 JTB Office	
Private Line		Shrine	
Subway Line		Temple	
Ropeway		Church	
Cableway		Hotel	
Monorail		Ryokan(Inn)	
Ramp — Toll Road		Hospital	
National Highway (15)		Bus Stop	
Trail		Spring	
Sea Route		Building	
Prefectural Boundary		Park	

JAPAN

0   100   200km

KYUSHU
Tanegashima Is.
Yakushima Is.
Amami-Oshima Is.
Tokunoshima Is.
Okinawa Is.
OKINAWA

OKINAWA p.163

Naha

Aguni Is.
Kerama Isls.
Tokashiki Is.

Miyako Is.
Ishigaki Is.
Iriomote Is.

THE SOUTHWEST ISLS. p.162

SEA OF JAPAN

SEA OF JAPAN

0   100   200km

Rebun Is.
Rishiri Is.

SEA OF JAPAN

Shakotan Pen. Otaru
Sapporo
L. Toya
Okushiri Is.
Muroran
Oshima Pen.
Hakodate
C. Esan
Tsugaru Straits

Oki Isls.

SAN-IN & SAN-YO p.134

Matsue
SHIMANE   TOTTORI

Tsushima Is.
Tsushima Straits

Iki Is.

YAMAGUCHI   HIROSHIMA   JHYOGO

OKAYAMA   KYOTO

Goto Isls.

Hakata

KANSAI p.106

SAGA   FUKUOKA

Kunisaki Pen.
C. Sata

Matsuyama   Takamatsu   Kobe

NAGASAKI

KAGAWA   OSAKA

Shimabara Pen.
Mt. Aso   OITA

EHIME   *Awaji Is.*

Amakusa Isls.
KUMAMOTO

TOKUSHIMA   NARA

KOCHI

Koshiki Isls.

KYUSHU p.149

SHIKOKU p.144

WAKAYAMA

KAGOSHIMA   MIYAZAKI

C. Ashizuri   *C. Shionomisaki*

Mt. Sakurajima

C. Toi

C. Sata

Yaku Is.   *Tanegashima Is.*

PACIFIC

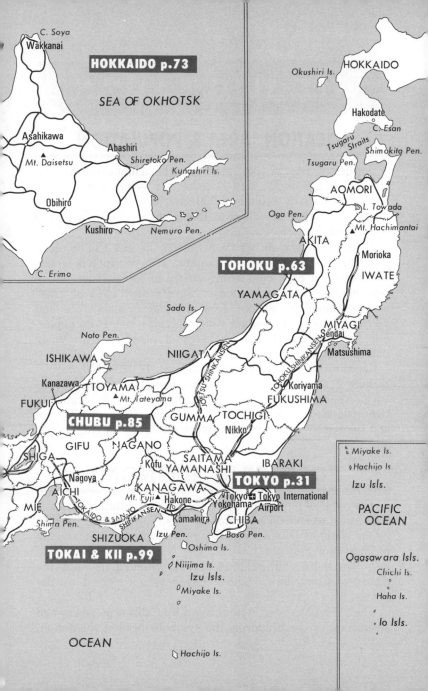

ALL ABOUT JAPAN

LOCATION, AREA & POPULATION

Japan consists of four main islands—Hokkaido, Honshū (the largest), Shikoku, and Kyūshū—as well as a number of smaller islands. It extends 3,000 km. from 45°33′ to 20°25′ latitude, a range equivalent to that from Quebec, Canada to Key West, Florida.

In longitude, Japan lies between 122°56′ and 153°59′ east. The total land area is 377,682 sq.km., 16% of which is fertile, the remaining 84% consisting mostly of forested mountainous regions. Japan is located on the Pacific " Ring of Fire" and consequently suffers from frequent earthquakes and volcanic activity, a pleasant side-effect of which is its numerous hot springs. It has an indented coastline with many natural harbors.

Japan's present population stands at 121,050,000 people, making it one of the world's most densely populated countries. Approximately half the population is concentrated in two main areas—the Kantō district centering around Tokyo, and the Kinki district with its large cities of Nagoya, Osaka, and Kyoto.

POLITICS & ECONOMY

The political power of the State consists of three branches: legislative, executive, and judicial. Legislative power is held by the National Diet, executive power by the Cabinet, and the juridical power by the Courts. The National Diet is divided into two houses—the House of Representatives and the House of Councilors—whose members are elected by the people.

The Prime Minister is nominated by Cabinet members and designated by the Emperor, the symbolic head of the nation.

The Liberal Democratic Party has been dominant for the past 30 years, and the Japan Socialist Party forms the main opposition. A system of local autonomy provides for local self-governing bodies such as Tokyo Metropolis, Hokkaido District, the two "fu" of Osaka and Kyoto, and 43 prefectures.

Japan's economy ranks second in the world in terms of its gross national product which amounted to 296,600 billion yen in 1984, while the annual per capital income in 1983 was 1,848,000 yen.

EDUCATION

Most Japanese children start their education at a nursery (up to 5 yrs. old) or kindergarten (3-5 yrs. old), though neither is compulsory. The present school system of 6-3-3-4 years was introduced in 1947, and is presently under review. Compulsory education consists of six years of elementary school and three years of junior high school. About 95% of junior high school graduates go on to senior high school, and 45% of senior high school graduates advance to 2-year colleges, 4-year colleges or universities. Education in Japan is highly competitive with the goal being to enter a prestigious university.

17

Increasing numbers of students are going to private schools, called "juku", in addition to regular high school classes, to prepare for university entrance examinations. Lately, even infants are being sent to these private schools to help them enter prestigious elementary schools.

These steps are taken because, in Japan, the school you go to has a direct effect on later life—the job and social position you will hold, and even whom you will marry.

RELIGION

● **Shintō**   Japan's original native religion, Shintō is a combination of nature and ancestor worship.

Many Shintō shrines were supported by the government

before World War II, but now all of them are maintained by offerings and donations.

● **Buddhism**   A religion of enlightenment, Buddhism was born in India about 25 centuries ago and came to Japan through China and Korea in the 6th century. Since then various new schools have developed in Japan, and lately, large lay Buddhist organizations. Japanese as a whole are magnanimous with regard to religion, many observing aspects of both faiths. They go to a Shintō shrine to celebrate births and marriages and to a Buddhist temple to observe funeral rites.

● **Christianity**   Introduced into Japan about 450 years ago, Christianity has weathered various vicissitudes, and is presently flourishing.

LIFE & LIVING

The standard of living of the Japanese people has been rising steadily for the past 40 years and the nation continues to reap the benefits of its rapid economic growth. The average family is adequately housed and is provided with modern utilities such as telephones, TV sets and an abundance of household appliances.

Many families have automobiles, and with leisure time increasing, people are beginning to enjoy the fruits of living in a modern, industrialized society.

Education and health services are highly developed, and imported medicines are available at drug stores in the larger cities.

Advanced transportation and information networks have narrowed the difference between lifestyles in different regions of the country, and there is now little difference between rural cities and the large metropolitan areas in many respects.

Although Japanese lead a modern life and Japan's cities have a western surface, there is a growing movement to reawaken interest in traditional customs and arts in an effort to retain them as part of Japanese life.

CLIMATE

Japan has a wide range in its climate, from the freezing winters of Hokkaido to the tropical summers of Okinawa.

The Pacific side of the country has higher temperatures and humidity while the Japan Sea side experiences heavy snowfalls and a generally cooler climate. Hokkaido has a short, cool summer and is unaffected by the rainy season or typhoons. The region from Tokyo to Ise is relatively warm throughout the year and has less rain than Kyushu or southern Shikoku. The areas facing the Inland Sea, between the San-yō district and Shikoku, enjoy fine weather most of the year with only a low rainfall.

The periods of the four seasons differ slightly in each district. Generally though, spring lasts from March to May, summer from June to August, autumn from September to November and winter from December to February.

The typhoon season is usually September with Japan's southern islands and Kyushu generally bearing the brunt of typhoons on their northern advance.

The rainy season is from mid-June to mid-July and brings with it a sharp increase in humidity.

19

MEAN TEMPERATURES (Centigrade) and AVERAGE RAINFALL (Millimeters)

CITY	TEMPERATURE / RAINFALL	JAN	FEB	MAR	APR	MAY	JUN	JUL	AUG	SEP	OCT	NOV	DEC	AVE.
SAPPORO	Mean	-4.9	-4.2	-0.4	6.2	12.0	15.9	20.2	21.3	16.9	10.6	4.0	-1.6	8.0
	Rainfall	114	92	78	65	59	76	80	131	142	115	104	101	97
SENDAI	Mean	0.9	1.3	4.2	10.0	14.9	18.4	22.2	23.9	20.0	14.3	8.7	3.7	11.9
	Rainfall	46	48	72	82	109	141	160	153	175	116	69	49	102
TOKYO	Mean	4.7	5.4	8.4	13.9	18.4	21.5	25.2	26.7	22.9	17.3	12.3	7.4	15.3
	Rainfall	54	63	102	128	148	181	125	137	193	181	93	56	122
NAGANO	Mean	-1.2	-0.4	3.1	10.2	15.5	19.4	23.6	24.5	19.9	13.3	7.2	1.9	11.4
	Rainfall	57	47	55	67	79	140	149	102	126	77	46	43	82
KYOTO	Mean	3.9	4.6	7.6	13.7	18.4	22.1	26.3	27.5	23.2	17.0	11.4	6.4	15.2
	Rainfall	57	67	108	163	156	247	250	176	206	118	75	45	139
HIROSHIMA	Mean	4.3	4.9	7.8	13.3	17.6	21.2	25.6	26.8	22.8	17.0	11.5	6.6	15.0
	Rainfall	53	65	101	174	161	254	269	124	188	104	72	40	134
KAGOSHIMA	Mean	7.0	8.2	11.2	16.1	19.8	23.0	27.2	27.7	24.9	19.6	14.3	9.2	17.3
	Rainfall	95	106	147	256	275	475	323	209	211	108	92	80	198
NAHA (OKINAWA)	Mean	16.0	16.4	18.0	21.0	23.7	26.1	28.1	27.8	27.1	24.3	21.3	18.1	22.4
	Rainfall	120	118	144	168	249	293	193	260	166	186	142	117	177

GETTING AROUND JAPAN

PORT TO CITY CENTERS

● *NEW TOKYO INTERNATIONAL AIRPORT: NARITA*
Limousine Bus: To The Tokyo City Air Terminal (TCAT) near Nihombashi: around 70 min., ¥2,500. A connecting bus to Tokyo Central Station is available for an additional ¥200. From Narita, buses also go to the Keiō Plaza Hotel via Shinjuku Station or to Haneda Airport for ¥2,700. To the Yokohama City Air Terminal (YCAT): 1 hr. 50min., ¥3,100.
Trains: *Keisei Railways* (private line): Take the shuttle bus to Narita Kūkō (airport) Station from in front of the terminal building: 6 min., ¥190. Board the "Skyliner" (Limited Express) to Keisei Ueno Station: 60 min., ¥1,810, which includes the seat reservation charge. There are toilets and spacious baggage racks on board. *Japan Railways* (JR): JR trains take longer and cost more than Keisei Railways but Japan Rail Passes (p.21) are honored on both JR trains and JR operated shuttle buses.
Taxi: 70-90 min. The average fare is around ¥18,000, including the expressway toll fee.

● *TOKYO INTERNATIONAL AIRPORT: HANEDA*
Haneda is now used mainly by domestic airlines and is the starting point for air travel within Japan.
Taxi: ¥5,000 to ¥7,000.
Monorail: From the basement of the terminal building to Hamamatsu-chō Station in downtown Tokyo: 15 min., ¥290. At Hamamatsu-chō Station transfer to JR or taxi.

● *OSAKA INTERNATIONAL AIRPORT*
The airport is close to the city and is the gateway to Osaka, Kyoto and Kobe.
Bus: To JR Osaka Station: 30 min., ¥380. To JR Kyoto Station: 55 min., ¥770. To JR Kobe Sannomiya Station:

40min., ¥620.
Taxi: To JR Osaka Station: ¥4,500. To JR Kobe Sannomiya Station: ¥8,000.

INTER-CITY TRANSPORTATION

● AIRLINES
Three major airlines operate regular domestic flights: Japan Air Lines (JAL), All Nippon Airways (ANA), and Japan Air System (JASC). Taking flights to regions not served by JR bullet trains will save time, but for areas within 600 km., the bullet train is often faster when transfer times between airports and city centers are taken into acount. Airfares are, for example, to Sapporo: ¥25,500; to Nagasaki: ¥31,100; to Okinawa: ¥37,300.

● RAILWAYS
Japan Railways (JR): JR has an extensive network covering over 21,400 km. on all four main islands. Its pride is Japan's fastest trains, the bullet trains commonly called "shinkansen". The Tōkaidō and San-yō Shinkansen trains run from Tokyo to Hakata in Kyushu along the Pacific coast of Honshū. From Ueno Station in Tokyo, the Tōhoku Shinkansen runs to Morioka and the Jōetsu Shinkansen runs to Niigata. Limited Express and Ordinary Express services operate frequently on most lines in addition to local trains. Long distance trains carry "Green Cars" (1st Class), sleeping cars, dining cars or buffet coaches. Public telephones are installed on Shinkansen trains. Extra charges, which vary according to the distance traveled, are required for using Shinkansen, Limited Express and Ordinary Express trains, sleeping berths and other reserved accommodations.

Japan Rail Pass: This pass is valid for the entire network of JR lines, including the Shinkansen, and is available only to foreign tourists visiting Japan for sightseeing purposes. To obtain the pass, an Exchange Voucher must be purchased and can only be purchased outside of Japan. They are available at JTB (Japan Travel Bureau) overseas offices or other authorized travel agencies in major cities throughout the world. After arriving in Japan, the pass can be obtained by turning in the Exchange Voucher at JR Travel Centers or at JTB offices. Seat reservations may be made at no extra cost. There are two types of passes: Green (1st Class) and Ordinary (Economy).

Japan Rail Pass	Green		Ordinary	
	Adults	Children	Adults	Children
7 days	¥35,000	¥17,500	¥25,000	¥12,500
14 days	¥58,000	¥29,000	¥41,000	¥20,500
21 days	¥76,000	¥38,000	¥53,000	¥26,500

● TIPS ON TRAVELING BY JR

Reservations: When using the Shinkansen and Limited Express trains or reserving any seats, extra tickets in addition to the fare tickets need to be purchased. Reserved tickets are sold on a "first-come-first-served" basis at major stations, JTB offices and leading travel agencies. All tickets are available 1 month before the boarding date.

Cancellation: Refunds for regular and express tickets are given, less ¥200 per ticket, within the period of validity. Cancellation fees for reserved seats are higher.

Excursion Tickets: These are available to most areas, and enable the bearer to get on and off trains freely within the stated area. They are an economical way to travel freely around a large area, such as Hokkaidō. Various kinds of tickets are available, such as "Wide", "Mini" and "Route" passes and are sold at JR ticket counters, JTB offices and leading travel agencies.

Private Railways: In addition to JR, many private railways are operated, and some which run between cities and tourist resorts operate deluxe excursion trains.

Subways: Operating in Tokyo, Yokohama, Nagoya, Kyoto, Osaka and Sapporo, subways are a convenient method of transport. Many of the leading hotels, department stores, shopping and entertainment areas are easily accessible by subway. Fares start at ¥120.

Boat Services: Various craft are used in inter-island services as well as excursion cruises. An interesting sea route for visitors is the one across the Inland Sea National Park. The Kansai Kisen Steamship Co., operates luxury liners which sail daily from Osaka to Beppu in Kyushu via Kobe, Takamatsu and other Inland Sea ports. The cruise is around 14 hrs., and the Special Class fare is ¥18,700.

Buses: Buses serve all districts and in large cities the sevices are frequent and the fares are inexpensive. However, destination signs are only written in Japanese. Buses are particularly convenient for touring sightseeing areas in the countryside. Timetables have seasonal variations.

Taxi: Outside railway stations and large hotels are the best places to catch taxis. Taxis cruise the streets in large cities and can be hailed. The basic charge is ¥470 for the first 2 km and increases with the distance traveled. Tipping is not customary. Generally, language is not a problem, but visitors are advised to carry the name of their destination written in Japanese.

Rental Cars: Cars are a convenient alternative to trains, especially for visiting more remote areas and can save a great deal of time. Visitors must produce their international driving permit when renting a car. (West Germany and some countries have no reciprocal agreement with Japan to honor an international driving permit.) The average rate for 24 hrs. with unlimited mileage, excluding gasoline is: ¥6,000 for a sub-compact; ¥11,000 for a compact; ¥12,000 for an intermediate; and ¥15,000 for a standard-sized car. Overseas offices of both Hertz and Avis can accept reservations for their affiliated rent-a-car companies in Japan.

MODEL COURSES

This section presents a selection of recommended courses that should provide something of interest for everyone.

● ENJOYING NATURE—CROSSING HOKKAIDO (6 DAYS)

Tokyo---(1 hr. 35 min. by air)---Kushiro====(2 hrs. by bus)====stay at Lake Akan====(2 hrs. by bus)====Lake Mashū====(1 hr. by bus) ====stay at Kawayu Spa====(2 hrs. 20 min. by bus)====Bihoro++++++++ (35 min. by JR)++++++++ stay in Abashiri ++++++++(1 hr. 35 min. by JR Express)++++++++ Rubeshibe ====(20 min. by bus)==== Onnetō Spa==== (45 min. by bus)====Sekihoku Ridge====(40 min. by bus)====Obako ====(20 min. by bus)====stay in Sōunkyō Gorge====(2 hrs. by bus) ====Asahikawa++++++++(1 hr. 45 min. by JR Limited Express)++++++++stay in Sapporo---(1 hr 25 min. by air)---Tokyo.

Day 1 Starting from Kushiro, visit Tsuru (crane) Park then Lake Akan, noted for its "Marimo" weed.

Day 2 Taking the Akan Panorama Course Bus with views of Lakes Penketō and Panketō and visit Lake Mashū and on to Kawayu Spa.

Day 3 Taking the same bus visit Bihoro via Bihoro Ridge then on to Abashiri. In season, visit the nearby Gensei Kaen (Wildflower Park). **Day 4** Visit Obako and Kobako and then on to the Sōunkyō Valley. **Day 5** To Asahikawa and Sapporo. If you have any energy left, a short tour to southern Hokkaido from Sapporo is a possibility. **Day 6** Return to Haneda.

● TOHOKU'S HOT SPRINGS AND HISTORICAL TOWNS (6 DAYS)

Tokyo (Haneda Airport)---(2 hrs. by air)---Aomori====(3 hrs. 20 min. by bus)==== stay at Lake Towada ====(2 hrs. 10 min. by bus)==== Goshogake Spa====(30 min. by bus)====top of Mt. Hachimantai==== (1 hr. 30 min. by bus)====Morioka▬▬▬(15 min. by JR Shinkansen) ▬▬▬Shin-Hanamaki====(25 min. by bus)====stay at Hanamaki Spa ====(20 min. by bus)==== Hanamaki ++++++++(45 min. by JR)++++++++ Hira-izumi++++++++(1 hr. 30 min. by JR)++++++++stay in Matsushima++++++++(35 min. by JR)++++++++Sendai++++++++(1 hr. by JR)++++++++Yamadera++++++++(40 min. by JR)++++++++ stay at Kaminoyama Spa ++++++++(1 hr. 15min. by JR)++++++++ Fukushima====(3 hrs. by bus)====Bandai Plateau====(1 hr. 30 min. by bus)==== Aizu Wakamatsu====(1 hr. by bus)==== Kōriyama ▬▬▬ (1 hr. 25 min. by JR Shinkansen)▬▬▬Ueno.

Day 1 To scenic Lake Towada. **Day 2** To Hachimantai Spa village then a drive across the plateau on the Aspite Line Road and on to Morioka. Stay at Hanamaki Spa. **Day 3** To Hiraizumi and

THE HAKONE OPEN-AIR MUSEUM

(Chokoku-no-mori) TEL.0460-2-1161 Ninotaira, Hakone-machi, Kanagawa-ken, 250-04 Japan

An outdoor sculpture museum located in the center of the Fuji, Hakone National Park. Surrounded by the beautiful mountain ranges of Hakone, this delightful museum assembles numerous modern and contemporary sculptures. The visitors can easily participate in the conversation with the sculptures. (Open daily, all year round)

The Picasso Pavilion

Located inside the Hakone Open-Air Museum, the museum presents ceramics, paintings, sculptures, and tapestries of the great artist, Pablo Picasso. Enjoy the intimacy with the works of Picasso. (Open daily, all year round)

Means of Transportation

Take the Tokai Line of JR or the Odakyu Railway to Odawara Station or Hakone-Yumoto Station, then the Hakone Tozan Railway to Chokoku-no-mori Station. Approximately 2 hours from Tokyo. (oneway)

THE UTSUKUSHI-GA-HARA OPEN-AIR MUSEUM

TEL.0268-86-2331 Utsukushi-ga-hara Daijo, Takeshi-mura, Chiisagata-gun, Nagano-ken, 386-05 Japan

Located in the most elevated and beautiful plateau of Utsukushi-ga-hara in the center of Japan. 2,000 meters above sea level, the museum stands in full view of the famous mountains in Japan. A day in the museum may be satisfied with the outdoor sculptures and the highland plants of the four seasons. (Open from the end of April to the middle of November, Closed during the winter)

Means of Transportation

Take the Chuo Line of JR to Matsumoto Station. A direct bus to the Utsukushi-ga-hara Open-Air Museum may be found in front of the station. Approximately 5 hours from Tokyo. (oneway) (Closed during the winter)

Chūsonji Temple then on to Matsushima Bay (try the local seafood dishes !). **Day 4**   Walk around downtown Sendai and visit Yamadera Temple. **Day 5**   Drive through the plateau on the Bandai Azuma Skyline Road. Hike around the plateau's lakes and marshes. Stop by Kaminoyama Spa with a view of Mt. Bandai. **Day 6**   A tour to the historical town of Aizu. Return to Ueno.

● *TAKAYAMA AND THE NOTO PENINSULA (5 DAYS)*

Tokyo▬▬(2 hrs. by JR Shinkansen)▬▬Nagoya┈┈┈(3 hrs. by JR Limited Express)┈┈┈ stay in Takayama ┈┈┈(1 hr. 40 min. by JR Limited Express)┈┈┈ Toyama ┈┈┈(45 min. by JR Express)┈┈┈ Tsubata┈┈┈(1 hr. 10 min. by JR Express)┈┈┈stay at Wakura Spa ┈┈┈(40 min. by rail)┈┈┈ Anamizu ═══(8 hrs. 25 min. by JR bus) ═══ stay in Wajima ═══(scheduled sightseeing bus)═══ stay in Kanazawa═══(55 min. by bus)═══Komatsu Airport┈┈(1 hr. 5 min. by air)┈┈Tokyo.

Day 1   Tour Takayama, soak up the atmosphere of "Little Kyoto".
Day 2   Travel by train to Wakura Spa, the gateway to Noto. **Day 3**   Rise early to catch the JR bus for Wajima. The bus stops at major places of interest, letting you get off and look around. **Day 4** In Wajima, visit the morning market, then take the scheduled sighseeing bus for Kanazawa. Visit Sōjiji Temple, Gammon and Senrihama Beach. **Day 5**   Tour Kanazawa then return to Tokyo. If time permits an alternative route returning to Tokyo is to go west on the Hokuriku Main Line to visit Yamanaka Spa and Eiheiji Temple and return via Fukui.

25

● *TOTTORI, MATSUE & KURASHIKI (5 DAYS)*

Tokyo┈┈┈(9 hrs. 30 min. by JR Limited Express sleeping car)┈┈┈ Kinosaki ┈┈┈(1 hr. 30 min. by JR Express train)┈┈┈stay in Tottori ┈┈┈(3 hrs. by JR Express train)┈┈┈Izumo ┈┈┈(12 min. by Taisha Line)┈┈┈Izumo Taisha Mae Station┈┈┈(1 hr. by Ichibata Railway) ┈┈┈stay at Matsue Spa┈┈┈(2 hrs. 40min. by JR Limited Express) ┈┈┈stay in Kurashiki┈┈┈(20 min. by JR)┈┈┈Okayama▬▬(4 hrs. by JR Shinkansen)▬▬Tokyo

Day 1   To Kinosaki on the overnight train. In Kinosaki, tour the city's spas. In the afternoon, go to Tottori and visit the sand dunes. **Day 2**   Sightseeing in Tottori. **Day 3**   To Izumo, visit Izumo Taisha Shrine. Next, by train past Lake Shinji to Matsue. **Day 4**   To Kurashiki, walk around the city. **Day 5**   Visit Okayama's famous gardens before returning to Tokyo.

● *HIROSHIMA TO MATSUYAMA ACROSS THE IN-LAND SEA (4 DAYS)*

Tokyo▬▬(5 hrs. by JR Shinkansen) ▬▬stay in Hiroshima ┈┈┈ (25 min. by train)┈┈┈ Miyajima-guchi ∼∼∼(10 min. by boat)∼∼∼

Miyajima Island ~~~~ Miyajima-guchi ┄┄┄┄(20 min. by train)┄┄┄┄ stay at Iwakuni ┄┄┄┄ Iwakuni New Port ~~~~(2 hrs. 25 min. by boat)~~~~ Mitsuhama Port ════(1 hr. by bus)════ Matsuyama ════(30 min. by bus)════ stay at Dōgo Spa ════(30 min. by bus)════ Matsuyama ════ (20 min. by bus)════ Matsuyama Airport┄┄┄(1 hr. 20 min. by air)┄┄┄ Tokyo.

Day 1 In the afternoon, sightseeing in Hiroshima, visit Peace Park and Hiroshima Castle. **Day 2** A trip to Miyajima Island, visit Itsukushima Shrine, and then to Iwakuni. **Day 3** Cross the Inland Sea and visit Matsuyama on Shikoku. Stay at Dōgo Spa. **Day 4** Return to Tokyo.

● *AROUND KYUSHU (9DAYS)*

Tokyo┄┄┄(1 hr. 45 min. by air)┄┄┄Fukuoka════(2 hrs. by bus)════stay in Karatsu ════(1 hr. by bus)════ Imari ┄┄┄┄(1 hr. by JR)┄┄┄┄ Hirado-guchi ~~~~(15 min. by boat)~~~~ stay in Hirado ~~~~(1 hr. sightseeing on Kujūkushima Island)~~~~Kashimae Pier ════(30 min. by bus)════ Sasebo ════(50 min. by bus)════ West of Saikibashi Bridge ════(1 hr. by bus)════ stay in Nagasaki ════(2 hrs. by bus) ════Unzen Park════(50 min. by bus)════stay in Shimabara~~~~(1 hr. by boat)~~~~Misumi════(25 min. by bus)════Kumamoto════(2 hrs. by bus)════Kusasenri-ga-hama, Aso-zan Nishi (West of Mt. Aso) ════(45 min. by bus)════stay in Uchinomaki════(40 min. by bus) ════Tateno════(50 min. by bus)════Takamori════(1 hr. 35 min. by bus)════stay in Takachiho┄┄┄┄(1 hr. 30 min. by JR) ┄┄┄┄Nobeoka ┄┄┄┄(1 hr. 20min. by Limited Express)┄┄┄┄Miyazaki════(30 min. by train)════ stay in Aoshima ════(15 min. by bus)════ Horikiri Ridge ════ Cactus Garden ════(15 min. by bus)════ Udo Shrine ════(15 min. by bus)════Aburatsu┄┄┄┄(1 hr. 45 min. by JR) ┄┄┄┄Kanoya ════(1 hr. 35 min. by bus)════ Sakurajima Island ~~~~(15 min. by boat)~~~~stay in Kagoshima┄┄┄(1 hr. 30 min. by air)┄┄┄Tokyo.

This course starts in Fukuoka and makes an "S" shaped tour of Kyushu. **Day 1** To the historiacl city of Karatsu. **Day 2** Visit Imari's potteries, then on to Hirado. Hirado Island is associated with Japan's early Christians. **Day 3** To Kujūkushima Island by boat and then on to Sasebo and Nagasaki, visiting Saikaibashi Bridge on route. Walk around Nagasaki's downtown area. **Day 4** To Unzen and Shimabara. **Day 5** Cross to Misumi by boat and on to Aso via Kumamoto. **Day 6** From Aso to Takachiho. **Day 7** To Nobeoka on the scenic Takachiho Line Road. Drive to Miyazaki around the beautiful coastline of Hyūga Bay. **Day 8** Go south along the Nichinan Coast, stopping at attractions on the way. Visit Sakurajima Island then on to Kagoshima. **Day 9** Sightseeing in Kagoshima before returning to Tokyo.

AREA GUIDE

❖

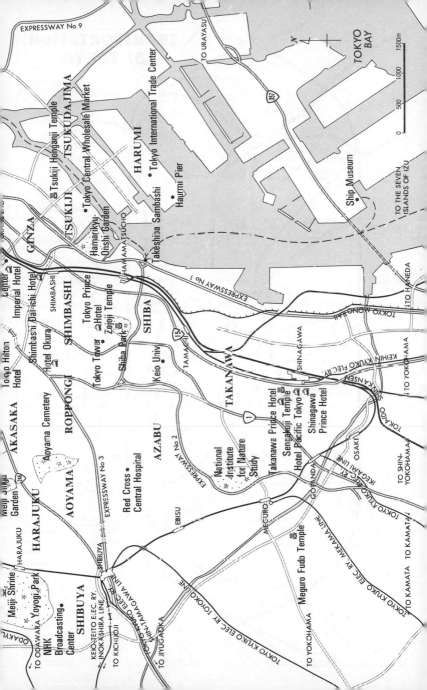

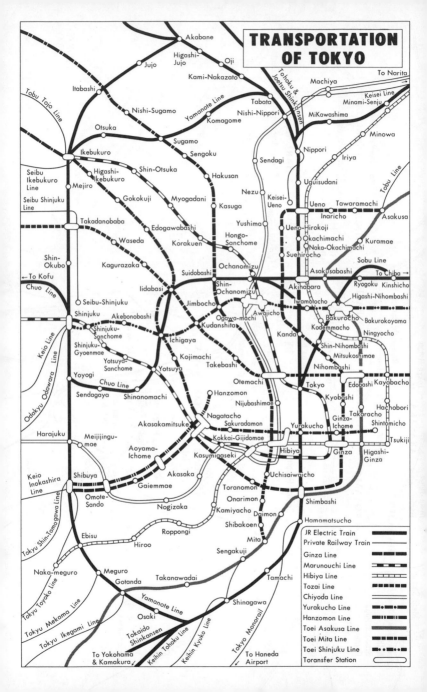

東　京
TOKYO

Tokyo is the political, economic and cultural heart of Japan. With a population of 12 million, it consists of wards, municipalities, towns and villages located on the mainland and outlying islands. Beneath its modern surface, tradition thrives—there's something for everyone in this great city.

TRANSPORTATION

Tokyo's transportation system consists of JR and private railways, subways, buses and street cars. Trains and subways are fast, economical and efficient. Trains to know are the Yamanote Line, circling the city center, and the Chūō and Sōbu Lines which cross the loop.

For access from Narita Airport to downtown Tokyo, see P.20.

TOUR HINTS

Bustling and lively Tokyo has a great diversity of sights and entertainments. For something of traditional Japan, see the original downtown areas around Asakusa and east of the city. Central Tokyo is modern and commercial, while cities of the west side are centers for fashion and entertainment. Guided tours are a convenient way to experience Tokyo's variety.

31

CENTER OF TOKYO

GINZA & MARUNOUCHI

Ginza boasts thousands of shops, leading department stores, galleries, bars and nightclubs. Sundays attract Tokyoites for a stroll around many blocks of boutiques and stylish stores. Marunouchi, the area around Tokyo Station, is Tokyo's commercial hub. In the evenings businessmen crowd the thousands of pubs and restaurants.

WHAT TO SEE

● *GINZA 4-CHOME CROSSING*
Ginza's center—featuring the Wakō and Mitsukoshi department stores, Nissan show-

room and San-ai building.

● **CHUO-DORI STREET** Ginza's main street, lined with famous stores. Clossed to traffic on Sundays and holidays — a stroller's paradise.

● **SUKIYABASHI CROSSING** Features the Sony Building with products displayed by Sony, Toyota, Suntory and Fuji Xerox.

● **TSUKIJI FISH MARKET** The largest wholesale fish market in Japan. Hectic trading starts at 5:00 a.m. on a market floor covering 21 ha.

● **TOKYO STATION** Over 3,000 trains and 670,000 people pass through this mammoth station daily. The Marunouchi side features a brick and stone building completed in 1914.

● **HIBIYA PARK** The first western-style park in Japan, with beautiful illuminated fountains and exotic trees. It covers 16 ha., and is known for its open-air plaza and Japan's oldest concert hall, the Hibiya Public Hall.

WHAT TO EAT

The narrow backstreets just off **Chūō-dōri Street** are filled with interesting restaurants and bars. Taste the finest traditional

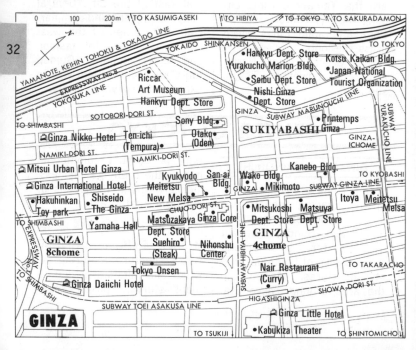

Japanese dishes, such as delicious *tempura* at Ten-ichi and *oden* at Otakō.

WHAT TO BUY

Ginza is renowned for its highclass department stores, conveniently located on Chūō-dōri Street and in front of Yūraku-chō Station. These and a myriad of other shops offer anything from the latest fashions to handmade Japanese arts and crafts. Mikimoto is world famous for its pearls, Kyūkyodō for calligraphy materials and the International Arcade for tax-free bargains.

ENTERTAINMENT

Evening performances at the theaters in Hibiya near Yūraku-chō Station begin around 7:00 p.m. Also, the alleys of 5 to 8 chōme abound with exclusive bars and clubs. Generally, Ginza's nightlife is quiet, with most places closed around 11:00 p.m.

AROUND THE IMPERIAL PALACE

In the very heart of Tokyo lies the Imperial Palace, home of the Emperor of Japan. Centered around the palace are the offices of the Japanese government and the National Diet — the Japanese parliament. The vast palace grounds are encircled by a network of railways and subway systems providing easy access to the palace and its immediate surrounding districts.

WHAT TO SEE

● **THE IMPERIAL PALACE** Formerly Edo Castle, the palace became the official residence of the Emperor after 1868. The palace grounds may be entered by the public only on January 2nd and on the present Emperor's birthday, April 29th. However, it is possible to stroll through the beautiful East Garden *(Higashi-Gyoen)*, which was opened to the public in 1968. Also of note is Nijūbashi, a classic iron bridge adorned with old-fashioned lights and leading to the front gate *(Otemon)* of the Imperial palace.

● **KITANOMARU PARK** Located in the northern part of the palace grounds and surrounded by moats, this park is a great place to relax. Nearby are several interesting museums. Also closeby is the

33

Chūō-dōri Street

Nippon Budōkan Hall where many well-known musicians, including the Beatles, have performed.

● **YASUKUNI SHRINE** Built in 1869, this shrine is a memorial to Japanese servicemen who died in the service of their country.

● **KOKURITSU GEKIJO (NATIONAL THEATER)** With two main theaters capable of seating 1,746 and 630 people, this building features many outstanding performances of *Kabuki, Bunraku* and popular music.

● **KOKKAI GIJIDO (THE JAPANESE NATIONAL DIET)** The heart of Japanese politics, consists of two houses: the House of Councillors on the right and the House of Representatives on the left.

WEST OF TOKYO

AKASAKA & ROPPONGI

Some of the liveliest nightspots in Tokyo are to be found in the downtown areas of Akasaka and Roppongi. There are numerous embassies here. Akasaka, near the Japanese National Diet and full of international business offices, is regarded by many as the "backroom" of the Japanese political and financial world. It has a variety of nightclubs, cabarets, discos and exclusive traditional teahouses. Roppongi is full of pubs, snacks and discos, where an international crowd of all ages is welcome.

WHAT TO SEE

● **HITOTSUGI-DORI STREET** Running from Aoyama-dōri to the TBS TV station, this street is lined with fine restaurants, bars, cafes and discos swarming with young people after dark.

● **SUNTORY ART MUSEUM** This houses a collection of folk art, genre paintings, clothing, furniture, tableware and other traditional artifacts.

● **WAVE BUILDING** Dedicated to multiart, Wave has 4 floors of records, books and videos, a computer graphics studio on the 5th floor, and a cinema in the basement.

● **AXIS** A shopping center for creative minds, with stores selling an endless list of interior decorations, textiles and tableware. It also has an exhibition space.

● **ARISUGAWANOMIYA COMMEMORATIVE PARK** Steeped

in history, this is a quiet park with a lake, stream and lovely trees.

● **PENTAX GALLERY** Established by the parent company of Pentax to celebrate 100 years of photography, it displays a huge collection of old and modern cameras and accessories.

● **TOKYO TOWER** This 333 m. high multipurpose tower, complete with observation deck, is an attractive landmark in Tokyo, from which on clear days can be seen the peak of Mt. Fuji.

WHAT TO EAT

Both Japanese and foreign cooking can be sampled in the many restaurants in this part of Tokyo. Hotel restaurants, although perhaps a little more expensive, have a relaxing atmosphere, and the inability to speak Japanese is not a problem. There are also lively bistros which serve excellent French dishes.

WHAT TO BUY

For top quality goods from around the world start at Akasaka's hotels. For traditional Japanese articles, such as *Geta* and *Kimono*, visit the more established and older shops. In Roppongi try Roi Roppongi for fashion, Axis for interiors, and Wave for records and videos.

ENTERTAINMENT

Both Akasaka and Roppongi have a wide variety of nightspots to suit the people from all walks of life who go there for a good night's entertainment. To be recommended in Akasaka is the Véglia discotheque. Roppongi boasts a great number of exciting places, especially discos. There is an entire building full of discos called the Square Building.

If all you want is a drink, why not try the Hard Rock Cafe "live house" bar or casual Bagpipe.

SHIBUYA, HARAJUKU & AOYAMA

Shibuya, on several train lines, is full of fashionable department and other stores, restaurants, pubs, fast-food stores and cinemas, and is a very popular playground for college and university students. Harajuku, also on the

Wave Building

Yamanote line, has many trendy boutiques and restaurants and is close to some of the renowned fashion houses in Aoyama, by Omotesandō Subway Station.

WHAT TO SEE

● **HACHIKO** Just outside Shibuya station, stands this small bronze statue of the faithful dog, Hachikō, which many people nominate as a meeting place. On weekends the little square is so crowded that it is often difficult to find the dog.

●**KOEN-DORI STREET** At the bottom of this 500 m. long street, which winds its way up to Yoyogi Olympic Stadium and Yoyogi Park, can be found the 8-story Taiseidō Bookstore, while further up the hill is Parco, one of Tokyo's leading fashion stores.

●**NHK BROADCASTING CENTER** This is located at the top of Kōen-dōri Street, and on certain days its studios are open to the public.

● **OTA MEMORIAL MUSEUM** This museum, specializing in *Ukiyo-e* (wood block prints), houses a collection of 12,000 original paintings and woodblock prints by famous artists such as *Utamaro*.

● **TAKESHITA-DORI STREET** Running down from Harajuku

Parco

Station, the boutiques which line this narrow little street are crowded with thousands of young people on the lookout for high quality fashion clothing at low prices.

●**MEIJI SHRINE** Located near Harajuku Station, this impressive shrine, dedicated to the Emperor Meiji by the people of Japan, lies hidden behind majestic trees and along peaceful pathways, which are thronging at New Year with thousands of people on their annual pilgrimage.

●**AOYAMA-DORI STREET** Running from Shibuya in the direction of Akasaka-Mitsuke, this wide avenue is lined with many fashionable boutiques, restaurants and cafes.

WHAT TO EAT

Shibuya and Harajuku boast a vast number of good restaurants, bars and cafes, both expensive and inexpensive, which cater for both office staff and students who abound in this part of Tokyo.

WHAT TO BUY

Harajuku and Shibuya boast some of Japan's finest fashion stores, where people go to find the top names in the fashion world. Leading the way are **Parco** in Shibuya and **Laforet Harajuku** in Harajuku. Besides these, **Kiddy Land** in Harajuku specializes in toys and hobbies, while the DIY enthusiast can find anything he requires at the unique **Tōkyū Hands** store in Shibuya.

SHINJUKU

The fact that more people pass daily through Shinjuku station than any other station in Japan is a good indication that Shinjuku has become one of Japan's busiest commercial and entertainment centers. Unlike Ginza and Akasaka, it gives the visitor a real insight into all aspects of Japanese society—rich and poor, old and new, refined and seedy. The modern skyscrapers of the west rise up in stark contrast to the alleyways of Kabuki-chō across the railway lines on the east.

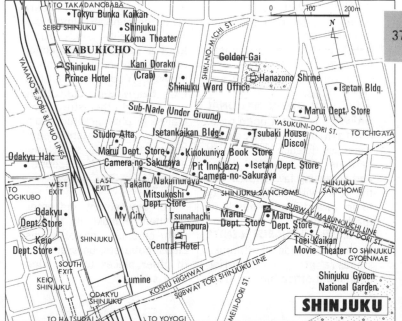

SHINJUKU

WHAT TO SEE

● **SHINJUKU STATION** The busiest station in Japan, this services the JR Yamanote, Chūō, Sōbu, Chūō Main, Subway Marunouchi, Toei Shinjuku, Keiō, Keiō New and Odakyū lines. It also contains some department and other stores.

● **STUDIO ALTA** Just outside Shinjuku Station's east exit, this building has a giant video screen, plus many boutiques and restaurants, and even a TV studio. It serves as a convenient rendezvous for people wanting to shop or find amusement in the area.

● **KABUKI-CHO** Less than 5 minutes' walk from the east exit of Shinjuku Station, Kabuki-chō is a prominent pleasure ground with everything from cinemas to pornography shops.

● **SHINJUKU GYOEN NATIONAL GARDEN** This vast open park, containing landscaped Japanese, French and English gardens with beautiful trees and sprawling lawns, provides the weary with the opportunity to get away from the bustle of the big city.

● **SHINJUKU HIGH-RISE CENTER** On the west side of Shinjuku stands a group of high-rise hotels and office blocks, from which you can take in a panoramic view of modern Tokyo.

WHAT TO EAT

In Shinjuku there are countless restaurants and bars with menus to suit both taste and pocket and often open until the "wee small hours" of the morning. Numerous bars serve Japanese food and *sake*, but the homesick may wish to have a taste of more familiar dishes, in which case **Takano World Restaurant** near Shinjuku Station's east exit is to be recommended.

WHAT TO BUY

Department stores, such as **Mitsukoshi** and **Isetan**, offer the shopper almost any kind of quality goods. **Kinokuniya** has a wide selection of books and magazines on its shelves. **Yodobashi Camera**, **Camera-no-Sakuraya** and several other stores specialize in photographic equipment, hi-fi, watches and electrical goods, sometimes at up to 30—40% discount.

ENTERTAINMENT

For amusement and entertainment, Kabuki-chō is alive with cinemas, discotheques, clubs, cabarets, bars and lots of other places for the pleasure seeker.

38

Yodobashi Camera

IKEBUKURO

To the north of Tokyo, Ikebukuro rivals Shinjuku and Shibuya as one of the city's busiest commercial centers. Ikebukuro station services several major JR and private railway lines, and together with the Sunshine Building, houses some of Tokyo's finest department stores, other smaller shops and restaurants.

WHAT TO SEE

● **SUNSHINE CITY** On the east side of Ikebukuro towers the tallest building in Asia, which houses some 60 stories of offices, shops and restaurants. Next to the Sunshine Building on the same site stands the World Import Mart which contains, amongst other things, an International Aquarium, a Planetarium and the Trade Centers of Governments from around the world.

Seibu Art Museum Located on the 12th floor of Seibu department store, this presents a unique and interesting variety of modern art exhibitions.

● **IKEBUKURO ENGEIJO** One of Tokyo's best known theaters, this features *Rakugo* (comic story-telling), *Manzai* (comic dialog), magic and acrobatics.

WHAT TO EAT

On both sides of the railway lines there are countless restaurants, both expensive and very cheap. The Sunshine City complex alone is filled with excellent eating houses which can also be found near the station. The west side of Ikebukuro, the atmosphere of which at times resembles that of Kabuki-chō in Shinjuku, abounds with bars full of salaried workers relaxing after a hard day at the office.

39

WHAT TO BUY

The huge **Seibu** department store and **Parco**, containing over 180 boutiques, together with **Tōbu**, **Marui**, **Alpa** and innumerable other stores, must make Ikebukuro one of Tokyo's best shopping districts for everything from luxury to everyday goods.

EAST OF TOKYO

ASAKUSA

Asakusa is the best known *"shitamachi"* — old downtown area—in Tokyo, as it has always been, and its special atmosphere has survived unchanged since the Edo era. These days, the town is full of visitors to the temple and surroundings, and with redevelopment taking place, its former vigor is being restored. A large number of seasonal festivals add to Asakusa's many attractions. Take the Ginza Subway Line to Asakusa Station.

WHAT TO SEE

● *SENSOJI (ASAKUSA KANNON TEMPLE)* The major deity of Tokyo's oldest temple is the *kannon* (Goddess of Marcy). Hōzōmon is one of the vermilion gates at the entrance to the grounds and features two guardian Deva kings. West of Hōzōmon stands the five story pagoda. Rebuilt in 1973, it is 48.32 m. high.

● *KAMINARIMON (GATE OF WIND AND THUNDER)* Built in 942 to assure crop fertility and world peace, this impressive gate's most remarkable feature is the 3.3 m, 100 kg red lantern hanging under its eaves.

● *NAKAMISE STREET* After passing through Kaminarimon Gate you are in a narrow street lined with shops. Here and on the intersecting streets are hundreds of souvenir stores as well as shops selling combs, fans, paper and other traditional crafts.

● *ASAKUSA CRAFTS CENTER* From wigs and special towels to cypress products and clothes for construction workers, this store sells every kind of hand-made product as well as the raw materials and tools.

● *SUMIDA RIVER* Boat tours start from a pier near Azuma Bridge. At the end of July, large crowds gather along the banks for a spectacular fireworks display.

● *KAPPABASHI* This is a street of shops dealing exclusively in kitchen supplies and utensils.

Kaminarimon

● **KURAMAE TOY DISTRICT**
From Asakusabashi to Umayabashi, this one long street is lined with shops carrying toys, dolls and stationery.

WHAT TO EAT

Asakusa is full of historic restaurants with all the character and atmosphere of Edo. **Daikokuya** is popular for *tempura*. If it's *sushi* you're after, go to *Sushiya-dōri* Street near Kaminarimon Gate. For *soba* there's **Nagaura** and **Namiki Yabusoba**. For something out of the ordinary, **Komagata Dojō** serves *dojōnabe* —a roach stew.

WHAT TO BUY

Nakamise Street is bursting with traditional souvenirs. A good place for toys is **Sukeroku**, while folding fans are available at **Arai Bunsendō**. **Fujiya** stocks decorative towels, and a great store for Japanese combs is **Yonoya**. Knives and swords can be purchased at **Kanesō**.

ENTERTAINMENT

Rakugo (comic storytelling) is performed at the **Asakusa Engei Hall**. Though it is in Japanese, visitors can appreciate the style and atmosphere of this traditional entertainment. *Rōkyoku* (*rakugo* with music) can be seen at the **Asakusa Mokubatei** theater.

UENO

Ueno, originally a quiet temple town, is a bustling city centered around its enormous station on the JR Yamanote Line, the gateway to Tokyo from the north. Ueno provides a tremendous variety of diversions. From the station, the "Ueno Park" exit takes you to a collection of museums, art galleries, and auditoriums set amongst trees and gardens. This is also the exit for Shinobazu Pond and Ueno Zoo.

WHAT TO SEE

41

●**UENO PARK** As well as the zoo, museums and galleries, the park contains **Kan-eiji Temple** and **Tōshōgū Shrine**. Ueno Park is one of Japan's most famous cherry viewing spots, and in spring, thousands of revellers picnic under the trees. On the west side lies Shinobazu Pond covered with lotus and lilies. In July, millions visit the pond, and with many in traditional dress and with lanterns decorating the trees, summer in Edo is briefly recaptured.

● TOKYO NATIONAL MUSEUM

This museum displays an incredible number of Asian works of art and relics and holds frequent exhibitions. Displays cover fields such as sculpture, traditional weaving and dyeing, metalwork, pottery, lacquerware and calligraphy. The Oriental pavilion houses a large collection of art treasures from throughout Asia.

● NATIONAL SCIENCE MUSEUM

This has everything from a dinosaur skeleton to a World War II Zero fighter plane and moon rocks. Weather permitting, on Saturday evenings visitors can take part in guided astronomical observations.

● SHITAMACHI LIFESTYLE EXHIBITION HALL

This is dedicated to the way of life of the common people who lived in *shitamachi*—downtown areas. There are replicas of typical apartments and houses as well as articles that were in everyday use.

● AMEYOKO

This is a bustling market area under the JR railway line selling practically everything at bargain prices.

Before closing at the end of the day, prices are discounted even further, and the market is very crowded especially at the end of the year.

WHAT TO EAT

The Hirokōji area provides a lot of good eating. The origin of *tonkatsu* (crumbed, deep-fried pork cutlets) is said to be the restaurant **Ponta**. For *soba*, try the popular **Rengyokuan**.

WHAT TO BUY

Near Hirokōji is the main shopping area. **Jūsan-ya** has sold beautiful wooden combs for lacquerwares.

ENTERTAINMENT

To see something of "downtown" entertainment, **Suzumoto Theater** has *rakugo* (traditional storytelling), comedy, juggling, impersonators and other burlesque performances as well as some traditional music. Nearby, the **Hommokutei Theater** features a different style of traditional story-telling.

KANDA & AKIHABARA

Kanda has been the home of Tokyo's merchants and craftsmen for hundreds of years. There are many restaurants and textile shops which retain their Edo period charm. Akihabara is popular with Japanese and tourists alike for its discount electrical goods stores.

WHAT TO SEE

● *TRANSPORTATION MUSEUM*
Over 20,000 vehicles, models and documents are exhibited to introduce the history of transportation in Japan.

● *SECONDHAND BOOKSTORES*
Over 100 stores in the area sell new, secondhand and antique books. A large book fair is held between mid-October and the end of November.

● *KANDA MYOJIN SHRINE* The god of this shrine is believed to influence commercial success, prosperity and marriage. Its festival in mid-May is one of the three big Edo festivals.

WHAT TO EAT

Kanda abounds with historic restaurants, like Kanda Yabusoba for buckwheat noodles or Botan for *torinabe* a superb chicken stew. Located in very traditional streets, these shops preserve the flavors and traditions of true Japanese cuisine.

WHAT TO BUY

In Akihabara's electrical center there are many stores to choose from, including tax-free and duty-free stores, and stores selling export models. Near the station, large stores include Yamagiwa, Minami, Ishimaru Denki, and Laox. Visiting several shops and comparing prices is a good idea. Between Kanda and Jimbō-chō Stations, there are many discount sports stores and secondhand bookshops.

TOKYO DISNEYLAND

Opened in 1983, the Tokyo version of Walt Disney's dream has much in common with its Florida and California counterparts. The 46-hectare park incorporates 5 theme lands: World Bazaar, Adventureland, Westernland, Fantasyland and Tomorrowland. There are several ticket options, so simply select one to suit your purpose.

TRANSPORTATION

16 min. from Nihombashi Station on the Tōzai line subway to Urayasu Station then 15 min. by bus direct to the Tokyo Disneyland Transportation Center. 35 min. by direct bus from the north exit on the Yaesu side of Tokyo Station. 50 min. by direct bus from Narita Airport. 45 min. by direct bus from Ueno.

43

Akihabara Electric Appliance Area

東京近郊
NEAR TOKYO

Within easy reach of Tokyo, there is a wealth of places ideal for day-trips or overnight stays. It's easy to fit in two or more attractions, like a trip to Mt. Fuji then a soak in Hakone's hot springs, or a visit to Yokohama combined with a look at historic Kamakura's temples and shrines.

NIKKO & ENVIRONS

A sacred site on a cedar-clad mountain, Nikko is a major attraction for both tourists and Japanese. Perfect in any season, it offers magnificent scenery, with splendid spots like Lake Chūzenji and Kegon Falls, and some of the most beautiful buildings in the world.

The national park also boasts numerous easily accessible hotspring resorts in majestic natural settings.

TRANSPORTATION

● *TO NIKKO* ＊Asakusa to Tōbu Nikko, I hr. 40 min. on the Limited Express Romance Car. Reserved seats only.
＊Ueno to Nikko, 2 hrs. 10 min. on the JR Tōhoku main line to Utsunomiya, then transfer to the Nikko Line.
● *TO KINUGAWA* Asakusa to Kinugawa Hot Springs, I hr. 55 min. on the Limited Express Romance Car. Reserved Seats only.
● *AROUND NIKKO* Tōbu buses leave Nikko for Yumoto Hot Springs via Shinkyō and Lake Chūzenji. It is 6 min. by bus to the Sacred Bridge, 20 min. on foot. By bus it's 50 min. to Chūzenji Hot Springs and I hr. to Yumoto Hot Springs.

To Kinugawa Hot Springs it's 2 hrs. 40 min.

TOUR HINTS

The central attractions at Nikko, the temple and shrines adjacent to the town, can be seen comfortably in 3 hrs.

Visitors should note that Oku-Nikko, including Yumoto Hot Springs and Senjōgahara, is in a heavy snowfall area and is closed during the winter.

45

NIKKO SANNAI

WHAT TO SEE

● **SHINKYO (SACRED BRIDGE)**
This is the first attraction on the way to Tōshōgū shrine. Vermilion lacquered, with gilt metal ornaments, this bridge throws a graceful curve over the quietly flowing Daiya River.

● **RINNOJI TEMPLE** Rinnōji is best known for its Sambutsudō (Temple of the Three Buddhas) reputedly built in 1648. The largest wooden structure in Nikko, it houses 3 gilded wooden statues of Buddha over 5 meters tall. The Traditional Japanese garden, Shōyōen, is also worth a visit.

● **TOSHOGU SHRINE** The single-most important attraction at Nikko, this masterpiece is dedicated to *Ieyasu Tokugawa* (1542-1616), the founder of the *Tokugawa* Shogunate government, and was completed in 1636.

At the start of the walk to the shrine, visitors pass under a 9 m. granite gate (Ichi no Torii or first torii). To the left of the path is a 5-story pagoda, 35 m. high. Built in 1818 it is lacquered in red and gold with a black door serving as the entrance.

Entry to the shrine is through Omotemon (Main Gate), also called Niōmon (Deva Gate) as it has statues of 2 guardian Deva Kings. Shinkyūsha (The Sacred Stable) comes into view next—the only unlacquered building in the area. It has various carvings of monkeys, and one panel features the celebrated Trio of Monkeys in poses signifying "Hear no evil, Speak no evil, See no evil".

Honchidō Hall is a Buddhist-style structure, famous for its "Crying Dragon" painted on the ceiling. Visitors clap their hands beneath it, and the echoes sound like the reverberating roars and moans of the dragon.

Yōmeimon (Gate of Sunlight). Certainly the most beautiful gate in Japan, it is lavished with intricate carvings, gilt and lacquer work carved by 130,000 craftsmen working on an unlimited budget. Beyond Yōmeimon is Karamon (Chinese Gate), painted white and gold.

To the east of the terrace between Yōmeimon and Karamon is the famous carving over a doorway of a Sleeping Cat whose presence is said to keep the building free of rats and mice. The central buildings at the shrine are the

Haiden (Oratory) and Honden (Main Hall) both richly decorated with paintings and elaborate carvings.

● *DAIYUIN* The mausoleum dedicated to *Iemitsu* who constructed Tōshōgū in honor of his grandfather *Ieyasu*. It resembles the Tōshōgū Shrine with everyting on a smaller scale — except its magnificence.

●*FUTARASAN SHRINE* Built in 1619, this is called the Head Shrine to distinguish it from the Inner Shrine on Mt. Nantai and the Middle Shrine on the shores of Lake Chūzenji.

WHAT TO EAT

As it is a major tourist area, there is no shortage of fine eating places in Nikko. For the vegetarian delight of *yuba* (dried bean curd), try Ebiya near the municipal office building. To sample some of the famed Chūzenji trout, go to the Lakeside Hotel.

WHAT TO BUY

Nikko is known for its excellent craftsmen. Especially good are the sculptures to be found at Mukai on the west approach to the main shrine and the tea ceremony accessories at Watanabe's near the Sacred Bridge.

WHERE TO STAY

There is plenty of accomodation in Nikko, both Japanese and western style. Among the latter, Nikko Kanaya Hotel, which overlooks the Sacred Bridge, is a classic and is where the Emperor of Japan and foreign VIP's stay. If you prefer hot springs, try Chūzenji Hot Springs or Yumoto Hot Springs.

47

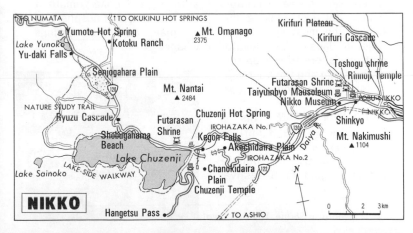

OKU-NIKKO

WHAT TO SEE

●**IROHAZAKA** This steep zig-zagging road runs to Chūzenji Hot Springs, giving panoramic views of the splendid colors of the trees in autumn. The 500 m. ascent and descent with its 48 continuous curves was named after the 48-word traditional *"Iroha"* song.

●**LAKE CHUZENJI** This lake is the result of an eruption of Mt. Nantai which forms a backdrop to the lake. Surrounded by mountains, the lake is 11.6 sq. km. in area, 21 km. in circumference. The spring cherry blossoms and the brilliant autumn foliage can best be seen from the excursion boats plying the lake.

●**KEGON FALLS** Kegon waterfalls plummet 100 m. into a wide basin. The water creates a beautiful mist, making this one of the most spectacular falls in Japan. An elevator carries visitors to the bottom of the gorge and the best view of the falls are from the lookout there.

●**CHUGUSHI SHRINE** This is the middle of the 3 shrines making up Futarasan. On July 31, thousands of people gather to join in a festival worshipping Mt. Nantai.

●**CHUZENJI TEMPLE** The main attraction here is a 1,000-year old wooden statue of Kannon with 1,000 arms carved by priest *Shōdō* out of a living tree.

●**RYUZU CASCADE** A series of pretty cascades through a forest of maples. Before the Yukawa River spills into lake Chūzenji, it drops 200 m., hits a black boulder and is divided into 2 streams. The fall's resemblance to a dragon gave rise to its name — *Ryūzu* (Dragon's Head).

●**SENJOGAHARA PLAIN** This is a vast, marshy plateau noted for its alpine plants which bloom from late spring to mid-summer. Hikers enjoy the popular Nature Study Trails here.

●**YUMOTO HOT SPRINGS** Nestled in the mountains, this spa lies 1,800 m. above sea level, at the edge of Lake Yumoto. It still has all the atmosphere of a small, quiet hot springs village.

Futabasan Shrine Yayoi Festival

KINUGAWA

WHAT TO SEE

● *KINUGAWA HOT SPRINGS*
Set amidst very picturesque scenery on the Kinugawa River, this spa is the most outstanding in the district. The town is lively well into the night, and the area is full of interesting sights.

● *KINUGAWA LINE* This is a 50 min. boat ride down the swiftly flowing Kinugawa River from the dock at Kinugawa Onsen Station to Otoro. An exhilarating ride, it takes in splendid scenery.

● *RYUO GORGE* A 3 km.-long rocky gorge, this is particularly popular in autumn when the crimson foliage contrasts with the rocky surroundings.

YOKOHAMA

Yokohama is the 2nd largest city in Japan and its 2nd largest port, but not so long ago it was just a sleepy fishing village. With the demise of the *Tokugawa* government's isolationist policy in 1859, it became an opening to the outside world and has developed dramatically with the influx of western cultures. Its links with the west are obvious in its buildings. With its Chinatown and large department stores, Yokohama is a popular place for shopping and dining.

TRANSPORTATION

Yokohama can be reached comfortably in 30-45 min. from Tokyo on any of five train lines: the JR Tōkaidō Line and Yokosuka Line are the fastest from Tokyo Station. The Keihin Tōhoku Line is a little slower.

The Tōkyū Tōyoko Line can be taken from Shibuya Station on the JR Yamanote Line. The Keihin Kyūkō Line can be reached from stations on the *Toei* Subway Lines. To get to Chinatown, Kannai Station, Motomachi, or Ishikawa-chō Station, the Keihin Tōhōku line is the most convenient.

TOUR HINTS

The most famous architectural sites in Yokohama are the historic western buildings. These buildings, scattered throughout Yokohama, can be easily seen in one day. During the spring and summer, there are a large number of festivals and tourist-oriented events. Yokohama's main attractions are located quite close to each other: Yamashita Park, Port Viewing Park, Marine Tower and Chinatown.

WHAT TO SEE

● **YOKOHAMA PORT** As well as a huge volume of merchant shipping, the port handles many large luxury liners that make Yokohama a port of call. A harbor cruise ship leaves from the jetty beside the permanently moored liner, the Hikawamaru.

● **YAMASHITA PARK** Lying along the waterfront, the park affords a fine view of the harbor, making it a popular spot for dating couples.

● **MARINE TOWER** Within walking distance of the park, this 106 m. tower commands extensive views over the city and harbor. It is possible on a clear day to see distant Mt. Fuji from here.

● **PORT VIEWING PARK** Situated on the upper west side of the Bluff, a prestigious residential area, this park certainly lives up to its name. Near the park is the Foreign Cemetery, with around 4,000 graves of early foreign residents of Japan.

● **YAMATE DATA MUSEUM** A wooden building of western design, this museum displays articles from the Meiji and Taishō periods, and many Ukiyo-e (woodblock prints).

● **CHINATOWN** A vermilion Chinese gate marks the entrance to this area which is best known for its cuisine and

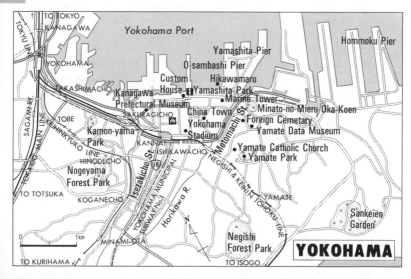

shops selling Chinese products and curios.

● *SANKEIEN GARDEN* Covering 170,000 sq. m., it is laid out around a large pond, with paths circling it. Its inner garden is one of the finest examples of traditional landscape design in the country.

The garden has many historic structures brought from other parts of the country. Rinshunkaku is the only remaining example of the villa architecture of Japan's feudal lords. This structure is typical of the transitional years between the Momoyama and Edo period; Chōshūkaku is a tea ceremony house built by the 3rd *Tokugawa* shōgun, *Iemitsu Tokugawa.*

● *YOKOHAMA STADIUM* The stadium seats 30,000 and is home to the popular pro-baseball team, the Yokohama Taiyō Whales. It also serves as a soccer and American football field, and large concerts are held regularly in the summer.

WHAT TO EAT

Yokohama ranks high in its offering of culinary delights. There is a wealth of restaurants both international and traditional. Chinatown alone has over 100 different restaurants. Try Manchinrō for great traditional Chinese cooking. Kōshō is renowned for its chicken *soba* (noodles). The buildings around Yokohama Station offer yet more international cuisine, while those in Sakuragi-chō or Isezaki-chō tend to be smaller and more individual in character.

WHAT TO BUY

Shopping in Yokohama is similar to Tokyo in that you can buy almost anything you want from anywhere in the world. Yokohama's most famous souvenirs are said to be the Chinese dumplings from Kiyōken, an equally famous store. Motomachi is a fashionable boulevard lined with boutiques and fine jewelry stores. It is particularly popular with younger shoppers.

51

WHERE TO STAY

The Hotel New Grand is one of the oldest in the city and has all the atmosphere and tradition of this port city. The Hotel Yokohama by contrast is very modern. Both offer fabulous harbor views. If you wish to stay in a typical Japanese lodging, you can get help in making reservations at the Tourist Information Center.

KAMAKURA & ENOSHIMA

Kamakura was the capital of Japan during the *Kamakura* period (1192-1333), when the military government of the *Minamoto* family held power. It was then a prosperous and powerful city but is now a tranquil spot and is probably the most interesting area near Tokyo for historic remains. The area has many ancient temples, shrines and a Great Buddha in very picturesque settings. Enoshima is a pretty, thickly-wooded island off Katase Beach. The nearby town and beaches are extremely popular in summer.

TRANSPORTATION

● *BY RAIL* Tokyo to Kamakura: 1 hr. on JR Yokosuka Line.; Shinjuku to Katase-Enoshima: 1 hr. 10 min. on Odakyū Line "Romance Car".
● *BY BUS* At Kamakura, buses and the Enoden Railway Line leave from the terminal at the east exit of Kamakura station for Enoshima and Fujisawa.

TOUR HINTS

All the major sights in Kamakura are within a 4 sq. km. area and can be seen easily in a day. The multitude of signposts in English make finding your way on foot very simple. The following suggested tour takes about 7 hrs. and takes in the major places of interest: From Kamakura Station, walk to Engakuji Temple, Kenchōji Temple, and Tsurugaoka Hachimangū Shrine. From here it's a 10 min. walk back to Kamakura Station.

Take the Enoden train to Hase Station walk to Hasedera Temple, Kōtokuin Temple (with the Great Buddha), and back to Hase Station. Enoshima Island can be seen comfortably in 1 or 2 hrs.

WHAT TO SEE

KITAKAMAKURA

● *ENGAKUJI TEMPLE* This temple dates from 1282 and is the headquarters of the *Rinzai* sect of *Zen* Buddhism. Its main gate is impressive, with carvings of lions and dragons.
● *MEIGETSUIN TEMPLE* This small temple is also called *Ajisaidera* (hydrangea temple), and in June the grounds are covered with the white and lilac blooms of hydrangeas.
● *KENCHOJI TEMPLE* The greatest of the *Zen* temples in

Kamakura and certainly the most beautiful, Kenchōji was founded in 1253. It was reputedly built as a symbol of authority for *Tokiyori Hōjō,* a regent to the 5th *shōgun.*

KAMAKURA STATION AREA

● *TSURUGAOKA-HACHIMANGU SHRINE* Built on a hillside overlooking the city, this shrine is a must on any visit. Founded in 1063, the present colorful buildings date from 1828. The bright red *torii* gate on the approach to the shrine is outstanding. At the bottom of the stone steps leading to the shrine is a

massive gingko tree-scene of the assassination of *Kamakura Shōgun Sanetomo* in 1219. The small museum in the main building houses armor, swords, masks and other historic items.

● *JUFUKUJI TEMPLE* Originally, this temple ranked third among the Five Great *Zen* Temples of Kamakura, and it is the oldest.

● *EISHOJI TEMPLE* Founded in 1636, this is the only nunnery remaining in Kamakura.

Summer sees the grounds blooming with flowers.

● *KAMAKURAGU SHRINE* The only shrine in Japan estab-

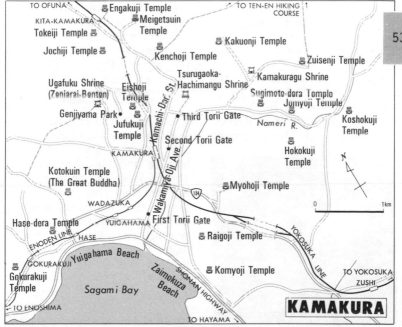

53

TO OFUNA
KITA-KAMAKURA
Tokeiji Temple
Jochiji Temple
Engakuji Temple
Meigetsuin Temple
Kenchoji Temple
Kakuonji Temple
TO TEN-EN HIKING COURSE
Zuisenji Temple
Tsurugaoka-Hachimangu Shrine
Kamakuragu Shrine
Ugafuku Shrine (Zeniarai-Benten)
Eishoji Temple
Sugimoto-dera Temple
Jomyoji Temple
Genjiyama Park
Jufukuji Temple
Third Torii Gate
Nameri R.
Koshokuji Temple
Second Torii Gate
KAMAKURA
Kotokuin Temple (The Great Buddha)
Hokokuji Temple
N
Komachi-Dori St.
Wakamiya-Oji Ave.
Myohoji Temple
WADAZUKA
0   1km
Hase-dera Temple
YUIGAHAMA
First Torii Gate
ENODEN LINE
HASE
Raigoji Temple
YOKOSUKA LINE
GOKURAKUJI
Yuigahama Beach
Gokurakuji Temple
Komyoji Temple
TO YOKOSUKA
ZUSHI
Sagami Bay
Zaimokuza Beach
SHONAN HIGHWAY
TO ENOSHIMA
TO HAYAMA

KAMAKURA

lished by an emperor. Every September *Takigi Noh* (*Noh* dramas performed in the light of flaming torches) are staged outdoors here.

● **ZUISENJI TEMPLE** In a quiet spot surrounded by hills, this is the largest temple in Kamakura and is famous for its trees and flowers.

● **ZENIARAI-BENTEN SHRINE** It is believed that money washed in the spring which bubbles up in the cave here will multiply. Consequently, there is no end to the number of visitors at this shrine.

● **KOTOKUIN TEMPLE** Here you will find the unquestioned symbol of Kamakura, the bronze statue (*Daibutsu* **Great Buddha**) sitting with a majestically serene expression in a pose representing steadfast faith. Cast in 1252, the figure weighs over 100 tons and is 13.35 m. high.

● **HASE KANNON TEMPLE** The 11-faced, 9 m. high *Kannon* (goddess of Mercy) carved

from a single camphor log in 721 attracts visitors here. On the way up to the main building are hundreds of tiny stone statues of *Jizō*, patron deity of children, pregnant women and travelers.

WHAT TO EAT

Restaurants in Kamakura are centered around the **Komachi-dōri Street** and **Wakamiya-ōji Avenue** area. Many of the restaurants are traditional in design and impart all the flavor of bygone eras. A delicious dish to try is *Shōjin-ryōri*, which emphasizes presentation and seasonal food and seems to fit the mood of Kamakura. An excellent place to try is **Hachinoki** near Kenchōji Temple. For *tōfu* cooking, **Hakuhō** near the Great Buddha is especially good.

WHAT TO BUY

A fine local product is **Kamakurabori**, hardwood covered with layers of black and red lacquer and highly polished. The process is applied to articles from plates to furniture. On **Komachi-dōri Street** and **Wakamiya-ōji Avenue**, stores sell the raw materials as well as the durable and artistic finished product.

54

The Great Buddha in Kōtokuin Temple

ENOSHIMA

WHAT TO SEE

● **ENOSHIMA** This is the island which gives its name to this popular resort town. 2.2 km in circumference, the whole island is sacred ground. Enoshima Shrine, the main attraction, has a nude statue of *Benten*, the Indian goddess of beauty and a Japanese deity for good-luck. The main beaches at Enoshima are Higashihama and Katase. Katase features an aquarium and Enoshima Marineland. Enoshima is always bustling with visitors and is very crowded on summer weekends.

WHAT TO EAT

On the bridge from the beach to Enoshima there are many small restaurants and food stalls. Shellfish cooked in the shell is popular and dried fish are sold as souvenirs.

FUJI, HAKONE & IZU

The Fuji-Hakone-Izu National Park contains some of the best scenery in Japan. With Mt. Fuji as the centerpiece, the Fuji area offers lakes, waterfalls and virgin forests. The highlands of Hakone boast a large number of hot-spring resorts and year-round recreational facilities. Izu Peninsula has a mild climate, abundant hot springs and a pretty coastline.

HAKONE

TRANSPORTATION

● **BY RAIL** * Tokyo to Odawara: 40 min. by JR shinkansen "Kodama".; 65 min. by JR Tōkaidō line Limited Express.
* Shinjuku to Hakone-Yumoto: I hr. 25 min. on Odakyū Line "Romance Car".
● **BY BUS** Shinjuku to Tōgendai: 2 hrs. I0 min. by Odakyū.
● **FROM ODAWARA** There are 5 different bus routes taking you either towards the Izu area or the Fuji area. Sightseeing buses also leave O-dawara.
● **HAKONE TOZAN RAILWAY** A 2-car train covers the I5 kms between Odawara and Gōra in 50 min. up steep grades on a very scenic route.
● **CABLE CARS** Available from Gōra to Mt. Sōunzan and from Komagatake-nobori-guchi to Komagatake Peak. There are

ropeways from Mt. Sōunzan to Tōgendai and from Hakone-en to Komagatake Peak.

WHAT TO SEE

● **HAKONE-YUMOTO HOT SPRINGS** One of the oldest towns and largest hot spring resorts in the district, Yumoto has a large number of traditional Japanese inns. From here the Hakone Tozan Railway goes to Gōra, the most popular resort area, with many well-known hot springs such as **Tōnosawa** and **Miyanoshita**.

● **GORA HOT SPRINGS** The 2nd largest in Hakone, and at 600 m. altitude, the area commands fine views. The town has a French-style garden, and the **Hakone Art Museum** with ancient paintings and porcelain.

● **OWAKUDANI VALLEY** Adding to the range of scenery in the area, this is a relic of the volcanic activity that created Hakone — a sulphurous valley with steaming fumeroles, hot water and boiling mud. **Chōkoku-no-mori** (Hakone Open Air Museum) contains galleries and sculptures, mostly modern, arranged in a garden.

● **ASHINOKO** (Lake Ashi)

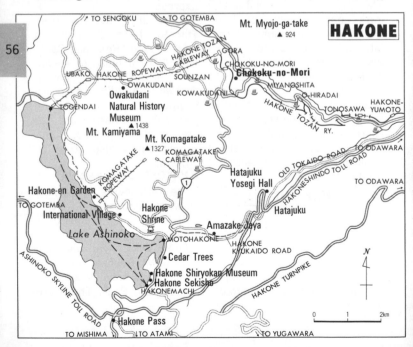

Lake Ashinoko

With famous views of Mt. Fuji, flame-red maples in autumn, and many excursion boats, this is a very popular lake. Hakone Shrine is set among ancient cedar trees overlooking Lake Ashi.

● *HAKONE SEKISHO* (Barrier Gate) Barriers were built in feudal times to separate different parts of the country and control travel. The Hakone checkpoint controlled the main road between the 2 capitals, Edo and Kyoto.

● *HAKONE SHIRYOKAN MUSEUM* This museum displays materials related to the checkpoint barrier, as well as firearms, armor and tools.

● *HAKONE KYUKAIDO ROAD* In feudal days, any road connecting east and west had to pass through Hakone. Hatajuku, famous for its inlaid woodwork, was a post town on this road. The atmosphere of the Edo era still lingers in Amazakejaya, a traditional tea shop there.

● *HAKONE GARDEN* This is a large recreation center with camping grounds, an International Village of 26 foreign houses, an aquarium, golf course, tennis courts and other facilities.

WHAT TO BUY

The best-known souvenir article produced here is the inlaid wooden ware known as Yosegizaiku. Visitors can see craftsmen producing it in Hatajuku. Odawarajōchin are lanterns, once essential for crossing the mountains, that also make interesting gifts.

WHERE TO STAY

An ideal visit to Hakone should include a stay in a hot springs hotel. Fujiya Hotel in Miyanoshita is popular with foreign visitors. For a stay in a traditional Japanese Inn, the old Edo-period hotel Naraya is excellent.

57

Hakone-Yumoto Hot Springs

FUJI

TRANSPORTATION

● **BY RAIL** * Tokyo to Mishima: I hr. 10 min. by JR Shinkansen "Kodama"; *Mishima to Mt. Fuji (New 5th Stage): 2 hrs. by Fuji Kyūkō Bus; *Shinjuku to Kawaguchiko: 2 hrs. 10 min. by JR Chūō Line Express and Fuji Kyūkō Line; *Kawaguchiko to Mt. Fuji (New 5th Stage): I hr.
● **BY BUS** Hamamatsu-chō to Mt. Fuji (5th Stage): 2 hrs. 45 min.; Shinjuku to Mt. Fuji (5th Stage): 2 hrs. 15 min. by Fuji Kyūkō Chūō-Kōsoku Express buses.
● **AROUND MT. FUJI** Fuji Kyūkō Buses are convenient. Their timetables have seasonal variations.

WHAT TO SEE

● **MT. FUJI** At 3,776 m., this is Japan's highest mountain and certainly one of the world's most beautiful. The Fuji-Yoshida Trail for the climb up, and the Gotemba Trail going down are the most popular of the 6 hiking trails.

Buses go to the 5th Stage on the north side and to the New 5th Stage on the south, both of which are half-way up the mountain. Hikers generally make the trip to the top with an overnight stay at one of the stone huts along the route in order to see the sunrise from the summit.

Climbers should equip themselves with warm clothing since the temperature at the summit is 20°C lower than at the base. The climbing season is during July and August.
● **FUJI FIVE LAKES** These are, in order of their position from east to west: Yamanaka, Kawaguchi, Sai, Shōji, and Motosu. The area has many recreational facilities. Especially popular with young people are those near Lake Yamanaka and Lake Kawaguchi. In addition to skiing and skating, winter activities include *wakasagi* (pond smelt) fishing through holes cut in the frozen surface of the lakes.

Shiraito Falls, located on the west of Mt. Fuji is a stately waterfall 20 m.-high and 200 m.-wide. Narusawa Ice Cave and Fugaku Wind Cave near Lake Saiko are lava caves with very low temperatures. Aokigahara is a dense, primeval forest where in parts, due to minerals, a compass will not function. Fujikyū High-Land near Lake Kawaguchi is an amusement park with a double-loop roller coaster and a skating rink.

IZU

TRANSPORTATION

● **BY RAIL** Tokyo to Atami: 50 min. by JR Kodama Express bullet train; Tokyo to Ito: I hr 50 min, Tokyo to Shimoda: 2 hrs. 50 min.; Tokyo to Shuzenji: 2 hrs. I5 min. by Odoriko Limited Express.

A bus service connects all resorts and places of interest on the Izu peninsula.

WHAT TO SEE

● **IZU PENINSULA** This is very popular year-round as a seaside recreation area for Tokyoites who flock to its beaches and hot spring resorts. Izu has a mild climate, pretty coastal scenery, delicious fresh seafood, and abundant recreational facilities and accomodation.

Atami, Ito, Atagawa, and Shimoda in eastern Izu, and Shuzenji in central Izu are lively resort towns with a multitude of hotels. In central Izu Yugano, Odaru, and Yugashima are much quieter resorts in forest areas.

Shimoda, a port and fishing town in the southeast is the major summer resort with white sandy beaches and clear water. At the southernmost point of the peninsula, the bluffs of Cape Irōzaki afford views towards the Izu islands. On the west coast, Dōgashima offers Izu's best scenery. This area, with its fantastic rocks jutting out of the sea, can best be seen by excursion boat.

● **IZU SEVEN ISLANDS** These islands, part of the Fuji volcanic chain, include 2 active volcanoes. Isolated until relatively recently, they are now popular summer holiday resorts. Oshima Island, the largest of the group, is accessible in 7 hrs. by boat or 40 min. by plane from Tokyo. It is well-known for its camellias which bloom in January and February.

The other six islands: Niijima, Shikinejima, Kōzushima, Miyakejima, Mikurajima and Hachijōjima are all serviced by boat from Tokyo. They offer excellent swimming and diving at a relaxed pace.

59

Mt. Fuji Skyline Road

BOSO

An easily-reached, but often overlooked area, the main attractions of the Bōsō Peninsula are its seaside resorts and mild climate. Bōsō lies southeast of Tokyo in Chiba prefecture, and its most popular resorts are Shirahama, Tateyama, Kamogawa and Katsuura.

TRANSPORTATION

The east side of Bōsō Peninsula is called Sotobō (outer Bōsō) and its west side is called Uchibō (inner Bōsō).
● **BY RAIL** * Tokyo to Ohara: I hr. 30 min, Katsuura; I hr. 50 min. Kamogawa: 2 hrs. I5 min. on JR Sotobō Line Limited Express. * Tokyo to Tateyama: 2 hrs. 5 min. on JR Uchibō Line Limited Express.

TOUR HINTS

The seaside in Bōsō attracts visitors all year, and there are many historic sites, as well as temples and shrines. From February to April the peninsula is blooming with poppies, daffodils, marguerites and other flowers. Popular places to stay are the many *minshuku* —private houses providing lodging and meals. A stay at a *minshuku* provides an insight into life in an ordinary Japanese home.

WHAT TO SEE

● *KUJUKURIHAMA BEACH* A 66 km. arc of sandy beach from Cape Taitō to Cape Gyōbu. The Pacific Ocean provides good waves for surfing here, and it is a popular bathing beach.
● *ONJUKU* It is known for its women divers called *Ama* and the large sand dunes along the beach. Women dive for seaweed and shells from May to the middle of September. Ohara is one of the largest fishing towns on the east side, popular in summer for fishing and swimming.
● *KATSUURA* This is one of the largest ports on the east side and a base for off-shore fishing. The port, crowded

The Morning Market at Katsuura

with fishing boats, is an interesting sight. The morning market has been running for 400 years and is a great attraction. Open from 6:00 to 11:00 a.m. everyday.

● *KATSUURA MARINE PARK* Open 9:00 a.m. to 5:00 p.m. throughout the year, this park features an underwater observatory.

● *KAMOGAWA* The main tourist center on the east of Bōsō, this town has many hotels and inns, and is a good starting point for further sightseeing. Kamogawa Sea World is a large marine and leisure center with a collection of fish and marine animals from around the world.

● *NAMEGAWA ISLAND* This features a large amusement center set in a tropical park, with great sea views. It is famous for it's Flamingo Show.

● *TATEYAMA* This is the entrance to southern Bōsō. A fishing center and dairy farming area.

● *CHIKURA* This is known for its flowers — in December rape plants bloom, and stocks, marigolds and freesias color the town.

● *SHIRAHAMA* This town is famous for its beach, picturesque seascapes, and lighthouse. Spring comes early to this resort, and its flowers are at their best from January to February.

61

CHICHIBU & TAMA

Chichibu-Tama with its great National Park is very popular with Tokyoites. A mountainous area with lakes and typical Japanese forests, it is a great place for hiking and camping.

TRANSPORTATION

● *BY RAIL* Shinjuku to Takao, 50 min. on the JR Chūō Line Special Fast train; 45 min. on the Keiō Line Super Express (Sun. and hols. only). Shinjuku to Sagamiko, 60 min. on the JR Chūō Main Line. Shinjuku to Musashi-Itsukaichi (Akigawa Valley), 1 hr. 10 min. on the JR Chūō Main Line. Ikebukuro to Chichibu, 1 hr. 20 min. by Seibu Chichibu Line "Red Arrow Super Express". Ikebukuro to Yorii, 1 hr. 30 min. by Tōbu Tōjō Line Express. Yorii to Nagatoro, 20 min. by Chichibu Railway.

TOUR HINTS

An ideal trip to the area might include a stay at a rural

inn with mineral springs in Chichibu or at a private lodge in the mountains. For sightseeing, warm clothes and walking shoes are recommended.

WHAT TO SEE

● **MT. TAKAO** Covered with thick natural forest, this 600 m. high mountain is a popular place for viewing autumn foliage. It also features an interesting nature study trail. On the 2nd Sunday of March, the *Hiwatari* (Fire Walking) Festival is held here. A priest and his followers walk barefoot over hot coals while praying for domestic peace, traffic safety and long life.

● **LAKE SAGAMI** This is an artificial lake on the Sagami River and is 11 km. in circumference. There are a lot of excursion boats here, and nearby are a Nature Park and Sagamiko Picnic Land.

● **SUMMER LAND** This large leisure center has 10 swimming pools including a heated wave pool. There is also an amusement park. 30min. by bus from Hachiōji.

● **AKIGAWA VALLEY** This scenic valley lies along the Akigawa River, a large tributary of the Tama River. It features unusual limestone formations and is popular for trout fishing.

● **NAGATORO** This is noted for its scenery, including sheer rock faces and unusually shaped rocks. Near the river are stone "pavements" —a famous formation caused by movements in the earth's crust and subsequent erosion. The cherry blossoms in spring and the azaleas in summer are particularly beautiful here.

● **CHICHIBU** Though close to Tokyo, Chichibu has all the atmosphere of a rural town. Its main attractions are the mineral springs along the river and the shrine with its large old trees. The Dec. 3 Night Festival here is well known in Japan for the procession of floats bedecked with lanterns and carts with decorative carvings. On festival day, the town brims with over 200,000 excited spectators.

62

Hatonosu Valley in Okutama

東　北

TOHOKU

Six prefectures make up Tōhoku, the northeastern part of Honshū, the main island. The district is an exceptional tourist attraction with its National Parks, mountains, lakes, peaceful farming valleys and numerous hot springs. It is rich in historic sites, and visitors are attracted to the district's annual festivals and abundant ski fields. Tōhoku's cities offer all modern amenities, but the region is better known for its age-old folk crafts and traditions.

TRANSPORTATION

● **BY AIR** From Tokyo's Haneda Airport, there are direct flights to Tōhoku's 4 airports. ✳ Haneda to Aomori: I hr. 50 min.; Misawa: I hr. I5 min.; Yamagata: 50 min.

● **BY RAIL** Sightseeing spots can be reached by branching off at the nearest station on the Tōhoku Shinkansen. ✳ Ueno to Kōriyama: I hr. 20 min.; Fukushima: I hr. 40 min.; Sendai: 2 hrs.; Morioka: 3 hrs. 20 min.; Shin-Hanamaki: 3 hrs. I0 min. by JR Yamabiko Shinkansen bullet train. ✳ Sendai to Yamagata, I hr. I5 min. by Rapid Train.

TOUR HINTS

Tōhoku has numerous places of interest, so a visit might include several areas from within the region. By starting and finishing at the cities with stations on the Shinkansen Line, you can use route buses connecting the cities. The tour season begins at the end of April, and the peak days are August 2 to 8 when the "Four Big Tōhoku Festivals" are held.

63

FUKUSHIMA & YAMAGATA

These prefectures form the south and central parts of Tōhoku. The entrance is usually Kōriyama station on the Shinkansen Line. Near here is **Aizu-Wakamatsu**, an Edo era castle town. Entering from Shiroishi Station in Miyagi

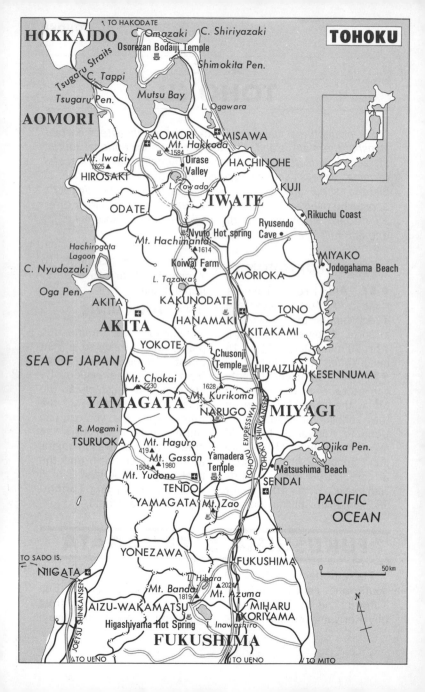

Prefecture, you are close to Mt. Zaō with its ski slopes and quiet hot springs.

FUKUSHIMA

WHAT TO SEE

● **KORIYAMA** The center of Fukushima. The Bandai-Atami hot springs resort area, with its many modern inns, is located nearby.

● **LAKE INAWASHIRO** 50 min. by bus from Kōriyama this, the 4th largest in Japan, lies at the foot of Mt. Bandai. There are 2 museums on the northern shore: Noguchi Hideyo Memorial Museum dedicated to the famed medical scholar, and Aizu Minzoku-kan, a folklore museum displaying items used by the local people in the feudal era.

● **AIZU-WAKAMATSU** This 700 year old castle town thrives as the political, cultural and commercial center of the district. The city's feudal past shows in its narrow winding streets, historical relics and mud-walled storehouses. I hr. by train from Kōriyama.

Tsurugajō Castle — A replica of this impressive castle was built on the original site and now serves as a museum. Other historic places include the beautiful traditional garden Oyakuen, and

Aizu Minzokukan Museum

Aizu Buke-yashiki, a large complex of reconstructed *samurai* houses and museums. The Aizu Sake Brewing History Museum and Sake Brewing Museum, where *sake* can be sampled, are excellent places to visit. Higashiyama Spa, 20 min. by bus from Aizu-Wakamatsu, is a modern, yet quaint hot spring resort.

● **KITAKATA** This town, features over 2,000 mud-walled storehouses. Originally used to store food and *sake,* they have also been used as living quarters, inns, and even as temples. 20 min. by train from Aizu-Wakamatsu.

● **BANDAI-KOGEN PLATEAU** A very popular mountain resort with beautiful lakes and ponds created by the eruption of Mt. Bandai in 1888. 35 min. by bus from Lake Inawashiro. Lake Hibara is one of Bandai's many lakes with a jagged shoreline and numerous

65

islets, it is a pretty place. Featuring many campgrounds and bungalows. **Goshi-kinuma** is named for its multitude of ponds, each with a slightly different hue.

Mt. Azuma This area is known for its hot spring resorts, most of which are in quiet surroundings with a few pleasant inns.

WHAT TO BUY

Tsuchiyu Hot Springs is famous for its traditional *Kokeshi* dolls. **Miharu dolls** have been produced since the Edo period and have a characteristic realistic shape. **Miharugoma dolls** (horse dolls), are produced in Miharu. **Aizunuri** (lacquerware) features delicate paintings in gold on a black or red background. Other Tōhoku specialties include **Aizu cotton**, **Akabeko dolls** (red papiermache cows), **decorated candles**, and **bamboo ware**. Most of these items are available at the department store in Fukushima Station.

YAMAGATA

WHAT TO SEE

● *ZAO QUASI-NATIONAL PARK*
Includes Mt. Zaō, reached by either road or ropeway from Zaō Spa. 45 min. by bus from Yamagata Station. The park offers skiing, hot springs and splendid mountain scenery, especially beautiful in autumn. Zaō's symbol is the silver thaw—trees coated with snow and ice which look like snow monsters.

● *THREE MOUNTAINS OF DEWA*
Part of the Bandai-Asahi National park, **Mt. Haguro**, **Mt. Gassan**, and **Mt. Yudono** are lofty peaks popular with skiers. As sacred mountains, they are worshipped by *Yamabushi* mountain ascetics.

● *MOGAMI RIVER* This river runs through Yamagata prefecture, irrigating the rice fields of the Shōnai plain. Boats operate year-round on the river from the dock near Furukuchi Station 1 hr. 40 min. by Express train from Yamagata Station, giving an opportunity to see the scenic Mogami Valley with its spectacular snowy winter landscapes.

WHAT TO EAT

Yonezawa beef has long been a favorite of the region, and is also eaten raw with soy sauce and ginger. Yamagata specialties include **soba** (noodles), **carp dishes**, and **pickles**. Yamagata is known as the home of **cherries**.

WHAT TO BUY

Well-known Yamagata products include **kokeshi dolls** and *Shōgi,* **chess sets** from Tendō, and **handicrafts** from Yonezawa.

Visitors can see chess pieces being made in craft shops in Tendō city. They are particularly popular as good-luck charms. Yonezawa handicrafts include **Sasano ittōbori** (dolls carved from wooden sticks), **Yonezawa textiles**, **Benihana dyed textiles**, and clay **Sagara dolls**.

MIYAGI & IWATE

Situated in the east of Tōhoku, these two prefectures offer a variety of sightseeing areas including Matsushima, the beautiful Rias Coast, and numerous hot spring resorts in the Ou mountains. The area is easily reached by Tōhoku Shinkansen.

MIYAGI

WHAT TO SEE

● *SENDAI* This is the economic and political center of Tōhoku. In the nearby mountains are the **Akiu Hot Springs** and **Sakunami Hot Springs**. From August 6 to 8 the city is crowded for the bright, colorful spectacle of the **Tanabata (Star) Festival**. **Aoba Castle** commands a magnificent view of the Pacific Ocean. **Zuihōden Hall** is an ornate mausoleum of the *Date* clan.

● *MATSUSHIMA* Hundreds of pine-clad islands are dotted in Matsushima Bay. This idyllic spot is one of Japan's **Scenic Trio** along with Miyajima near Hiroshima and Amanohashidate in the San-in District. Regular sightseeing boats are available. 40 min. by train from Sendai.

● *NARUGO SPA* 45 min. by JR express train from Furukawa Station, this old hot springs town is also known as the home of *kokeshi* doll craftsmen.

● *OJIKA PENINSULA* Jutting

67

Matsushima Islands

out into the Pacific east of Ishinomaki Bay, the forests and coastline of this peninsula are very scenic. Many islands are dotted around the peninsula and off the southern tip is the thickly wooded **Kinkazan Island**, home to monkeys and deer.

WHAT TO EAT

Fresh seafood is abundantly available. April to October is the season for eating the famed **Matsushima oysters** straight from the shell, and year round pickled oysters are available. Try **Sasa Kamaboko** which are bamboo leaf fish cakes (fish paste spread on a cedar spit and steamed).

WHAT TO BUY

Miyagi handicrafts include Sendai dressers, **Sendai-hira** (high quality fabrics), **Umoregi** woodcrafts, **Narugo Kokeshi** dolls, and **Narugo-nuri** lacquerware.

Narugo Kokeshi Dolls

IWATE

WHAT TO SEE

● **MORIOKA** The capital of Iwate prefecture is an old castle city featuring the **Hachimantai Plateau**, **Rikuchū Coast**, **Lake Towada** and **Lake Tazawa**. On June 15, about 90 brilliantly decorated draught horses known as **Chagu Chagu Umako** are paraded through the city.

● *HANAMAKI* This is the home town of the noted literary figure *Kenji Miyazawa*. It is the gateway for railway lines leading to the Rikuchū coast. 10 min. by train from Shin-Hanamaki Station.

● *TONO* This peaceful farming village was made famous by the book of folk tales "Tōno Monogatari" (Legends of Tōno). 50 min. by train from Shin-Hanamaki Station.

● *CHUSONJI TEMPLE* 25 min. by bus from Ichinoseki Station via Hiraizumi Station. Set in thick woods on the side of a mountain, this large temple is well known for its National Treasure, **Konjikidō Hall**—a glittering mausoleum covered in gold leaf.

● *KOIWAI FARM* The largest private dairy farm in Japan. 30 min. by train and bus from Morioka.

● *HACHIMANTAI PLATEAU* Situated among volcanic mountains ranging over the Iwate-Akita border, this area is a paradise for nature and hot spring lovers and for skiers in winter. I hr. 45 min. by train from Morioka.

● *RIKUCHU COAST* This uniquely beautiful Rias coastline extends 200 km. north to south. Its northern half features overhanging cliffs, while the southern half is a submerged coast with headlands, fiords and small quiet bays.

WHAT TO EAT

Along the Rikuchū Coast you can enjoy oysters, scallops, salmon, sea squirts and sea urchins.

A delightful novelty in Morioka is **Wanko soba**. I or 2 mouthfuls of noodles are placed in your bowl at a time and after you slurp them down, the server, with rhythmical shouts, replaces them with more — until you reach your limit.

WHAT TO BUY

Morioka's specialty is **Nambu tekki** (ironware), and its kettles are widely known. In the city of Hanamaki, you can find **Kimbeko** — figures of cows coated with gold dust.

AKITA & AOMORI

69

Rich in mountains, lakes, and forests, Akita and Aomori have their own distinctive cuisine, traditions, accents and songs. The region can be reached via the Tōhoku Shinkansen Line, transferring to Limited Express at Morioka.

AKITA

WHAT TO SEE

● *AKITA* The prefectural capital thrived as the main castle town of the *Satake* clan for 2 centuries until the Meiji Restoration in 1868. Akita's products include textiles, silver and gold ware, rice and cherries.

Senshū Park marks the site of the now ruined *Kubota* Castle. The park is known for its cherry blossoms and azaleas and for the spectacular **Kantō Festival** when young men try their hand at balancing long bamboo poles hung with up to 50 paper lanterns. **Hirano Masakichi Art Museum** in Senshū Park has a fine collection of paintings by *Tsuguji Fujita.*

● **OGA PENINSULA** I hr. 10 min. by train from Akita and transfer to buses to get around. Jutting out 20 km. into the Sea of Japan, this peninsula offers outstanding natural beauty. The sheer cliffs with their caves and grottos, can be seen by cruise boat.

On New Year's Eve, the Namahage Festival is held. In this unique event groups dressed as ogres roam from house to house, shouting gruff reprimands to sluggards but are nonetheless received courteously.

Oga Spa, on the northern side of the peninsula, serves as a base for sightseeing in the area and offers a variety of overnight accomodation. I hr. by bus from Oga.

● *HACHIMANTAI PLATEAU* Typical traditional back-country resorts, Fukenoyu Spa and Goshogake Spa are well known for their "Ondoru" or Korean-style steam baths and steam boxes.

Lake Tazawa, the deepest lake in Japan, has transparent blue water and is a popular resort for leisurely vacations.

● *KAKUNODATE* This is a pretty castle town with many 350-year old *samurai* and merchant houses still intact. I hr. by train from Morioka.

● *YOKOTE* Another old castle town with a morning market.

One day every year during Yokote's snowy winter, *Kamakura* (igloo-like snow shelters) are built by the city's children. I hr. by train from Akita Station.

WHAT TO EAT

An Akita specialty: new rice, steamed and mashed, is pasted on cedar spits and grilled over a charcoal fire. **Kiritampo** are these same rice dumplings boiled with chicken and vegetables. **Shottsuru** is vegetables and pickled fish stewed in a special sauce. Akita is famous for its rice, and from great rice comes some of Japan's finest *sake.* For something entirely different, when in Kakunodate try **Iburizuke** — smoked and pickled radish!

WHAT TO BUY

Osugi-warabe are dolls made of Akita cedar, with the 3-cornered straw hats characteristic of the Akita region. **Mage Wappa**, thin strips of cedar, are shaped into a variety of receptacles. Kakunodate is the best place for **Kabazaiku** — cherry bark crafts.

Kiritampo

AOMORI

WHAT TO SEE

● **AOMORI** The prefectural capital is nationally famous for its apples and the summer Nebuta Festival. Munakata Shikō Memorial Art Museum displays woodblock prints and wall paintings by this renowned Aomori artist.

● **HIROSAKI** This is an old castle town which has preserved much of its traditional appearance and atmosphere. There are many old houses and stores along its narrow winding streets and several large temples. A Neputa festival is held in the city from Aug. 1 to 7. Hirosaki Castle Park contains various cultural and sports facilities as well as the castle. Iwakisan Shrine is known for its annual event called *"Oyama sankei"*. People with lighted torches climb the mountain throughout the night to watch the sunrise from the shrine at the summit. 30 min. by train from Aomori.

● **HAKKODA MOUNTAINS** These are a series of peaks rising to the south of Aomori city. They are a natural wonderland with lakes, marshy plains and hot spring resorts. Sukayu Spa, a unique hot spring resort with only one inn, features mixed bathing pools that can accomodate 1,000 people. There is a bus route from Aomori to Lake Towada via Hakkōda Mountain, but it is closed during winter. Oirase River flows north from the eastern shore of Lake Towada through a thickly wooded valley. Though the beauty of this natural treasure with its waterfalls, rapids, rocks and lush greenery can be partly enjoyed from a bus window, it is best appreciated on foot. The most popular stage of a 14 km. riverside trail is the 2.5 hr. hike from Ishigedo to Nenokuchi. 2 hrs. 35 min. by bus from Aomori.

● **LAKE TOWADA** This beautiful crater lake, is especially pretty in autumn when the surrounding mountains are ablaze with reds and golds. Sightseeing boats operate

71

between mid-Apr. and early Nov.

● **SHIMOKITA PENINSULA** Mt. Osorezan on the peninsula is famous for the blind women who act as mediums for the dead.

● **TSUGARU PENINSULA** From the peninsula, the Seikan Tunnel, the world's longest undersea tunnel, connects Honshū with Hokkaido.

WHAT TO EAT

Himemasu are the delicious small trout from Lake Towada, eaten raw or baked with salt. There is a large market for apples in front of Aomori Station, and the best season is Oct. to Dec. Among the plentiful seafood available, squid from the Tsugaru Straits and Mutsu Bay scallops are especially popular. Tsugaru is rich in folk music, and the sound of the shamisen can be enjoyed.

WHAT TO BUY

In Hirosaki you can find Tsugaru-nuri, a glossy, multi-coated lacquerware and Kogin-zashi, hemp cloth stitched with cotton thread. Also popular are Hatobue, dove-shaped whistles and Takoe kites colorfully decorated with sketches of Japanese warriors.

FOUR BIG TOHOKU FESTIVALS

● **AUG. 2-7 : AOMORI NEBUTA FESTIVAL** Large floats covered with figures of soldiers are pulled through the city while hundreds of dancers shout in unison.

● **AUG. 5-7 : AKITA KANTO FESTIVAL** Paper lanterns are tied to rungs at the top of 10 m..bamboo poles with 9 cross-poles. Colorfully dressed youngsters try their hand at balancing them on their foreheads, shoulders and hands. At night, the festival scene is flooded with light.

● **AUG 6-8 : SENDAI TANABATA FESTIVAL** A colorful 700-year-old parade includes streamers, poles decorated with strips of paper, paper cranes and intricate paper designs.

● **AUG 6-8 : YAMAGATA HANAGASA FESTIVAL** The highlight is the 7—9:00 p.m. parade. Large, enthusiastic groups wearing traditional *yukata* and carrying flower-adorned hats stream through the city, shouting "*Ha-Yassho-Makasho!*", led by a sumptuously decorated festival float.

北海道

HOKKAIDO

The northernmost island of Japan, Hokkaido is similar in latitude to the state of South Dakota in the U.S. and the south of France. Renowned for its wide open spaces and great natural beauty, its unrivaled landscape abounds with vast forests, lush gardens of sub-arctic flora, marshlands stocked with numerous species of birds and other wildlife, lakes of crystal-clear water and hot springs.

TRANSPORTATION

● *BY AIR* Tokyo to Hakodate: I hr. 15 min.; Sapporo: I hr. 25 min.; Asahikawa, Obihiro or Kushiro: I hr. 35 min.; and Memambetsu: 2 hrs. 50 min.

● *BY RAIL* Tokyo to Sapporo: 16 hrs. by JR express service with undersea tunnel link between Aomori and Hakodate (Seikan-Tunnel). 11 hrs. by the Tōhoku Shinkansen and express train via Morioka.

● *GETTING AROUND* Extensive rail and bus services, plus air links between major cities. Also, ferry services to islands and peninsulas. Self-drive is a popular alternative.

TOUR HINTS

For a complete tour, leave yourself about I week for each of Hokkaido's 3 main districts, *Dōnan* (south), *Dōto* (east) and *Dōhoku* (north). However, using Hakodate, Sapporo and Kushiro as bases, it's possible to take in the major points of interest around Tōya, Shikotsu, Sōunkyō and Akan. The best time to travel is from the beginning of May to September, as it has no rainy season and is less humid than other parts of Japan. In the winter, the Sapporo Snow Festival is a must.

73

SAPPORO

The rapidly developing capital city of Hokkaido, Sapporo is the focal point of the island's politics, economy and culture. Uniquely laid out with wide, tree-lined boulevards and huge parklands, Sapporo often serves as a gateway to other parts of the island.

WHAT TO SEE

● **ODORI PARK** Dividing the northern and southern parts of the city, this wide promenade, bordered with beautiful flowerbeds, is the venue for Sapporo's annual **Snow Festival**, during which Odōri boulevard is the home of some huge ice sculptures of people, famous buildings and mythological figures.

HOKKAIDO

Rebun Is. WAKKANAI — C. Soya
Wakkanai Airport
Rishiri Is.
Sarobetsu Natural Flower Garden
TOYOTOMI
HAMATOMBETSU
OTOINEPPU
Teuri Is.
Yagishiri Is.
OKOPPE
NAYORO
MOMBETSU
RUMOI
SHIBETSU
SEA OF JAPAN
FUKAGAWA
ASAHIKAWA
Sounkyo Gorge
C. Kamui
Ishikari Bay
Asahikawa Airport
2290 ▲ Mt. Daisetsu
Shakotan Pen.
OTARU
Okadama Airport
FURANO
Mt. Tokachidake ▲ 2077
SAPPORO
Jozankei Hot Spring
NISEKO
Nakayama Pass
HIDAKA
IKEDA
L. Toya
L. Shikotsu
Chitose Airport
OBIHIRO
Mt. Showa-Shinzan ▲ 407
Noboribetsu Hot Spring
Obihiro Airport
Okushiri Is.
Uchiura Bay
Oshima Pen.
Onuma Park
HIROO
Trappist Convent
Hakodate Airport
SAMANI
HAKODATE
C. Erimo
MATSUMAE
Tsugaru Straits

● **CLOCK TOWER** Mounted in the Russian-style Municipal Memorial Hall, this famous landmark reminds people of the old colonial days of 1881 when it was erected.

● **BOTANICAL GARDENS** These have sections of virgin forest and more than 6,000 species of plants from around the world, and also contain the University and the Ainu Museums.

● **TANUKI-KOJI STREET AND SUSUKINO** Running from east to west in the center of the city, Tanuki-kōji Street's more than 300 shops and restaurants are a hive of activity during the day. Susukino, on the other hand, comes to life at night with thousands of bars and cabarets.

● **MT. MOIWA** From the summit of this hill, which is an ideal place for hiking and skiing, there's a bird's-eye view of Sapporo and its surrounding districts. Accessible by ropeway and chairlift.

● **MARUYAMA PARK** This park lies 4 km. southeast of Sapporo Station and is filled with a great variety of trees of plum, cherry, pine and cedar. It also contains zoological gardens, a 400 m. athletic track, a baseball diamond and tennis courts.

● **HITSUJIGAOKA PLATEAU** 35 min. by bus from Sapporo Station. Lined with cottonwood trees, this peaceful meadow is the grazing ground for different breeds of livestock, mostly sheep (hitsuji). Here you can taste Mongolian-style barbecued

SEA OF OKHOTSK

C. Shiretoko

L.Saroma
L.Notoro   Shiretoko Pen.
ABASHIRI
    Koshimizu Natural   Kunashiri Is.
     Flower Garden
Memambetsu Airport
L. Kussharo
     L. Mashu
L. Akan
      Nakashibetsu
       Airport   Notsuke Pen.
                    C. Nosappu
Kushiro Marsh Fields NEMURO

Kushiro Airport

KUSHIRO

N

PACIFIC OCEAN

0   40   80km

mutton (Genghis Khan).

WHAT TO EAT

Sapporo is where you can enjoy many different dishes, especially seafood. Susukino and Tanuki-kōji street are the best places. Rāmen Yokochō, as its name suggests, is a narrow alley full of only Rāmen shops, serving typical Sapporo Rāmen, which is a little salty and rich with garlic and butter. Odōri Park is lined with stalls selling food such as boiled potatoes and corn-on-the-cob. You can have your fill of draught beer and Genghis Khan cooking in the Sapporo Beer Garden, or taste delicious ice cream at the parlor of one of Japan's most famous dairies, Yukijirushi.

WHAT TO BUY

The department stores in front of Sapporo Station offer the shopper anything from top Japanese designer fashion to products particular to Hokkaidō. Some splendid fashion boutiques can be found between Odōri and Tanuki-kōji Street are interspersed with much older, traditional shops. For marine products, visit the market at Nijō-Ichiba.

SAPPORO

TO OTARU — HAKODATE MAIN LINE — TO HOKKAIDO UNIV. — TO ASABU
0   200m   Keio Plaza Hotel
SAPPORO
Century Royal Hotel   Sapporo Terminal Bldg.
Sogo Dept. Store
TO CHITOSE & ASAHIKAWA
Washington Hotel II
Washington Hotel   Kokusai Hotel
Tokyu Hotel   SAPPORO   Tokyu Dept. Store
Botanical Gardens of Hokkaido Univ.
Hokkaido Pref. Government
Yukijirushi Parlor   Zenniku Hotel
Hotel New Otani
Old Hokkaido Government Bldg.
SUBWAY NAMBOKU LINE
Sapporo Beer Garden
City General Hospital   Grand Hotel   Hotel Rich
Clock Tower
City Hall   Chuo Bus Terminal
NISHI-JUICHOME   Odori Park   ODORI   Marui Imai Dept. Store   TV Tower   BUS CENTER MAE
TO KOTONI   SUBWAY TOZAI LINE   Hotel Alpha   Odori Bus Center   TO SHIN-SAPPORO
CHUO-KUYAKUSHOMAE   Mitsukoshi
STREET CAR   NISHI-SANCHOME   NISHI-YONCHOME   Dept. Store
Prince Hotel   Parco
Tanuki-Koji St.   Nijo Market
SUSUKINO
STREET CAR
SOSEISHOMAE   Tokyu Inn   SUSUKINO
TO NISHI-YONCHOME   TO MAKOMANAI

DONAN

Dōnan extends from Sapporo, south to the southern gateway of Hakodate, west to Cape Erimo, and as far north as the southern part of Mt. Daisetsu. More developed than other parts of Hokkaido, it still has many features of interest to the visitor, including lakes, hot springs and rugged coastline.

TRANSPORTATION

●**BY RAIL** Hakodate to Sapporo via Muroran or Otaru. 4 hrs. 10 min. by JR express.

●**BY BUS** Lake Tōya and Lake Shikotsu can be taken in by direct bus service from Sapporo. Buses also run to Shakotan Peninsula and Cape Erimo, depending on the weather conditions.

TOUR HINTS

For *Dōnan*, Hakodate, Sapporo, Lake Tōya, Noboribetsu and Jōzankei should be used as bases for their surrounding districts.

HAKODATE

WHAT TO SEE

● **HAKODATE** The southern gateway to Hokkaido, Hakodate is a thriving fishing port and has several tourist attractions. The early birds can take in the day's catch of seafood and local farm produce at the Asaichi (Morning Market).

Motomachi, the old port area of the city, is a very interesting place to stroll around. Still displaying remnants of the old harbor, this hilly part of Hakodate with its cobblestone streets has many relics of old European and American style houses and the Haristos Church. The summit of Mt. Hakodate, accessible by a 5 min. ropeway, commands a spectacular view of the port especially at night.

●**GORYOKAKU** A Dutch style fortress shaped like a five-pointed star, which was completed in 1857, this is now a park, and its tower affords a fine view of the modern port city.

●**TRAPPIST CONVENT** 50 min. by bus from Hakodate lies the

77

Haristos Church

Trappist Convent, curently the home of some 70 Trappistine nuns engaged, amongst other things, in livestock and dairy farming. Their butter and candy are famous throughout Japan.

● **YUNOKAWA SPA** A 30 min. streetcar ride from Hakodate Station, Yunokawa Spa is the oldest hot spring resort in Hokkaido.

● **ONUMA NATIONAL PARK** This is one of Hokkaido's best scenic spots and provides facilities for activities such as camping, hiking, boating, fishing, skiing and skating. An excursion boat takes visitors to the swamps and islands of the lakes, including Lake Onuma.

WHAT TO EAT

The Daimon district in front of the station is the best place to taste local dishes, including ika-sōmen, delicately sliced pieces of freshly caught raw squid. Butter and candies from the Trappist Convent can also be purchased here.

TOYA & NOBORIBETSU

WHAT TO SEE

● **JOZANKEI SPA** I hr. 5 min. by bus from Sapporo, this hot spring resort, with many love-ly hotels and surrounded by thickly wooded mountains, is famous for the seasonal colors of its foliage in summer and autumn.

● **LAKE TOYA** A sightseeing boat connects the four small islands on this beautiful lake and the lake shore. 2 hrs. by train from Hakodate.

● **LAKE SHIKOTSU** I hr. 20 min. by bus from Sapporo. Hidden away among soaring cliffs, this beautiful caldera lake of clear, blue water, which never freezes over in winter, is well stocked with trout. A 40 min. sightseeing cruise is available.

● **MT. SHOWA SHINZAN** As this is still a very active volcano (situated near Lake Tōya and formed between 1943 and 1945 by a series of earthquakes) be sure to check with local guides before attempting to climb it.

● **MURORAN** This is the industrial hub of Hokkaido. It is also a port with ferry links to Aomori on mainland.

Noboribetsu Spa, I5 min. by bus from Muroran. One of the largest hot spring resorts in Hokkaido, it boasts I I hot springs of various kinds, including sulphur, simple thermals and common-salt. The attractions include a Bear Ranch and the spouts of

Jigokudani (Hell Valley). Poroto Ainu Kotan, a former Ainu settlement, containing a museum and restored Ainu dwellings, is located in Shiraoi, 25 min by train from Noboribetsu. From **Nakayama Pass** you can get a good view of Mt. Yōtei, nicknamed Ezo Fuji because of its resemblance to Mt. Fuji.

● *CAPE ERIMO* Tomakomai to Samani: 2 hrs. 40 min by train. Samani to Cape Erimo: 1 hr. by bus. The steep cliffs of Cape Erimo, which runs south from Mt. Hidaka, are frequently battered by raging seas over which towers a lighthouse. The rocks below boast various types of colorful coral.

OTARU

WHAT TO SEE

● *OTARU* This is a lively port city with stone storehouses lining its canals and many other Meiji period buildings, giving it the flavor of an old harbor town. Herring fishing once thrived here, and the good old days before the herring disappeared are reflected by **the Nishin Goten Hall** (Herring Palace). In winter, Niseko mountain offers excellent skiing with good facilities. Apres-ski enjoyment can include a hot spring bath.

● *SHAKOTAN PENINSULA* This peninsula features spectacular views of the rugged shoreline, full of sea-eroded rocks and imposing cliffs. **Cape Shakotan** and **Kamui** on the peninsula's northern tip command great views of the Sea of Japan. Otaru to Cape Kamui: 1 hr. 50 min. by bus.

WHAT TO EAT

Otaru folk are proud of the freshest seafood for making *sushi*. **Sushiyoshi** and **Ebizushi** are recommended.

WHAT TO BUY

At the **Sankaku Ichiba Market** on the left side of Otaru Station, over 60 stalls sell everything from clothes to fresh fish. Try **Sujiko** (salmon eggs with soy sauce) or **baked fish** at the market's restaurants. Open from 4:00 a.m. to 8:00 p.m. and closed on Sundays. For souvenirs, seafood and glassware are very popular.

Otaru Canal

DOTO

The Chishima volcanic range forms a backbone to *Dōtō* (Eastern District), which is divided into 4 sub-districts: Tokachi, Kushiro, Nemuro, and Abashiri. The district is a major tourist attraction and is full of interesting changes of scenery, with volcanos, deep blue lakes, and primeval forests.

TRANSPORTATION

Areas such as Lake Akan, Lake Mashū and the Shiretoko peninsula are not served by rail lines, so the regular sightseeing buses and route buses are the most convenient when traveling around *Dōtō*.

TOUR HINTS

June to September is the best season for sightseeing in *Dōtō*, as the temperature is pleasant and wild flowers are in bloom. Recently, visits in winter to see the beautiful red-crested white cranes and Japanese cranes (called *Tanchō*)are becoming popular as well. The most popular course is one beginning in Asahikawa in Dōhoku (the Northern District). It includes Sōunkyō and takes in Abashiri, Lake Kussharo, Lake Mashū, Lake Akan and on to Kushiro.

ABASHIRI & AKAN

WHAT TO SEE

● *ABASHIRI* This is the largest city on the coast and is a thriving fishing and agricultural center. Abashiri Folklore Museum contains items covering the culture of the Orokko and Giriyark, two races who inhabited the Abashiri district. Moyoro Shell Mound is part of the remains of a village where some of the original inhabitants of the area once lived.

The Orochon fire festival is held here in July. A bus goes to an observation platform on Mt. Tento, which offers panoramic views over the mountains, lakes and sea.
● *KOSHIMIZU WILD FLOWER GARDEN* In a narrow strip between the sea and Lake Tōfutsu, this garden contains more than 50 varieties of flowers which bloom from spring to autumn. In winter, the sea here is covered with pack ice which eventually forms an icefield for as far the eye can see. Another attraction is the swans flying

overhead on their winter migration from Siberia to Lake Tōfutsu. 35 min. by bus from Abashiri.

● **LAKE KUSSHARO** is a large caldera lake with hot springs gushing up on the south and east shores. Kawayu Spa lies at the northern foot of Mt. Iō. Abashiri to Kawayu: I hr. 50 min. by train.

● **LAKE AKAN** This is well known for a rare, spherical green weed called marimo which has the ability to rise and fall in the water of its own accord. A I hr. 25 min. boat cruise includes *marimo* viewing. The Marimo Festival is held here in October. 2 hrs. 10 min. by bus from Kushiro.

● **LAKE MASHU** This beautiful lake features sapphire-blue water, transparent to a depth of 35.8 m. Since the lake is often shrouded in fog, it is regarded as being mysterious.

No outlet from the lake has ever been found, which adds to its eerie atmosphere. I hr. by bus from Kawayu Spa.

The Tokachi River meanders through fields around the quiet resort, Tokachigawa Hot Springs.

WHAT TO EAT

Abashiri is a fishing port and offers plentiful seafood with popular specialties like *Kegani* (crab) and sea-urchin. Tokachi Nabe, also known as Salmon Nabe, is a famous hot-pot dish from the Tokachi Hot Springs area.

Chunks of salmon, vegetables and *tōfu* are boiled in a soy sauce soup. Ask for it at traditional Japanese inns. Tokachi Rose is the local wine specialty. It is not available for sale, but can be tasted in various places. From mid-September to the end of October is the season for Akiaji (salmon), and stands are set up to cook and sell it in Chiyoda-entei bank and near Obihiro.

WHAT TO BUY

Nipopo dolls, carved by local prison inmates, are popular Abashiri souvenirs. At Lake Akan, Koropokkuru are wooden dolls representing a deity said to live under the

81

Lake Mashū

leaves of the *Fuki* bush.

SHIRETOKO & NEMURO

WHAT TO SEE

● *SHIRETOKO PENINSULA* 40 min. by train from Abashiri, this remote area of great natural beauty has a rich variety of alpine plants and birds, small lakes and forests. There is a picturesque walking trail around Shiretoko Five Lakes, and the peninsula offers many open-air hot spring baths. Sightseeing cruises provide an opportunity to see the coastline with its sheer cliffs and waterfalls.

● *NEMURO* 2 hrs. 20 min by train from Kushiro. Occupying all of the Nemuro Peninsula is this port and fishing city. Cape Nosappu, 45 min. by bus from Nemuro, features a large expanse of swampy ground carpeted with rare species of wild flowers which are a blaze of color in spring and summer. Lake Fūren 25 min. by bus from Nemuro, is known for the visits of swans, numbering up to 20,000, from Oct. to Mar. Nemuro-Shibetsu, 2 hrs. by train from Nemuro, is noted for Notsuke Peninsula (also called Odaitō), Japan's largest sand spit, 28 km. long. The central part of the peninsula

Sōunkyō Gorge

features a desolate area with Todowara — decayed pine trees. The bay of Notsuke, embraced by the peninsula, is famous for its clams and shrimp catch.

● *KUSHIRO* This is the center of northern fisheries and the only unfrozen trading port in Hokkaido. Not far from the city is a vast swampy region inhabited by the extremely rare Tanchōzuru or red-crested white cranes.

WHAT TO EAT

Fresh seafood, including lobsters, scallops, sea urchins and other shellfish is served. The crab market in front of Nemuro Station is a good spot to visit.

Teppō-jiru — crabmeat and vegetables boiled in *miso* (soy paste) is highly recommended. Large artificially-grown oysters are the treat in Akkeshi. In Kushiro, crab and salmon are popular, and a market in front of the station sells them cheaply.

DOHOKU

Dōhoku (the Northern District) incorporates the central district of Daisetsu and Sōunkyō, the areas facing the Sea of Japan and Sea of Okhotsk and the outlying northern islands. Spring arrives very late here, and for 6 months of the year the district suffers fierce arctic winds and heavy snowfalls.

TRANSPORTATION

Asahikawa is the entrance to the Daisetsu and Sōunkyō regions. The overnight train is often preferable to the daytime express for the long trip to Wakkanai, which is also reached by air from Sapporo. From Wakkanai, planes fly to Rishiri and Rebun, or the ferry from Wakkanai harbor is a pleasant alternative.

TOUR HINTS

"The end of Japan" aptly describes this district. Apart from Sōunkyō, a popular tourist center with good transport services and plentiful accomodation, the area is largely undeveloped, but has a raw, uncultivated beauty. Most of the area is accessible by local train lines. Small inns, pensions and youth hostels are available. Note that trains are infrequent and temperatures are low!

DAISETSU & SOUNKYO

WHAT TO SEE

● *ASAHIKAWA* Hokkaido's 2nd biggest city, this is the transport center of the region. Many historical sites associated with the Ainu are easily accessible from the city. At the start of February, the Ice Festival begins and snow and ice sculptures can be seen.

● *DAISETSUZAN NATIONAL PARK* The valleys here are fringed with well-appointed spas such as Tenninkyō, Shirogane, Shikaribetsu and Sōunkyō. Sōunkyō, 2 hrs. by bus from Asahikawa, is set in the center of a vast ravine with steep cliffs and waterfalls adding to the majestic scenery.

● *FURANO* On a fertile plain, the area is blanketed with blooming lavender in mid-June. Furano wine is the specialty here. Furano is also the starting point to sightsee parts of Daisetsuzan National Park. I hr. 20 min. by train from Asahikawa.

83

SOYA & REBUN

WHAT TO SEE

● **WAKKANAI** This city is the northernmost tourist spot in Japan, I hr. by air from Sapporo. The hill behind the city is Wakkanai Park which commands a view of the city and Cape Noshappu and Rishiri and Rebun Islands.

● **SAROBETSU GENSEI KAEN (WILD FLOWER GARDEN)** In the center of the Sarobetsu Plain, this garden contains many species of sub-artic flowers, blooming in June and July. Wakkanai to Toyotomi Spa, 50 min. by train. Then a 15 min. bus ride brings you to the Garden.

● **RISHIRI ISLAND** This is home to seabirds and also features the conical Mt. Rishiri. An island tour bus is available.

● **REBUN ISLAND** This island has abundant alpine flora on its gentle slopes. Rishiri and Rebun can be reached in 20 min. by air from Wakkanai.

WHAT TO EAT

In Wakkanai seafood is plentiful and restaurants serve crabs *(Kegani and Tarabagani)*, shrimp, sea urchin, salmon and raw salmon eggs. In front of the station you will find Kanimeshi (rice with crabs), and Uni-don (rice with sea urchin). Rishiri also has abundant fresh seafood and vegetables.

Sea urchins are the specialty here, in July and August. Hot-pots such as Dobin-mushi (boiled sea urchin) and Uni-don are popular, along with soups like Hama-nabe (seafood), and Sampei-jiru. Rishiri kombu (a variety of seaweed) is a popular souvenir. In Rebun, seafood such as codfish, Uni-don, Hama-nabe and Mizutaki (boiled sea slugs) are popular, along with raw Soi fish dishes and Namanori Soba-noodles with raw seaweed.

WHAT TO BUY

In Rishiri and Rebun, tinned smoked sea urchin and Rishiri kombu (seaweed) make good souvenirs.

Cape Sōya : The Northernmost

中　部

CHUBU

In this book "Chūbu" refers to the central part of Japan, excluding the Tōkai region which is dealt with in the next section. In the Chubu area, there are many attractions for visitors, including alpine scenery, spas, towns of historical interest, and a wide variety in its excellent local cuisine.

NIIGATA & SADO

This region is directly accessible from Tokyo by both the Jōetsu Shinkansen and the Kan-etsu Highway. Its beauty ranges from the high, snowcapped mountains around the port of Niigata to the folklore of the island of Sado. Seafood abounds in this part of the country.

TRANSPORTATION

● **BY AIR** Infrequent flights from places such as Osaka, Fukuoka and Sapporo land at both Niigata and Sado airports.

● **BY RAIL** Ueno to Niigata: 2 hrs. 10 min. by Jōetsu Shinkansen.

● **BY JETFOIL** Niigata to Ryōtsu in Sado: 1 hr.

In both Niigata and Sado there are scheduled bus routes plus sightseeing coaches. Also, in Sado you can hire bicycles for traveling within small areas, but only the very adventurous should consider cycling all around the hilly terrain of this H shaped large island.

TOUR HINTS

The port city of Niigata is the gateway to Sado island. Tulips are one of the prefecture's symbols and are at their best from the end of April through May. For eating out, winter is the best season, especially for food from the northern parts of the country.

Sado island's peak sightseeing time is July and August, when many festivals, such as *Bon-odori*, take place. You can also enjoy the pleasures of swimming and fishing in Sado's beautiful waters, or indulge in some other amusements of local character.

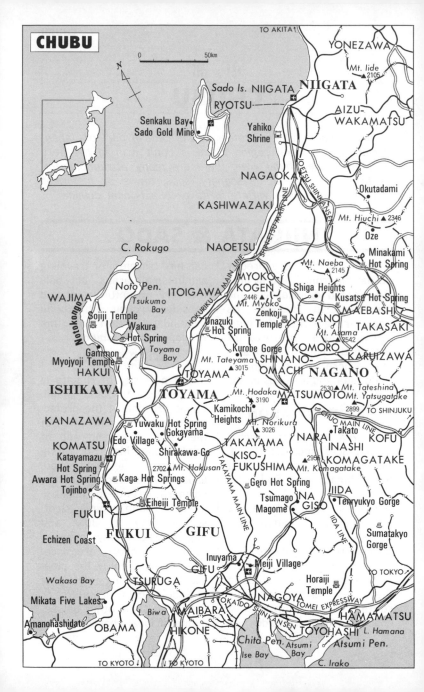

NIIGATA

WHAT TO SEE

● **NIIGATA DUNES** To the north of Niigata city, these run for 2.6 km along the Japan Sea between Kaihin and Hiyoriyama Parks. Nearby are an aquarium and the Japan Sea Tower. 20 min. by bus from Niigata Station.

● **LANDOWNERS' RESIDENCES IN ECHIGO** This area is filled with the residences of some wealthy landowners. Their houses and gardens exemplify the beauty of Japanese architectural and landscaping styles.

WHAT TO EAT

Both Niigata and Sado are blessed with an abundance of seafood and, because of the high quality of the local rice, excellent sake. Try some Wappa-meshi (flavored rice with seasonal fish served in cedarwood bowls).

SADO

WHAT TO SEE

● **RYOTSU** As it is the main port of Sado, it has many places to stay and lots of souvenir shops. Between spring and autumn, visitors can see Sado-okesa, a festi-

Sado-Okesa Dance

val of local ballads and dancers wearing tall bamboo hats. Also, **Ondeko** can be seen at the *Okesa* Hall.

● **SADO GOLD MINE** The small fishing village of Aikawa was the scene of a gold rush in the early 17th century. Today many reminders of that time still remain. In Sōdayū-kō, the largest of the mine shafts in the area, the severe working conditions of the trade are reproduced by mechanical displays. Take a taxi at Aikawa, 1 hr. 10 min. by bus from Ryōtsu.

● **SENKAKU BAY** This part of the island boasts the beautiful coastal scenery of **Soto-kaifu**, with 2 km. of steep cliffs and bluffs. Age-jima, which can be reached by boat from Tassha, affords the best views along its quiet paths.

87

SHINSHU

Shinshū is the name of the mountainous inland region of Chūbu. It consists mainly of Nagano Prefecture, which is a very popular area for hiking in summer and skiing in winter. Many charming, western-style boarding houses named "pension" are scattered around here, catering mainly for the thousands of students who come here on summer camps.

TRANSPORTATION

The best way of getting to Shinshū is by train. The major railway lines are the Chūō Main Line from Shinjuku or Nagoya, and the Shin-etsu Main Line from Ueno, with special trains added during the peak season.

● **BY AIR** Osaka to Matsumoto: 1 hr. 10 min.

● **BY RAIL** * Shinjuku to Matsumoto: 3 hrs. on the Limited Express "Azusa"; * Ueno to Karuizawa: 2 hrs. ; to Nagano: 3 hrs.; to Myōkō-kōgen: 3 hrs. 40 min. on the Limited Express "Asama".

* Nagoya to Kisofukushima: 1 hr. 35 min.; to Matsumoto: 2 hrs. 20 min.; to Nagano: 3 hrs. 10 min. on the Limited Express "Shinano".

Local buses run from train stations within the area, but schedules are seasonal.

TOUR HINTS

Your itinerary and activities will, of course, depend on the season you choose to visit Shinshū. In summer you can enjoy many sports and leisure activities, including a trip along the old Kisoji Road. If you want· to take in some great views of the Northern Alps you should go to Kami-kōchi, Mt. Hakuba or take the Tateyama-kurobe Alpine Route. In winter there are countless ski resorts with spas and accomodation to suit both taste and budget.

NAGANO, MATSUMOTO & SHIGA

WHAT TO SEE

● **NAGANO** The capital of Nagano Prefecture, this city is noted for **Zenkōji Temple**, which was built originally in 642 and reconstructed in 1707. The temple houses 3 Buddhist statues, including *Amida* (Amitahba) *Nyorai*. The main statue is exhibited to the public every 7 years, the next such year being 1991.

● **SHIGA-HEIGHTS** This beautiful hot spring resort situated in the mountains attracts thousands of holidaymakers all year round. In summer it serves as a cool retreat from the oppressive heat of the cities, while in winter it becomes one of Japan's most popular ski resorts.

● **MATSUMOTO** This is the second largest city in Nagano Prefecture and serves as a major transportation link between Shinshū and other areas. With **Matsumoto Castle** as its focal point, the city has many reminders of old feudal Japan, including the **Japan Folk Customs Museum**, the former **Kaichi School**, the **Japan Ukiyo-e Museum**, the **Matsumoto Folk Crafts Museum** and many other buildings. For those staying overnight in Matsumoto, **Asama Spa** is highly recommended.

WHAT TO EAT

The speciality of the Shinshū region is **Soba** (buckwheat noodles). It is produced mainly in the Togakushi Heights, Norikura Heights and Matsumoto Basin areas. Delicious handmade Shinshū *Soba* is usually eaten cold in a soup with a soy sauce base.

KARUIZAWA

WHAT TO SEE

● **KARUIZAWA** Situated 1,000 m. above sea level, the city enjoys cool, dry summers, and is one of Japan's most fashionable inland holiday resorts. Regarded as a place where the wealthy relax in the summer time, Karuizawa has many private holiday villas in beautifully tranquil surroundings.

Karuizawa Ginza and Kyū-Karuizawa also abound with fashionable boutiques and restaurants, which are familiar names in Tokyo and Osaka, and these are normally bustling with hundreds of young people.

● **KARUIZAWA ICE-SKATING CENTER** As well as ice-skating, one of the major attractions of this center is the Ice Festival, featuring 40 or so ice sculptures, including locomotives, buildings and other figures familiar to Japan. The festival runs for one week, beginning on the last Saturday in January.

89

Karuizawa

● *SHIRAITO FALLS* 3 m. tall and 70 m. wide, these are really a beautiful sight in spring when the surrounding trees are in full bud and in autumn when they have changed their hue. The clear waters fall like silver threads. 30 min. by taxi from Karuizawa.

● *MT. ASAMA* Still an active volcano, this magnificent mountain adds to the great natural beauty of the whole area. Its billowing fumes can be seen on the train ride between Karuizawa and Komoro on the Shin-etsu Main Line.

● *ONI OSHIDASHI* During the great eruption of Mt. Asama, huge masses of black lava flowed down the northern side of the mountain covering an area 3 km. from east to west and 12 km. from north to south. 1 hr. by bus from Karuizawa.

● *KOMORO KAIKOEN PARK* Built in the ruins of the old Komoro Castle dungeons, this vast park covers most of the grounds of the former castle and its surrounding mountains and valleys.

Ruins of the third gate and the castle tower as well as other points of interest still remain. 25 min. by JR from Karuizawa.

WHERE TO STAY

Karuizawa boasts lots of hotels and inns that are noted for their tradition and for their architectural design. Some even constitute worthy sightseeing spots in themselves. **Mampei Hotel** (Kyū-Karuizawa) opened in 1894 as a western-style hotel for foreigners. Its magnificent wooden main building contains many pieces of stained glass and antique furniture.

Hotel Kajima-no-mori (Kajima-no-mori) is a very attractive hotel with a lot of tradition.

Karuizawa Prince Hotel (south of Karuizawa Station), the largest modern hotel in Karuizawa, has 416 chalets scattered throughout its surrounding forest.

Tsuruya Ryokan (Kyū-Karuizawa) Providing first-class service and traditional Japanese cooking, many long-term guests stay at this *ryokan*. **Oiwake Aburaya Ryokan** (Oiwake-juku) was once the official *ryokan* for the *Daimyō* of the Edo period.

KISO & INA

WHAT TO SEE

● *KISOJI ROAD* Containing many old properties of the

Edo Period which have been carefully restored and maintained, the main attractions of this area are Magome and Tsumago with its old latticework buildings.

Magome is the birthplace of the great novelist *Tōson Shimazaki*. Some of the buildings which have connections with him still remain and are popular with visitors. 40 min. by bus from Nagiso Station.

Tsumago was designated as an area to protect buildings. Nowadays, many of the area's old houses have been turned into family boarding houses and souvenir shops. Walk the 7.4 km nature trail from Magome or take the 10 min. bus from Nagiso.

Narai, which is similar to Tsumago, many of the old houses and shops in the area have also been designated as protected buildings. Known as "Narai of the Thousand Inns", it was one of the old post towns of 300 years ago. Several buildings of traditional architectural style, including the former home of *Nakamura* (famous for his lacquerware combs), are open to the public. 40 min. by JR from Matsumoto.

● **TAKATO** Formerly a castle town, this was once the center of the Ina Valley area until the Meiji Restlation. Its history and traditions go back 700 years. This city is a main attraction of old Inaji Road. Nowadays, it is a quiet town, the streets of which boast many buildings of a bygone era. The former Kasuga Castle site is famous for its 1300 cherry trees. 20 min. by bus from Inashi Station

● **TENRYU-KYO GORGE** To be recommended here is the 20 km. boat trip along the river.

The highlight of the trip comes after Suizinbashi Bridge, when the boat takes you past steep cliffs, down fast flowing rapids into the Garyū-kyō Gorge. The best scenery is in Tenryū-kyō Gorge, where the green waters of the river curve gently around imposing, rugged rocks of dark granite. A shorter boat trip of 12 km. runs from Tenryū-kyō to the lower reaches of Karakasa.

The main attraction is the variety of fish caught, cooked and served along the way by the boatman. 3 hrs. 40 min. by JR from Toyohashi to Ichida.

91

Ryokan at Narai

HOKURIKU

With a blend of beautiful scenery, culture and history, the Hokuriku district, which stretches from the Japanese Alps to the Japan Sea, offers visitors a wide range of activities including fishing, hiking, camping and skiing.

TRANSPORTATION

● **BY AIR** Tokyo to Komatsu: I hr.; to Toyama: I hr.

● **BY RAIL** * Western Hokuriku from Kanazawa: by Tōkaidō Shinkansen, Tokyo to Maibara: 3 hrs. 30 min.; and from Maibara on the Limited Express "Kaetsu" and "Shirasagi" to Tsuruga: 30 min.; to Kanazawa: 2 hrs.

* Eastern Hokuriku from Kanazawa: by Jōetsu Shinkansen, Ueno to Nagaoka: I hr. 40 min.; and from Nagaoka on the Limited Express "Raichō", "Hokuetsu" and "Shiratori" to Toyama: 2 hrs. 20 min.

* For Takayama, take the Tōkaidō Shinkansen to Nagoya and change to the Limited Express "Hida"; Nagoya to Takayama: 3 hrs.

Most overnight express and Limited Express trains provide for sleepers. In Hokuriku, use the Hokuriku Main Line and local lines. In Kanazawa,

Noto and along the Echizen coast, buses are convenient.

TOUR HINTS

Hokuriku is noted for its rather inclement weather and frequent heavy snow falls. However, Noto and the Echizen coast receive much less snow than other parts of the district due to the warm Tsushima currents. Modern inns with excellent facilities can be found at the spas of the region, such as Kaga Hot Springs. Along the Echizen coast and at Wakasa, private boarding houses are very good.

KANAZAWA

Often referred to as "Little Kyoto" because of the atmosphere of its twisting, narrow streets, the castle town of Kanazawa is famous for its potteries, dyed fabrics, cooking and folk ballads.

WHAT TO SEE

● **KANAZAWA CASTLE** Built in 1592 by the *Maeda* clan, most of the castle's structures have since been destroyed. Today only the *Ishikawamon* Gate and one *samurai* house remain intact.

● *KENROKUEN GARDEN*

Adjoining the grounds of Kanazawa Castle, this spacious garden provides a nice place for a stroll in its hills and around its ponds. In winter the trees here are protected from heavy snowfalls by ropes called *Yuki-tsuri*. 10 min. by bus from Kanazawa Station.

● *SEISONKAKU*

Built by *Nariyasu Maeda* to house his mother in her old age, this fine building deserves a visit. Its many elegant rooms include an audience room with magnificent transoms and the majestic "Blue Room". Situated in the Kenrokuen.

● *MYORYUJI TEMPLE (NINJA-DERA)*

This temple was built in 1643 also by the *Maeda* clan. By all outward appearances, it would seem to be only a 2-story building, but in fact its clever design belies its 4 storys, which contain 23 rooms and 29 steps. Throughout the temple, there are hidden devices thought to have been used by *Ninja,* secret agents and masters of disguise in the feudal days. 10 min. by bus from Kanazawa Station.

● *OLD SAMURAI RESIDENCES*

Many old *samurai* residences and storehouses still remain

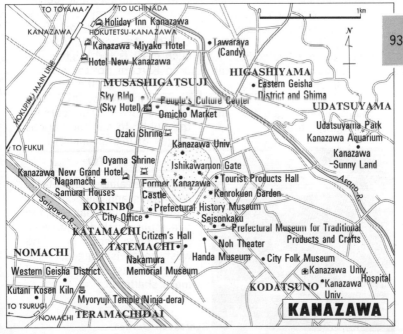

KANAZAWA

in Kanazawa and west of Kō-rinbō, especially in 1-Chōme Naga-machi.

● *EDO-MURA (EDO VILLAGE)*
Located at Yuwaku Spa, this village contains about 20 buildings, constructed during the Edo period. They include the former mansion of the counsellor of the lord *Maeda*. A tour of the village gives the visitor a good idea of what life was like in the Edo period. 50 min. by bus from Kanazawa Station.

WHAT TO EAT

Kanazawa has a great variety of excellent cooking, which includes local dishes from land and sea. **Kōbako Crab**, available from December to March, is one of the most delicious seafoods.

Jibuni is a dish of wild duck or chicken served with raw mushrooms, spring onions, other vegetables and wheatgluten bread.

Gori, a grotesque looking but very succulent fish which can be eaten fried, raw or in *miso* soup, is another well-known dish. **Gorijiru**, boiled *Gori* with *miso,* is especially delicious.

Chōseiden, square rice cakes made from the finest rice and sugar, should satisfy those with a sweet tooth.

WHAT TO BUY

Kanazawa owes the development of its various traditional crafts to the influence and protection of successive feudal lords. One such craft is **Kaga Yūzen** (dyed fabric) with its characteristic design and subtle array of colors, delicately shaded off from outside to inside. Another such craft is the brightly colored **Kutani pottery**, which can be seen at the **Prefectural Art Museum**. Some local potteries lay on tours for the public to see the various stages of this ancient craft.

NOTO

Covered almost entirely by mountains and hills, and surrounded by the Japan Sea, the peninsula is noted for its wild, picturesque scenery. The west coast is rugged, while the east coast is indented and more sheltered.

Kenrokuen Garden

WHAT TO SEE

● **MYOJOJI TEMPLE** This is one of the great temples of the district, with its main hall and other buildings registered as Important Cultural Properties. 15 min. walk after a 25 min. bus ride from Hakui Station.

● **NOTO KONGO** This scenic, 14 km. stretch of coast line between Fukura and Togi is noted for its beautiful sea views and fantastic rock formations. Excursion boats are available for sightseeing around the Gammon Cave. 1 hr. 20 min by bus from Hakui.

● **SOJIJI TEMPLE** This was originally one of the two headquarters of the *Sōtō* sect of *Zen* Buddhism along with the Eiheiji Temple in Fukui Prefecture. Founded in 1321, but destroyed by fire in 1898, the temple has only a sanctum and two other structures left intact. 45 min. by bus from Wajima.

● **WAKURA SPA** This idyllic spa is in a great setting at the tip of Cape Benten which juts out into Nanao Bay. 1 hr. 10 min. by JR from Kanazawa.

● **TSUKUMO BAY** Located east of Ogi, this bay features a 4 km. indented shoreline and interesting rock formations. Its green islands set in an expanse of blue combine to present a magnificent scene. 1 hr. 20min. by JR from Wakura spa.

● **WAJIMA** This city is noted for its lacquerware, called **Wajimanuri**, which consists mainly of household utensils. In Kawai-chō Street, there is a bustling market every morning selling fresh fish and farm produce. A similar open-air market is held in the precincts of Sumiyoshi Shrine from around 3 p.m. daily. 2 hrs. 20 min. by JR from Kanazawa.

WHAT TO BUY

Wajima Lacquerware, which has a long history and tradition, is known for the robustness and elegance of both its utility and artistic products. Several intricate processes, such as techniques to sink the gold and silver foil into the lacquer, have been highly developed, and the result is very high quality lacquerware.

ECHIZEN

WHAT TO SEE

● **KAGA HOT SPRINGS** These are a group of popular spas, each with its own distinct character. Awazu has the appearance of an old town, while Katayamazu is marked by modern high-rise hotels on the lakeshore. Yamashiro has many traditional inns with latticed entrances, and Yamanaka is picturesquely set among green hills. 30 min by JR from Kanazawa.

● **EIHEIJI TEMPLE** This has a 700 year history as one of the headquarters of the *Sōtō* sect of *Zen* Buddhism. There are 70 buildings in its extensive grounds, each connected by corridors that extend into a cedar forest. Overnight accommodation is available. 45 min. by Keifuku Railway from Fukui.

● **AWARA HOT SPRING** Accessible by bus in 15 min. from Awara-Onsen Station, this is one of the most celebrated resorts in the Hokuriku district. It has many large traditional inns, most with elaborate landscape gardens, standing in the fields.

● **TOJIMBO** Reached by bus in 40 min. from Awara Spa, Tōjimbō features rocky projections along the seashore. These igneous rocks have large, square columns soaring up to 90 m. Tōjimbō Tower serves as an observation deck to look down on the inlets and rock formations and the nearby beaches.

● **ECHIZEN COAST** Situated in

Tōjimbō

western Fukui Prefecture, this coast runs for 100 km. from the Kaga Coast to Tsuruga Bay, with Echizen Point at its center. It forms the main part of the Echizen Kaga Coast Quasi National Park with sheer bluffs and a pounding sea.

WHAT TO EAT

Echizen Crabs are the celebrated seafood in Echizen, usually boiled and eaten with vinegar. Male crabs are said to be better in taste and price, but prices for the crabs generally are becoming exorbitant.

TOYAMA & TATEYAMA

WHAT TO SEE

● **TOYAMA** One of the main cities along the Japan Sea Coast, Toyama is noted for its manufacture of patent medicines, and medicine peddlers have been part of Toyama since the 17th century. 45 min. by JR from Kanazawa.

● *UNAZUKI HOT SPRING* Situated on the Kurobe River in the heart of the Northern Japan Alps, this is one of the best resorts in the Hokuriku district and serves as a base for excursions to the Kurobe Gorge. 1 hr. by Toyama Chihō Dentetsu Railways from Dentetsu Toyama Station.

● *TATEYAMA* This is the name of the mountains to the west of the Kurobe Dam: Mt. Oyama, Mt. Bessan and Mt. Jōdo. These fine mountains have been the object of worship since ancient times. The Tateyama-Kurobe Alpine Route is a sightseeing route starting from Tateyama Station to Shinano-ōmachi Station (JR) in Nagano Prefecture through the Northern Alps. 1 hr. by Toyama Chihō Dentetsu Railways from Toyama to Tateyama.

● *KUROBE GORGE* This deep gorge, on the upper reaches of the Kurobe River, is noted for the beauty of its rapids and overhanging cliffs. A perfect trip in summer or autumn, the gorge can be seen from the Kurobe Gorge Railway running between Unazuki and Keyakidaira in 1 hr. 30 min..

● *GOKAYAMA & SHIRAKAWA-GO* These are remote villages with old 3 or 4-storied houses known for their steeply pitched thatched roofs. The inhabitants have maintained a system whereby several families all live together in these large wooden houses. 1 hr. 35 min. by bus from Takaoka.

HIDA & TAKAYAMA

WHAT TO SEE

● *TAKAYAMA* This city features many old, traditional houses, some of which have been turned into museums. Chief places of interest are Takayama Jin-ya, the former residence of the *Shōgun* officials, the Kusakabe Folkcraft Museum, and Hida Minzokumura, a village with old local houses. An annual attraction is the Takayama Festival in Apr. and Oct. The festival floats are exhibited at the Takayama Floats Pavillion.

WHAT TO BUY

Almost every souvenir shop in Takayama sells Shunkei-nuri Lacquerware and Ichii-ittōbori wood carving, the best known products. For pottery fans, there are 3 kinds of local pottery: Shibu-kusa, Koito and Yamada.

97

WAKASA & OMI

Wakasa is the southwestern part of Fukui Prefecture, facing the sea. It is known for its spendid coastline which includes both cliffs lashed by high waves and quiet inlets with white sand beaches and green pine trees. Beyond the mountains behind Wakasa is the Omi area, a "lake country" with beautiful scenery and a rich storehouse of historical and cultural remains.

WAKASA

WHAT TO SEE

● **MIKATA FIVE LAKES** This is an ideal recreational area formed by the five lakes of Kugushi, Suigetsu, Mikata, Suga, and Hiruga. They are part of the Wakasa Bay Quasi National Park, which extends from Kehi-no-Matsubara to Amano-Hashidate in Kyoto Prefecture. Excursion boats are available. 35 min by JR from Tsuruga to Mikata.

● **OBAMA** This is the main town of the district and is well-known for its lacquer ware called Wakasa-nuri, products of centuries old craftsmanship and skill. The 8 old temples in the town all preserve treasures designated as National Treasures. The town with its many old houses can be toured enjoyably on rental bicycles. I hr. by JR from Tsuruga.

● **AMANO-HASHIDATE** This is known as one of the 3 finest views in Japan, along with Miyajima Island in Aki (Hiroshima) and Matsushima Islands in Mutsu (Sendai). It is a 3.6 km. sandbank which effectively divides Miyazu Bay, 15 m. wide at its narrowest point. It is covered with a thick grove of pines and this strip of bright green stands out even at a distance. 2 hrs. 20 min. by JR from Kyoto.

● **LAKE BIWA** This is the largest fresh-water lake in Japan with an area of 694 sq. km. Its scenic beauty can be seen from the regular sightseeing boats that tour the lake.

Amano-Hashidate

東海・紀伊
TOKAI & KII

The Tōkai region and Kii Peninsula, between Nagoya and Osaka, both abound in breathtaking stretches of coastline. Tōkai, a major route to the west in feudal times, is steeped in history, while Kii Peninsula, including Ise, Shima and Nanki, is renowned for its pearl farms and religious shrines.

SHIZUOKA & NAGOYA

Shizuoka and Hamamatsu cities enjoy a mild climate and are surrounded by beautiful, gentle scenery. Nagoya, Japan's 4th largest city, is also surrounded by lovely valleys and attractive historical sites.

TRANSPORTATION

Traditionally an important link in transportation routes, Nagoya is a major stop between Tokyo and the south, with rail links all the way to Kyūshū.

● **BY RAIL** ＊ Tokyo to Shizuoka: I hr. 30 min.; Hamamatsu: 2 hrs.; Nagoya: 2 hrs. on the Tōkaidō Shinkansen.

In Nagoya subways, buses and taxis will take you most places you want to go, while several suburban railway lines connect the city with its surrounding areas.

TOUR HINTS

With its extensive transportation network, this area is very convenient for travel in a short time. It abounds with accomodation which is often booked up in spring and autumn.

SHIZUOKA & HAMAMATSU

WHAT TO SEE

● **SHIZUOKA** This is the capital city of Shizuoka Prefecture which is renowned for its tea production and its huge crop of mandarin oranges. Toro, 20 min. by bus from Shin-Shizuoka Station, is the ancient hamlet which dates back 2,000 years. Nihondaira Plateau, 35 min. by bus from Shin-Shizuoka Station(5 min. walk from Shizuoka Station). From this plateau, especially Udosan Hill, there is a grand view of the sea and mountains.

Kunōzan Hill, 35 min. by bus from Shin-Shizuoka Station with many stone walls facing the sun, is well known for its *ishigaki* (stone wall) strawberry cultivation and is the site of the famous Tōshōgū Shrine. Built in 1617 in honor of *Ieyasu Tokugawa* (1542-1616), the first of the *Tokugawa* Shōguns, it is here that *Ieyasu's* remains were first interred before being removed to a mausoleum in Nikko later the same year.

●*OKUOI VALLEY* Situated in the upper reaches of the Oi River, this deep valley together with its lake makes a fine setting for a trip on the steam locomotive which runs along the river. Sumata-kyō Gorge Spa (at the end of the trip by steam locomotive along the Sumata River), can be found this bright and colorful hot spring resort, which boasts some of Tōkai's best autumn scenery. 3 hrs. by train and bus from Shizuoka Station.

●*HAMAMATSU* This city is famous for its musical instrument and motorcycle works, some of which can be visited upon request.

Kanzanji Spa, located on

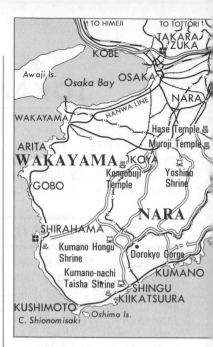

the eastern shores, is large hot spring resort.

Lake Hamana itself has important eel fisheries, and bordered with beautiful pine trees, it is a pleasant spot to enjoy a variety of water sports. 30 min. by bus from Hamamatsu Station.

WHAT TO EAT

In the Okuōi valley area it is possible to taste wild game, including boar and venison. On the other hand, Lake Hamana boasts eels, oysters and snapping turtles. Mikawa is excellent for all kinds of seafood.

NAGOYA

WHAT TO SEE

● **NAGOYA** A leading industrial city with a castle as its focal point, Nagoya is especially noted for its chinaware, timepieces, machinery and chemical products. Nagoya Castle, built in 1612 and reconstructed in 1959, features a 5-story "donjon" topped by a pair of golden dolphins. While the 5th floor commands a fine view, the lower floors house a display of castle treasures. Higashiyama Park contains a zoo, botanical gardens and a playground. Atsuta Shrine, 5 min. by JR from Nagoya. Thought to have been built originally in the 3rd century and containing the *Kusanagi-no-tsurugi,* part of the emperor's regalia, this is one of Japan's most sacred *shinto* shrines.

● **MEIJI VILLAGE** 1 hr. 5 min. by bus from Nagoya. You can find here more than 50 old buildings which serve as a reminder of the Meiji Period (1868-1912).

● **SETO** 45 min. by Meitetsu Railway from Nagoya. Famous for ceramics, Seto's brick

101

chimneys give the city its peculiar atmosphere.

WHAT TO EAT

Kishimen, flat Japanese noodles which can be eaten either in hot soup or with a cold sauce, is a speciality of Nagoya. *Udon* (noodles) boiled in *miso* soup is also popular. The chicken (*kashi-wa*) used in this type of *udon* is another of the local specialties.

WHAT TO BUY

Nagoya has many fine department stores and fashion boutiques and also boasts Japan's largest underground shopping mall at Sakae Station. Local crafts, such as china and glassware (*Shippōyaki*), make very good souvenirs of this part of Japan.

WHERE TO STAY

Being a large city, Nagoya provides visitors with a wide choice of places to stay. Some of the bigger hotels include **Hotel Nagoya Castle**, with a view of ·the castle, **Nagoya Kankō Hotel** on the main street, and **Nagoya Terminal Hotel** which has direct connections with Station.

ISE & SHIMA

This area is a tourist mecca, and Ise Jingū Shrine has traditionally been a very popular place for people from all over Japan. Shima Peninsula is famous for its cultured pearls and, surrounded by the sea, is a very scenic spot.

TRANSPORTATION

● *BY RAIL* Kintetsu Nagoya to Kashikojima: 2 hrs.; Kintetsu Namba (Osaka) to Kashikojima: 2 hrs. 30 min. on the Kintetsu Line.
● *BY BUS* The Mie Bus Network, departing from Ise and the Kintetsu Railway Line, link most of the popular sightseeing spots.

TOUR HINTS

A popular route around the area, involving only one or two overnight stays, begins with a visit to the Ise Jingū Shrines and then on to Toba and Kashikojima Island.

ISE & TOBA

WHAT TO SEE

● *ISE JINGU* Visited annually by about 7 million tourists and

Ama Women Divers

worshippers, Ise Jingū consists of two shrines: Naikū (Inner Shrine), 20 min. by bus from Ise-shi, dedicated to the Great Sun Goddess, and Gekū (Outer Shrine), 10 min. by bus from Ise-shi, dedicated to the Goddess of Food, Clothing and Dwellings.

● *FUTAMIGAURA BEACH* 20 min. by bus from Ise-shi. Noted for its twin "wedded" rocks joined by a long twine rope, this beautiful beach is the scene of spectacular sunrises.

●*TOBA* From Toba Bay it is possible to take a 50 min. boat trip to see the complete process of pearl cultivation and pearl diving by *Ama* women divers on Mikimoto Pearl Island. The island is also connected to the mainland by Pearl Bridge. Pearl Museum features a display of various materials related to pearls, including the biography of *Kōkichi Mikimoto,* who lived on the island and in 1893 became the first person ever to succeed in producing a cultured pearl.

Toba Aquarium includes a variety of marine life such as dolphins, whales and penguins. 7 min. on foot from Toba Station.

WHAT TO EAT

Located between Nagoya and Ise is Matsuzaka, which is famous for its beef. There is the local specialty of Akafuku (rice cakes covered with sweet bean paste). In Toba you can sample many kinds of steamed seafoods and Isorice cooked with ear and turban shells.

WHAT TO BUY

Not surprisingly, pearls are the most popular souvenirs of the region. They are sold in many shops, but it might be more advisable to buy from the reliable ones on Mikimoto Pearl Island.

SHIMA

WHAT TO SEE

●*AGO BAY* With over sixty islands scattered throughout the bay and a rugged coastline, this offers the finest scenery of Shima peninsula.

Kashikojima Island is well known for its many cultured pearl farms. **Nemuno-sato** is a newly developed leisure resort in a setting of rich grasslands and orchards where you can enjoy a variety of sports and recreation facilities. 35 min. by Kintetsu Railway from Kashikojima Station.

NANKI

Nanki in the southern part of Kii peninsula abounds with holiday resorts, hot springs and mountainous scenery. The central region of Nanki is the home of several historical legends, including Mt. Kōya, the worshipped mountain.

TRANSPORTATION

● **BY AIR** Tokyo to Shirahama: I hr. 45 min. (Ferries also run from Tokyo).

● **BY RAIL** If you use Nagoya or Osaka as your base, you can take an excursion on the JR Kisei Main Line which goes all the way round Kii Peninsula. *Nagoya to Kii-Katsuura: 4 hrs. 10 min.; from Osaka 3 hrs. 40 min. on the JR Express Line. Also, Kōyasan can be reached by taking the Nankai Kōya Line for I hr. 40 min. from Namba Station in Osaka.

TOUR HINTS

The major sights of this area can be toured comfortably in 4 days. If you want to visit **Mt. Kōya**, you should allow yourself another overnight stay.

WHAT TO SEE

● **WAKAYAMA** 50 min. by JR from Tennōji in Osaka, this is the gateway to Nanki, and with its castle it used to be a strategic town for the *Tokugawa* clan. **Wakayama Castle**, 10 min. by bus from Wakayama-shi, serves as a reminder to the local inhabitants and visitors of a bygone age when the *Tokugawa* clan were at the height of their power. **Wakanoura**, 25 min. by bus from Wakayama-shi, is a thriving seaside resort, often alluded to in poetry, and has a reputation for being one of the most beautiful spots around Wakayama.

● **SHIRAHAMA HOT SPRINGS** A well known hot spring resort, Shirahama Spa enjoys a lovely mild climate and affords views of the ocean. Visitors might like to take a short trip on a glass-bottom boat to see some colorful coral and other marine life.

● **KUSHIMOTO** I hr. by JR from Shirahama. The best scenic attractions of this port on the southern tip of Kii Peninsula are Hashikui-iwa (Bridge Pier Rocks) and the high cliffs of Ushio Point.

● **KATSUURA HOT SPRINGS** This is a unique spa with hot springs emerging from very unexpected places, and its inns with their own individual styles are overnight stops for most visitors to Nanki. Nachi: 30 min. by bus from Kii-Katsuura. Noted for its 133 m.-high waterfalls and the nearby 7th century Seigan-Toji Temple and 4th century Kumano Nachi Shrine, Nachi offers the tourist several things of interest in the one spot.

● **DOROKYO GORGE** I hr. 10 min. by bus from Kii-Katsuura to Shiko. On the upper reaches of Kumano River and noted for its great natural beauty, Dorokyō Gorge stretches upstream for over 30 km. If you want a bit of excitement, a jet boat trip down the gorge should do the trick!

● **MT. KOYA** Accessible by cable car in 5 min. from Nankai Railway's Gokurakubashi Station, the top of this mountain is the site of a monastery, which was founded in 816 by Kōbō-Daishi or Kūkai, one of the greatest priests and scholars of the Shingon sect of Buddhism. The monastery comprises 20 temples surrounded by tall trees and is visited every year by about a million pilgrims. As there are no inns here, visitors usually stay overnight at Shukubō, a temple abode where the faithful may put up for the night.

WHAT TO EAT

105

One of the most interesting ways to taste the local Nanki food is the Station Lunch. While you take in the beautiful scenery of Nanki, you can indulge in some of the best dishes of the region, including delicious sushi. Why not try Kodai-suzume-zushi (hand-rolled sushi with pickled baby porgy) at Wakayama, Mehari-zushi (riceballs wrapped in pickled mustard leaves) at Kii-Katsuura and Shingū, or tender beef at Taki and Matsuzaka.

Dorokyō Gorge

KANSAI

Kansai, which includes Kyoto, Nara, Osaka, and Kobe is the cradle of Japanese culture and civilization and contains many well-known historical and scenic attractions. Kyoto and Nara, in particular, are well-known tourist meccas.

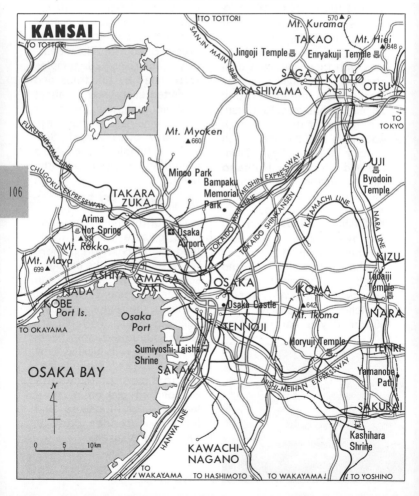

KYOTO

Kyoto is a classical city. It was the capital of Japan for more than 10 centuries until 1868 and it still retains a lot of its Edo period appearance and charm. Kyoto is rich in cultural assets, including 2 Imperial villas, 200 *Shintō* shrines, 1,500 Buddhist temples and over 60 beautiful gardens.

TRANSPORTATION

Tokyo to Kyoto: 2 hrs. 50 min. on the Tōkaidō Shinkansen *Hikari* bullet train. In Kyoto, buses are the most convenient form of transportation. There are also JR and 4 private rail lines (Hankyū, Keihan, Kintetsu and Keifuku) connecting major points in the city with the suburbs. Plenty of taxis are available.

TOUR HINTS

With so many things to see in Kyoto, it's best to focus on a few representative attractions. Many sightseeing spots are within easy walking distance of each other or just a short taxi ride away. When entering temple and shrine buildings, visitors are required to change into the slippers provided at the entrance. Kyoto can be roughly divided into 6 sections: Rakuchū (central), Higashiyama (east) Rakuhoku (north) Rakusei (west), Nishiyama (west mountain) and Rakunan (south).

RAKUCHU

WHAT TO SEE

● *HIGASHI - HONGANJI TEMPLE*
This temple was founded in 1602 by *Ieyasu,* the first *Tokugawa* shōgun, to rival Nishi-Honganji Temple. The present structures date from 1895, and Higashi - Honganji is one of the main temples of the *Jōdo-Shinshū* sect. Opposite the great 2-story front gate is the Daishidō (Founder's Hall), an elaborately decorated double-roofed wooden structure. East of the temple, the Shōseien Garden (also known as *Kikokutei*) is a well-known landscape garden with small groves of cherry and plum trees and wisteria vines.
● *NISHI - HONGANJI TEMPLE*
This is one of Kyoto's finest temples and one of the best examples of Buddhist architecture. Founded in 1272, it is the present headquarters of

107

the *Jōdo-Shinshū* sect. It features 5 buildings designated as National Treasures and many works of art, examples of the showy, decorative style of the Momoyama period.

The 3-storyed **Hiunkaku Pavilion** in the temple grounds combines 3 different architectural styles and is richly decorated with paintings in every room. It is regarded as one of the architectural masterpieces of the Momoyama Period.

● *NIJOJO CASTLE* Built in 1603 by *Ieyasu Tokugawa*, this castle served as his residence when he visited Kyoto from Edo (now Tokyo). Its buildings are national treasures with splendid architectural beauty and richly decorated interiors.

● *KYOTO IMPERIAL PALACE* (Kyoto Gosho) has 2 distinguished buildings — **Seiryōden** was originally used as living quarters for the Emperor and was later set aside for ceremonial use only. It was destroyed repeatedly by fire and the present building dates from 1855. **Shishinden** (Ceremonial Hall) has a similar construction and was used for state functions such as the enthronement of the Emperor and the New Year's audience. For large-group

visits to the Imperial Palace advance permission is required. Enquiries can be made at travel agencies.

● *NISHIJIN* This is a cluster

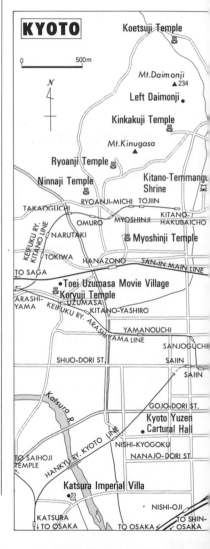

KYOTO

of over 1,500 offices and workshops connected with the silk-weaving industry. It is especially famous for its pre-dyed silk fabrics which have enjoyed an excellent reputation for centuries. **Nishijin Textile Hall** displays various Nishijin products including *Kimono.*

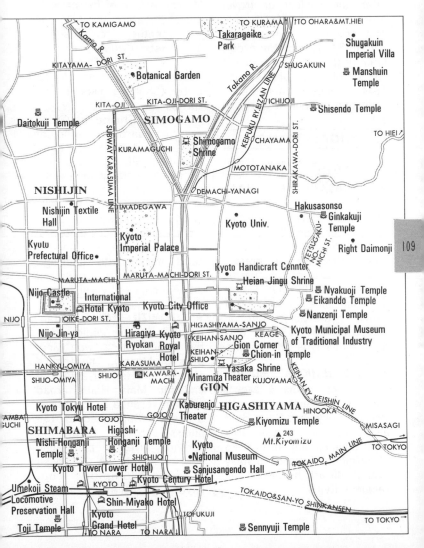

● **TOJI (KYO-O-GOKOKUJI) TEMPLE** Well-known for its 55 m. high, 5-story pagoda built in 1644, this pagoda is emblematic of Kyoto and is often the subject of travel brochure covers. The temple was originally founded and built in 794 by imperial order, later destroyed, and was not completely restored until 1644. It houses an immense collection of ancient works of art.

HIGASHIYAMA

WHAT TO SEE

● **SANJUSANGENDO HALL** (Renge-Oin), established in 1164 and restored in 1266, is named for the 33 spaces between the pillars in its elongated structure. It houses 1,001 wooden *Kan-non* statues, and 500 smaller ones on each side of the chief image — the *Senju Kan-non* carved in 1254. It is the only hall of this type left in existence.

● **KYOTO NATIONAL MUSEUM** This is one of the 3 largest museums in Japan along with those in Tokyo and Nara. Built as a repository for treasures from temples and shrines, its 17 exhibition rooms display over 2,000 art, historical and religious items.

● **GION - MACHI** is the best known of the traditional *geisha* quarters in Kyoto and is also noted for its theaters— Minamiza and Kaburenjō. Minamiza, one of the nation's oldest theaters (built in the 17th century) features all-star-cast *Kabuki* performances every December. Kaburenjō stages its *Miyako Odori* (Cherry Dance) in the spring.

Yasaka Shrine, regarded as the guardian shrine of Gion, is noted for its large Gion Festival. Gion Corner, on the 11th floor of Yasaka Kaikan Hall in Gion, offers demonstrations of tea ceremony and flower arrangement, performances of *bunraku* (puppets), *gagaku* (ancient court music with dancing), *Koto* (Japanese harp) and traditional dances by *geisha* and *maiko*.

● **KIYOMIZU TEMPLE,** established in 798, is dedicated to the 11-headed *Kan-non* (Goddess of Mercy). The temple stands on Higashiyama Hill and the Main Hall's broad wooden veranda juts out over a canyon. Supported by 139 pillars, 15 m. high, the veranda gives a panoramic view of Kyoto. A Japanese proverb "Jumping from Kiyomizu Veranda" means

Sanjūsangendō Hall

to make a drastic decision. The narrow path leading up from the temple gate is lined with small shops selling *Kiyomizuyaki* (pottery).

● **HEIAN JINGU SHRINE** was established in 1895 to commemorate the 1,100th anniversary of the founding of *Heiankyō* as the capital of Japan. Most of its buildings are smaller scale replicas of the first Imperial Palace. The shrine has a beautiful pond-centered garden, popular for its cherry blossoms in spring and irises in early summer. Its Jidai Festival is one of Kyoto's 3 famous festivals along with the *Aoi* and *Gion* Festivals.

● **KYOTO MUNICIPAL MUSEUM OF TRADITIONAL INDUSTRY** Demonstrations by artisans and craftsmen can be seen here. The center also exhibits traditional Kyoto arts and crafts including bamboo, silk, paper crafts, pottery and lac-querware.

● **NANZENJI TEMPLE** This is well-known for its *Sammon* Gate built in 1628. Its Main Hall has 16th century screen paintings by artists of the *Kanō* School — one of the top schools of painting at that time. The *Hōjō* Garden in the temple grounds features symmetrically arranged rocks and white sand designed in typical *Karesansui* style. Restaurants specializing in *yudōfu* (boiled tōfu) dishes can be found in the neighborhood.

● **HAKUSASONSO** This is a pleasant pond garden laid out in 1915. Nyoigatake Hill rising in the background serves as *shakkei* — a piece of borrowed scenery for the garden.

● **GINKAKUJI (JISHOJI) TEMPLE** (Temple of the Silver pavilion) was originally built in 1482 as the country villa of *Yoshimasa Ashikaga,* the military ruler in the 15th century. He intended to have the outer walls of the pavilion covered with silver foil, but due to his sudden death, the plan never saw fruition. Hence it remains "Silver Pavilion" in name only. On his death, the villa was converted into a temple. Its gardens are perhaps the most attractive in Kyoto. They are laid out on 2 levels: the upper is a rock garden (Karesansui) and the lower is a pond-centered walking garden.

● **TETSUGAKU-NO-MICHI** (Path of Philosophy) This is a walking path along the canal originating in Lake Biwa. The walk from Nyakuōji Shrine to Ginkakuji Temple takes 40 min. and has many benches for strollers to sit and admire the beauty of the seasons and ponder the name of the path.

RAKUHOKU

WHAT TO SEE

● **SHISENDO TEMPLE** was built in 1641. The name means "Hall of the Great Poets" and it displays the poems and portraits of 36 Chinese poets. The hall is also noted for its Chinese garden with a man-made waterfall and streams.

● **SHUGAKUIN IMPERIAL VILLA** Originally built by the *Tokugawa* Shogunate in 1659 as a retreat for ex-Emperor *Gomizuno-o*, the villa consists of 3 summer houses, each built in a large garden on a different level, within a total area of 28 ha. The gardens are the largest and most elegant of Kyoto's numerous pond-centered, strolling gardens. In 1884, control of the villa was transferred to the Imperial Household Agency.

Daisen-in(Daitokuji Temple)

Advance permission in person is required from the Kyoto Office of the Household Agency for visits to the villa.

● **MT. HIEI** rising to the northwest of Kyoto, is known for Enryakuji Temple, standing in a thick grove of cypress trees on the summit. I hr. by bus from Kyoto Station. The large, vermilion lacquered Central Hall is a national treasure. The temple, easily accessible by cable car, was founded in 788 by Priest *Dengyō-Daishi,* founder of the *Tendai* sect of Buddhism.

● **LAKE BIWA** is the largest fresh-water lake in Japan, and many sightseeing boats operate here. There are many places of interest around its shores, including Shigaraki, a town famous for its pottery, and Ogoto Hot Springs. On the south shore stands Ishiyama Temple, where *Murasaki Shikibu* is said to have written her classic romance, The Tale of the *Genji* clan, a literary masterpiece.

● *SANZEN-IN TEMPLE,* I hr. by bus from Kyoto Station, was built at Ohara as a residence for the brothers and sisters of deifice Emperors. The site was chosen since Ohara had been considered a holy place from ancient times by believers in *Jōdo,* the pure land or Buddhist heaven. The temple consists of a beautiful mansion and gardens set in secluded hills.

● *DAITOKUJI TEMPLE* One of Kyoto's most important temples, this is the headquarters of the *Rinzai* sect. Originally constructed in 1319, most of the present buildings were rebuilt in the 16th century. The grounds contain many smaller buildings built in memory of various deceased military commanders, and several tea-ceremony rooms and rock gardens.

RAKUSEI

WHAT TO SEE

● *KINKAKUJI (ROKUONJI) TEM-PLE* (Temple of the Golden Pavilion) Set in a beautiful landscape garden, this temple was formerly a *Shōgun's* villa. Once covered with gold foil,

KYOTO'S 3 BIG FESTIVALS

Among Kyoto's many ancient festivals, these three are "musts".

● *AOI FESTIVAL* Originating in the 6th century, the festival reproduces the imperial processions made to the shrines in feudal days as a sign of homage. A procession of people wearing costumes of the Heian aristocracy parade from Kyoto Palace to Shimogamo and Kamigamo Shrines. May 15.

● *GION FESTIVAL* Starting on July 1 and continuing for a month, this huge festival took its present form in the Edo era, when the sumptuously decorated floats first made their appearance.

● *JIDAI FESTIVAL* Begun in 1885, this is a colorful historical pageant with 17 groups clad in costumes depicting Japan's history from the Meiji era back to the Heian era. October 22.

Aoi Festival

Kinkakuji Temple

the temple was destroyed by fire in 1950. The present replica succeeds in preserving the temple's grandeur.

● **RYOANJI TEMPLE,** established in 1450, is well-known for its rock garden which depicts the sea and a group of islands. Typical of *Karesansui* (dry gardens), it has a simplicity and purity stemming from the principles followed in *Zen* meditation.

● **NINNAJI TEMPLE** Built in 888, the temple always had an Imperial prince as its superior until 1868. Originally, there were around 60 buildings, but most were destroyed by a series of rebellions so that only a wooden image of *Amitabha* as an object of veneration remains.

● **MYOSHINJI TEMPLE** Built in 1338, this is one of the main temples of the *Rinzai* sect. It has one of the most elaborate designs of any *Zen* temple,

and has 43 sub-temples as well as the main gate and various halls.

● **KORYUJI TEMPLE** Built in 603, this is one of Japan's oldest temples. The buildings were reconstructed in 1165, but most of the Buddha statues in the temple houses were carved in the 7th and 8th centuries. One statue in particular has historically attracted a lot of devotees — the *Miroku Bosatsu,* with its mild pensive expression, ranks among the best figures from this period.

● **TOEI UZUMASA MOVIE VILLAGE** has a large outdoor set representing a section of a typical feudal town.

● **KATSURA IMPERIAL VILLA** is said to have been built in 1642 by 2 brothers of *Enshū Kobori,* a noted tea ceremony master. It includes a masterpiece of Japanese landscape gardening which combines all the different styles of the period, together with various halls and teahouses. To see the villa, permission must be obtained in advance from the Kyoto Imperial Household Agency.

● **SAIHOJI (KOKEDERA) TEMPLE** was founded in 731 and later reconstructed by *Musō Kokushi,* a distinguished *Zen* priest, who also laid out the temple's garden. The garden's lower level is a typical example of a stroll garden, designed to give the impression that the pond has a geographical connection with the mountain in the background.

The upper level is a rock garden. The entire lower garden is covered with over 100 species of green and yellow moss — hence the temple is called *Kokedera* (Moss Temple). 45 min. by bus from Kyoto Station.

● *ARASHIYAMA* is the area around *Togetsu* Bridge, 30 min. by bus from Kyoto Station, which spans the River Oigawa. Its beautiful scenery, with pines, cherry and maple trees along the river, has long been celebrated in poems and songs.

● *SAGANO,* the area beginning on the far side of the bridge, at the base of the mountains, contains many temples, villas and places of historical interest. It takes about 5 hrs. to see most of them, like Tenryūji Temple and Okōchisansō Villa.

● *HOZU RAPIDS* An interesting trip to make from Kyoto is to shoot the rapids of the Hozu River from Kameoka to Arashiyama, a 2 hr. trip covering about 16 km. This excursion, in flat-bottomed boats, is delightful in spring when cherry trees are in bloom and equally attractive in summer and autumn.

RAKUNAN

WHAT TO SEE

● *TOFUKUJI TEMPLE* A 5 min. walk from JR's Tōfukuji Station. One of the *Rinzai* sect's main temples, Tōfukuji was built over a period of 19 years, starting in 1236.

There are 37 buildings in extensive grounds and the huge 2-story main gate is one of the most important *Zen*-style gates in Japan. It is an excellent example of medieval architecture, and its location outside the center of Kyoto saved it from the fires that destroyed most of the old capital.

● *FUSHIMI INARI SHRINE* A 15 min. walk from Tōfukuji Temple. Since ancient times, Japanese farmers have

115

Katsura Imperial Villa

believed the fox to be the messenger of the god of harvests, and there are around 40,000 shrines dedicated to it.

Fushimi Shrine consists of 5 shrines on the slopes of Mt. Inari and it is the focus of this popular belief. The shrine is actually dedicated to the Goddess of Rice and Food. A unique feature of the shrine is the 10,000 red *torii* gates, donated by devotees, which form a tunnel about 4 km. long.

● **DAIGOJI TEMPLE,** established in 926, is a celebrated temple of the *Shingon* sect. Built on the side of a mountain, it consists of the upper *Daigo* at the summit and the lower *Daigo* at the base. They comprise more than 70 buildings, including a 5-story pagoda, one of the oldest existing structures in Kyoto. It is also noted for its beautiful old cherry trees. 45 min. by bus from Kyoto Station.

● **MAMPUKUJI TEMPLE** This is a *Zen* temple established in 1661 by the Chinese priest *Ingen.* Built in the style of the Chinese Ming Dynasty, it is one of the few purely Chinese style temples in Japan. A 5 min. walk from JR's Obaku Station.

● **BYODOIN TEMPLE** This is well-known for its *Hō-ō-Dō*

(Phoenix Hall) and is typical of the temples of the *Fujiwara* period (897-1185). The hall was designed to represent a mythological Chinese bird in the act of descending to earth. The body is represented by the central hall, the wings by the lateral corridors and the tail by the rear corridor. The whole effect is one of amazing architectural symmetry. A 10 min. walk from JR's Uji Station.

WHAT TO EAT

Kyōryōri (Kyoto-style cuisine) is a distinctive style that developed from Kyoto's unique geography and customs. It features subtle flavors and seasonal ingredients to give a sense of the passing of the seasons. Food is presented in a series of small servings, with the shape and color of receptacles and food harmonizing perfectly.

Course dishes are often expensive, but boxed lunches are very reasonable and a good way to sample Kyoto's

Tōfukuji Temple

superb cuisine. **Shōjinryōri** originated in China and is a form of vegetarian cooking popularized by Buddhist priests of the *Zen*-Sect. It can be tried at **Izusen** at Daitokuji Temple and at **Ikkyū** near the temple's gate. **Kaisekiryōri** is the light meal served before a tea ceremony. A feast for the eyes, it consists of a series of delicate portions of a variety of food, beautifully presented. Try **Hyōtei** in Okazaki.

Another specialty is **Nishin Soba** — buckwheat noodles with soft, boiled herring. Try **Matsuba** in Shijō Minamiza. **Imobō** is dried cod boiled with shrimp and potato. Try **Hiranoya** in Maruyama Park.

WHAT TO BUY

Pride of craftsmanship flourishes in Kyoto and is represented in a wide variety of traditional products. Kyoto has 3 special areas providing convenient shopping: **Kawaramachi, Shin-Kyōgoku,** and **Shijō** Streets, all in the center of the city.

Kiyomizuyaki is the name of Kyoto's porcelain and pottery, noted for its elegance. **Kyō-shikki** (Lacquerware) : Kyoto's lacquerware is known for its quality, elegant designs and sturdy construction and is

considered the highest form of this craft. Especially famous is *maki-e* — elaborate gold and silver lacquerware.

Bamboo Crafts : Kyoto bamboo is long, glossy and durable and various techniques were developed centuries ago for rendering this high-quality bamboo into useful and artistic objects.

Combs and **Ornamental Hairpins** include *Kushi,* the highest quality, and *Kanzashi* — tortoiseshell or blacklacquered wooden hairpins. There are a variety of other traditional products such as fans — 90% of Japan's fans are produced in Kyoto. **Nishijin** (silk) and **Yūzen** (dyed *kimono*) are also specialties of Kyoto.

WHERE TO STAY

Kyoto has plenty of large hotels like the **New Miyako Hotel** near Kyoto Station, but to completely appreciate the city's charms a stay at a traditional inn is recommended. They offer quiet hospitality and the serenity of traditional rooms and gardens. **Tawaraya** and **Hiiragiya** are famous high-class inns. For those interested in *Zen,* several temples in *Shukubō* offer lodging, such as the **Myōshinji Temple Tōrin-in.**

NARA

The Nara region played an important role in Japan's arts, crafts, literature and industries. In scenic surroundings with a restful, timeless atmosphere, the city is rich in cultural treasures related to Buddhism that predate those in Kyoto, since from 710, Nara was for 84 years Japan's first permanent capital.

TRANSPORTATION

Nara is best reached via Kyoto or Osaka. Kyoto to Nara: 40 min. by Kintetsu Kyoto Line Limited Express. From Osaka Namba: 30 min. by Kintetsu Nara Line Limited Express. In the Nara area, the Kintetsu Railway and Nara Buses which leave from Kintetsu Railway's main stations are convenient.

TOUR HINTS

Recommended on any visit to Nara are Tōdaiji Temple and Tōshōdaiji Temple and if time permits, Asuka, with its ancient tombs.

Nara can be seen comfortably in a day-trip, but it's a good idea to take time to walk around its parks, town and temples and enjoy its special atmosphere.

NARA CITY

WHAT TO SEE

● **NARA PARK** is also known as "Deer Park" for the 1,000 or so tame deer that roam freely here. Many of the city's historical structures are located in and around the park.

● **KOFUKUJI TEMPLE** was moved from Asuka and rebuilt on its present site in 710. Only a few of the original 175 buildings have survived, and they include a 3-story pagoda dating back to 1143, a 5-story pagoda from 1426, and *Tōkondō* (Eastern Main Hall), built in 1415 — all registered as National Treasures. Sarusawa Pond, near the temple, is well known for the reflection cast on its surface by the temple's 5-story pagoda — one of the most popular sights in Nara.

● **NARA NATIONAL MUSEUM** houses a valuable collection of ancient works of art, including Buddhist art objects dating from the Nara period (710-784).

● **TODAIJI TEMPLE** The first thing that attracts your attention here is the magnificent *Nandaimon* Gate, 25 m. - high at the main entrance. Tōdaiji was founded in 752 and is well-known for its Daibutsu — the world's largest bronze statue of Buddha, cast in the mid-8th century. It is enclosed in the Daibutsuden, the world's largest wooden structure. Near this building is the Shōsōin Treasure Repository which contains 8th Century art objects as well as a collection from abroad. Sangatsudō Hall, the oldest Tōdaiji structure, has a splendid flowing line to its roof. The hall contains an elaborately decorated garret, and 3 magnificent ceilings set off the Buddhas in its sanctuary. The main object of reverence is the celebrated dry-lacquered Fukūkensaku Kan-non, surrounded by 14 other statues. The statue's diadem is bedecked with various jewels, including 20,000 pearls. The clay images of *Nikkō-Bosatsu* and *Gakkō-Bosatsu* surrounding the statue are regarded as most representative of the exquisite workmanship and art of the Nara period.

● *KASUGA SHRINE,* founded in 768, is dedicated to 4 *Shintō* deities and is one of the most celebrated shrines in Japan. The approach to the shrine is lined with 1,800 stone lanterns and there are also 1,000 small metal lanterns hanging from the eaves.

● *KASUGA WAKAMIYA SHRINE,* near Kasuga Shrine, features a Kaguraden (Hall for Sacred Dancing) where *Shintō* music and dances are performed when a donation is made.

● *YAKUSHIJI TEMPLE* was originally founded in 680, but apart from its 3-story eastern pagoda, all the temple buildings only date from the 13th century because of the frequent fires and earthquakes that hit the temple. The vermilion colored western pagoda was reconstructed in 1981.The Main Hall houses 3 Buddhist statues typical of the Nara period. 20 min. by bus from Nara Station.

● *TOSHODAIJI TEMPLE* was established in 759 by *Ganjin,* an illustrious Chinese priest of the Tang Dynasty. The headquarters of the *Ritsu* sect, its Main Hall is consid-

Yakushiji Temple Kondō

FESTIVALS IN NARA

● **WAKAKUSAYAMA HILL BURNING** At 6:00 p.m. on Jan. 15, the grass covering the hill is set alight and the entire hill is soon ablaze, making a grand sight.

● **TODAIJI TEMPLE FESTIVAL** Mar. 12, is celebrated to praise the virtue of *Honzon Jūichimen* (the 11-faced) *Kan-non* and to repent of sins. Omizutori Festival (Drawing Water Festival) is an important part of the Mar. 12 ceremonies. At 2:00 a.m. the following morning, water is drawn from the Wakasa Well at Nigatsudō Hall and after a magnificent procession it is brought to Tōdaiji's Main Hall. Dattan Mar. 12 – 14. Priests holding pine torches run around in the temple's sanctum.

● **TAKIGI NOH** at Kōfukuji Temple May 11, 12. Outdoor *Noh* and *Kyōgen* performances are held here starting around 4:00 p.m.

Omizutori Festival

ered one of the most valuable structures of the late Nara period. Its chief statue is the 3.3 m. *Birushana-Butsu,* a National Treasure, surrounded by other wooden statues — all examples of exquisite workmanship. The Kōdō (Lecture Hall) houses many treasures including the wooden, 2.4 m. *Miroku-Bosatsu.*

Although it has undergone several reconstructions, the hall is important as the only remaining example of palace architecture from the Tempyō period (729-749). In the Mieidō (Founder's Hall) is enshrined a dry-lacquer statue of *Ganjin,* regarded as

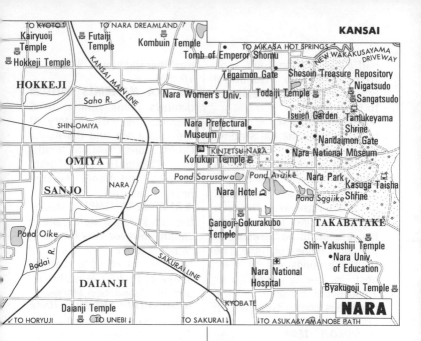

Map labels:

TO KYOTO↑   TO NARA DREAMLAND↑↑
Kairyuoij Temple   Futaiji Temple   Kombuin Temple
Hokkeji Temple   Tomb of Emperor Shomu
TO MIKASA HOT SPRINGS
NEW WAKAKUSAYAMA DRIVEWAY
HOKKEJI
Tegaimon Gate   Shosoin Treasure Repository
KANSAI MAIN LINE
Saho R.   Nara Women's Univ.   Todaiji Temple   Nigatsudo
Sangatsudo
SHIN-OMIYA
Nara Prefectural Museum   Isuien Garden   Tamukeyama Shrine
Nandaimon Gate
KINTETSU-NARA
OMIYA   Kofukuji Temple   Nara National Museum
Pond Sarusawa   Pond Aruike   Nara Park
SANJO   NARA
Nara Hotel   Pond Sagiike   Kasuga Taisha Shrine
Pond Oike
Bodai
Gangoji-Gokurakubo Temple   TAKABATAKE
SAKURAI LINE
Shin-Yakushiji Temple
Nara Univ. of Education
Nara National Hospital
DAIANJI   Byakugoji Temple
Daianji Temple   KYOBATE
NARA
TO HORYUJI   TO UNEBI↓   TO SAKURAI↓   TO ASUKA&YAMANOBE PATH

one of the greatest portrait statues in Japan. 20 min. by bus from Nara Station.

● **HORYUJI (IKARUGA-DERA) TEMPLE** This is rich in architectural and sculptural works of art. The temple is divided into 2 sections: the *Tōin* (East Temple) and *Saiin* (West Temple). The major structures in the *Saiin* are the *Nandaimon* (Great South Gate), rebuilt in 1483, the Great lecture Hall dating from 990 and a 5-story pagoda. The *Yume-dono* (Hall of Dreams) is a beautiful octagonal structure built in 739. The Main Hall, housing several Buddhist images, is the oldest wooden structure in the world. A 5 min. bus ride from JR Hōryūji Station.

ASUKA & YAMANOBE

WHAT TO SEE

● **YAMANOBE PATH** One of the oldest roads in Japan, this runs almost straight for 35 km. for Nara to Sakurai Station via Tenri, 20 min. by JR from Nara. Along the way, the path offers a lot of historic sites, ancient tombs, temples and Buddhist stone statues. The usual walking course is the 15 km. from Tenri to Sakurai, but if you have only half a day, try the 7 km. walk from Tenri to Isonokami Shrine and from Yanagimoto to Miwa Station.

● **HASEDERA TEMPLE** A 25 min. bus ride from Sakurai Station, this temple was founded in 686 and is the 8th of the 33 holy *Kan-non* temples for pilgrimage in western provinces. Set in Mt. Haseyama, the area is rich in fine scenery and hence used to be a resort of the court nobles of Nara. The temple grounds are at their best in spring when over 7,000 peonies bloom and the numerous cherry trees are in blossom.

● **MUROJI TEMPLE,** founded in 681, contains various National Treasures such as the *Kondō* (Golden Hall), the Main Hall, and the central image of *Shaka Nyorai*. The temple itself stands in a copse of cedars and has an unusually solemn atmosphere. Perhaps it used to be a seminary. 15 min. by bus from Kintetsu Murōguchi-Ono Station.

● **ASUKA** was the first capital designated by the *Yamato* Court. The area is full of ancient tombs of emperors, ruins of large temples, and mysterious stone buildings. Most of the points can be reached by bus from Kintetsu

Kashiharajingūmae Station in 10 min.

● **ASUKA MATERIALS MUSEUM** displays items related to 6 themes: the early history of the Asuka era and the Asuka Court, stones, ancient tombs, the *Takamatsuzuka* Tomb, temples, and *Man-yōshū* (the ancient Japanese poems).

● **ASUKADERA TEMPLE** This is the oldest full-scale temple in Japan, however very little of it remains today — only a small hall in which the central image of Buddha is enshrined and the foundation stones.

● **ISHIBUTAI ANCIENT TOMB** This is said to be the tomb of *Soga-no-Umako*. It is a good example of 7th century tombs, with its square base and round top. Bereft of its earth top, the stone ceiling and side walls are exposed. The tunnel to the tomb is over 8.4 m. long.

● **TACHIBANADERA TEMPLE** is said to be the birthplace of prince *Shōtoku Taishi* (574-622), an ancient politician. The monastery once occupied a vast area and had corridors with gates, a pagoda and many buildings, but now only the *Kondō* (Prince's Hall) and the hall of *Kan-non* remain.

● **TAKAMATSUZUKA ANCIENT TOMB** This is a small circular tomb with a diameter of 18 m.

In 1972 beautiful frescos were discovered here. Copies of these frescos and other materials related to the tomb are displayed in the **Takamatsuzuka Fresco Museum.**

WHAT TO EAT

Narazuke Pickles, pickled eggplants and cucumbers, are a local specialty and can be purchased at **Mori Rōho** in front of Tōdaiji Temple's South Gate and several other places. **Warabi Mochi** (bracken-starch pastry), balls of starch covered with soy flour, will melt in your mouth. Try the tea shops around Nara Park.

Miwa Sōmen are thin noodles made by exposing the kneaded and rolled dough to the winter wind. The result is thin, white, deliciously chewy noodles. **Chameshi** is cooked rice with roasted soybeans in boiled tea. Try **Yanagi Jyaya** near Kōfukuji Temple. **Kakinoha Zushi** is the sushi peculiar to Yoshino. Rice with vinegar and topped with pickled mackerel is wrapped in persimmon leaves and pressed.

WHAT TO BUY

Nara produces most of Japan's ink *Sumi* . Many old stores along Sanjō-dōri Street such as **Kōbaien** and **Genrindō** specialize in ink and calligraphy brushes. Nara is the birthplace of Japanese calligraphy and writing brushes and all other materials are expertly hand-made. **Akashiya** sells *Shika-no-makifude,* a beautiful writing brush dyed in 5 colors.

Nara Dolls are characterized by roughcut chisel work and bright colors and are made in a variety of forms. **Akahadayaki** is the area's solid and chunky pottery. Tea utensils are the most common items produced. Most souvenirs can be found in the **Nara Commerce** and **Tourist Building** near the Kintetsu Railway Nara Station.

WHERE TO STAY

Nara abounds in cozy traditional *Ryokans* such as the famous **Shikitei** and **Kikusuirō** and the old inn in Nara Park, **Edosan.** Those around JR Nara Station are very reasonably priced. Hotels include the **Nara Hotel** and **Hotel Fujita Nara.** Some temples will accept guests.

123

Nara Ittōbori Wooden Carvings

OSAKA

At one time the nation's capital, Osaka is now Japan's third largest city in terms of population (currently 2,648,000). It is the commercial and industrial center of western Japan and also takes pride in its traditional stage arts such as *bunraku* and *jōruri*. Moreover, Osaka is a major transportation hub, both international and domestic, thus making it convenient for visiting the nearby ancient capitals of Nara and Kyoto.

TRANSPORTATION

● **BY AIR** Visitors to Japan can arrive at Osaka International Airport direct from abroad or can fly there from other domestic airports. Frequent flights from Tokyo to Osaka take just I hr., with a 30 min. bus link to the city center.

● **BY RAIL** Tokyo to Shin-Osaka: 3 hrs. 10 min.; From Kyoto: 20 min. by Tōkaidō Shinkansen. Shin-Osaka to Osaka: 5 min. by JR. For getting around, you can choose between the many subway lines, buses and taxis.

TOUR HINTS

Visitors to Osaka will almost certainly feel the intense commercial atmosphere of the city, in which many of the old wholesalers retain their businesses. There are, however, several places of interest for the sightseer which give the city an atmosphere totally different from the other major cities such as Tokyo. To see something of these contrasts, try a walk to both the modern **Kita** (northern) district near Osaka Station and the older **Minami** (southern) district around Namba, 10 min. by subway from Umeda (Osaka Station).

KITA

WHAT TO SEE

● **UMEDA** The area around Osaka Station is a thriving business and entertainment center. There are several theaters and department stores here, including **Acty Osaka**, while nearby on **Hankyū-Higashi-dōri** can be found lots of department and other stores. Underground is the **Umeda Chika Center**, a vast shopping complex featuring many souvenir shops, fruit and vegetable markets, teahouses and restaurants and connecting with several of the major department stores and Hankyū Sambangai Shopping Arcade.

● **OHATSU TENJIN SHRINE** Hidden amongst the numerous bars, clubs and Japanese restaurants of the bustling Sonezaki Shinchi district stands this lovely old shrine, which was the setting for the *Sonezaki Shinjū* (lovers' suicide at Sonezaki), a famous *Jōruri* which was dramatized by *Monzaemon Chikamatsu*, the most popular playwright of the Edo period.

● **NAKANOSHIMA** Located on a small island between the

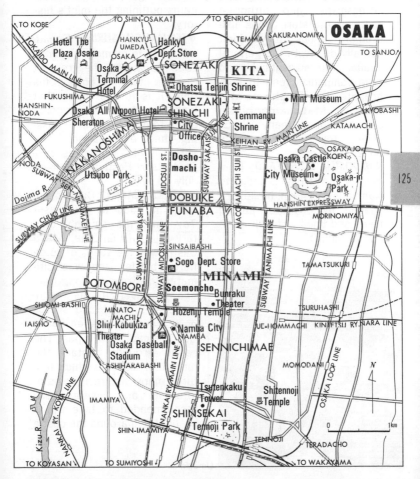

Dōjima and Tosabori Rivers, Nakanoshima is a civic center containing many prefectural and municipal government buildings, including the City Hall, and the Osaka Grand and Osaka Royal Hotels.

● *DOBUIKE* This has traditionally been Osaka's wholesale district for clothing and accessories, and although some of the stores look like ordinary shops, they don't actually deal with the general public. Pharmaceutical and drug companies tend to congregate in Dōshōmachi, while in Matchamachisuji can be found many shops selling toys, fireworks and dolls.

● *MIDOSUJI BOULEVARD* Running south from Umeda to Namba is this 4 km. boulevard shaded by beautiful ginkgo trees and lined with tall highrise buildings.

● *THE MINT* The only mint in Japan, this was founded in 1871 on the banks of the Yodo River. A part of the Mint garden is open to the public during the cherry blossom season, while the Mint Museum houses a collection of Japanese and foreign coins together with other items outlining the mint's history.

● *TEMMANGU SHRINE* Founded in 949 in memory of *Michizane Sugawara,* the greatest Chinese literary scholar of his time, it is to this shrine that large numbers of students come to pray for help in passing their examinations. The shrine is also where the *Tenjin Matsuri* Festival is held on July 24 and 25.

● *OSAKA CASTLE* Built originally in 1586 by *Hideyoshi Toyotomi,* the nation's military ruler of that time, Osaka Castle was the scene of some fierce battles and was ultimately destroyed a long time ago. However, it was reconstructed in 1931 and serves as a reminder of when Osaka was the capital of Japan. The castle grounds contain the municipal museum which features many historical items of interest, and visitors are recommended to take the 1 hr. boat trip around the castle

Umeda

and Nakanoshima.

MINAMI

WHAT TO SEE

● *SHINSAIBASHISUJI* This is one of the city's best shopping areas and is filled with department and other fashionable stores, such as Sony, Parco and Shinsaibashi BAL, which are very popular with young people. The northern end of the area contains several traditional wholesale establishments, dealing in clothing and other items.

● *SOEMON-CHO* Formerly the busiest of Minami's five *geisha* districts, Soemon-chō is nowadays a bustling amusement center, illuminated by bright neon signs attracting customers to its many restaurants, cabarets and bars. Teahouses used to stand side by side along its streets, but now only Yamatoya remains to tell of the past.

● *DOTOMBORI* This is also a popular amusement quarter, where a variety of Japanese stage productions are performed in the theaters lining the street. Of these, the National Bunraku Theater, featuring several *bunraku* and *jōruri* performances a year, is probably the best known. Besides the theaters, there are lots of excellent restaurants, where the gourmet will feel very much at home.

● *SEN-NICHI-MAE* Yet another part of the city renowned for entertainment and amusements, Sen-nichi-mae abounds with cinemas, *Pachinko* parlors, game centers, cabarets and nightclubs.

Look out for the moss-covered *Mizukake Fudō* statue standing in the Hōzenji Temple adorned with many paper lanterns.

● *NAMBA* Within walking distance of Sen-nichi-mae, Namba is a major junction for suburban railways, including the Nankai and Kintetsu Lines. The area around Namba boasts several department and other stores. Dōguya-Suji specializes in equipment and utensils used in restaurants and cafes. These plastic food models make interesting souvenirs to take home. In the area are the Shin-Kabuki Theater, Osaka Baseball Stadium and the Prefectural Gymnasium.

● *SHITENNOJI TEMPLE* This was founded in 593 by prince *Shōtoku Taishi*, and its stone *torii* gate, the oldest in Japan, has stood since 1294. The temple buildings, including the Main Hall, Lecture Hall and a five-story pagoda, were restored in later years. The layout of the temple buildings resembles that of the Hōryūji Temple near Nara.

● **TSUTENKAKU TOWER** A well known landmark of Osaka is this 103 m.-high tower which has an observation deck commanding a fine view of the city and its environs. The area around the tower, Shinsekai, is very much downtown Osaka and is filled with numerous inexpensive bars.

● **SUMIYOSHI SHRINE** Situated near Sumiyoshi-Kōen Station, this shrine is said to have been founded by the Empress *Jingū* in the early 3rd century. Although rebuilt in 1808, the shrine is designated as a National Treasure, and on June 14 the *Otaue Shinji* (rice planting festival) is held here.

SUBURBS OF OSAKA

WHAT TO SEE

● **BAMPAKU KINEN KOEN** (World Exposition Memorial Park) Accessible by a 10 min. bus ride from Senri-Chūō Subway Station. It was on this site that the World Exposition was held in 1970. The vast park is now a recreational and cultural center, containing vari-

Dōtombori

ous exhibition and performance halls, a Japanese garden and sports grounds. The park's facilities include the Expo Commemoration Hall, the National Museum of Ethnology, the Japan Folk Crafts Museum and Expo Land, all of which are closed on Wednesdays.

WHAT TO EAT

Osaka is often referred to in Japanese as *Kuidaore* which means that Osaka people spend their money on food until they go bankrupt. This does not mean, however, that all the restaurants in Osaka are expensive. On the contrary, restaurants in which you can enjoy good food at very reasonable prices are plentiful.

There are certain differences between cooking in Osaka and other parts of Japan. One difference is the soy sauce which is very lightly salted. Another is Osaka-zushi which, unlike Tokyo, is pressed into a square shape and is topped with marinated fish. Other Osaka specialities include **Porgy Rice** and **Ta-koyaki** (octopus and vegetables fried in balls of flour) which can be bought from stalls on the streets. Most restaurants are centered around **Soemon-chō**, **Dōtombori**, and **Sen-nichi-mae**. It's worth taking a look at some of the many restaurants, pubs and cafes in the 8-story *Kuidaore* building in **Dōtombori**, where all tastes are catered for.

WHERE TO STAY

Being such an important commercial center and a large city, Osaka has a wide range of hotels, inns and youth hostels to accommodate anyone from the high-powered businessman to the hitchhiker. First-class international hotels include the **Hotel Plaza** and the **ANA-Sheraton Hotel Osaka**. Many sightseers choose to stay at the **Osaka Terminal Hotel** because of its convenient location.

KOBE

Kobe, the capital of Hyōgo Prefecture, is one of Japan's largest ports, handling more than 14,000 ocean-going vessels a year. It has for many years been a major gateway into Japan, and with its large foreign population, it has a cosmopolitan atmosphere.

TRANSPORTATION

Tokyo to Shin-Kobe: 3 hrs. 30 min. by Shinkansen. Both Sannomiya and Shin-Kobe Stations are linked by frequent bus services. Sannomiya Station has a direct 40 min. bus link with Osaka International Airport. The JR,

Hankyū and Hanshin Railways all run between Sannomiya Station and neighboring cities. In the city, buses and taxis are plentiful.

TOUR HINTS

Being a major international port, Kobe presents the visitor with some interesting sights. Sightseers can often be seen at the port itself and in **Sorakuen Garden**. Shoppers should make straight for **Sannomiya** in downtown Kobe where there are countless stores, often filled with visiting crew members on the lookout for good bargains.

Many Chinese restaurants are located in **Nankin-machi**, while restaurants of various international flavors can be found in the **Kitano** district.

KOBE CITY

WHAT TO SEE

● **KOBE PORT** Naturally, this is the major feature of the city and a constant hive of activity, with passenger and cargo liners coming and going all the time. It ranks with Yokohama and Hakodate as one of the oldest ports in Japan. Boasting more than a dozen piers, the best known are **Naka** (Central) **Pier** and **Maya Pier**.

● **PORT TOWER** Standing 108 m. high on Naka Pier and resembling a *tsuzumi* (Japanese hand-drum), the Port Tower has a revolving observation platform commanding a panoramic view of the port city.

● **MOTOMACHI STREET** Running between Motomachi and Sannomiya Stations, this covered shopping street is lined with quality stores, restaurants and tea-houses. The street also has a department store at each end, **Mitsukoshi** on the west and **Daimaru** on the east.

● **SANNOMIYA** This is Kobe's most popular central shopping district. Its busiest streets include Flower Road and Sannomiya Center-*gai*, while underground is fashionable *Sanchika* Town. The modern tall buildings along the covered Center-*gai* arcade, such as Sony Plaza, Center Plaza and Sun Center, contain a myriad of fashion boutiques, restaurants and cafes.

● **TOR ROAD** Leading to Kitano, it lends this part of the city a somewhat exotic flavor. The road is lined with stylish restaurants, coffee shops, antique shops and boutiques tastefully displaying a wide range of imported items.

● **KOBE COMMERCE & TRADE CENTER BUILDING** Standing 26 stories tall and housing many international business offices, this major landmark of Kobe is one of western Japan's highest buildings. Its Sky Lounge serves as an excellent

Kobe City

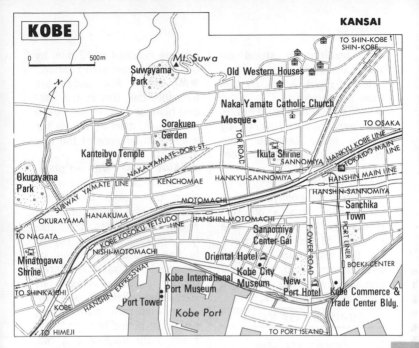

KOBE

0 ___ 500m

Mt. Suwa

Suwayama Park

Old Western Houses

Naka-Yamate Catholic Church

Mosque

Sorakuen Garden

TOR ROAD

Ikuta Shrine

SANNOMIYA

TO OSAKA

HANKYU KOBE LINE

TOKAIDO MAIN LINE

Kanteibyo Temple

NAKA-YAMATE-DORI ST.

HANKYU-SANNOMIYA

HANSHIN MAIN LINE

Okurayama Park

SUBWAY YAMATE LINE

KENCHOMAE

HANSHIN-SANNOMIYA

Sanchika Town

OKURAYAMA

HANAKUMA

MOTOMACHI

HANSHIN-MOTOMACHI

PORT LINER

TO NAGATA

KOBE KOSOKU TETSUDO LINE

NISHI-MOTOMACHI

Sannomiya Center-Gai

F. OWER ROAD

Minatogawa Shrine

HANSHIN EXPRESSWAY

Oriental Hotel

Kobe City Museum

BOEKI CENTER

TO SHINKAICHI

KOBE

Port Tower

Kobe International Port Museum

New Port Hotel

Kobe Commerce & Trade Center Bldg.

TO HIMEJI

Kobe Port

TO PORT ISLAND

TO SHIN-KOBE
SHIN-KOBE

131

observatory.

● **KOBE CITY MUSEUM** Here the visitor can find a wide collection of items relating to the archaeology, history and folklore of Kobe. It is combined with the Kobe City Museum of *Namban* Art in which there is an exhibition of Japanese paintings and art objects of the 16th and 17th centuries during which Kobe experienced a strong European influence.

● **KITANO** It was here that many foreigners used to live during the Meiji and Taishō periods (19th and early 20th centuries). Some of the old Western-style houses are well preserved and several are open to the public.

● **SORAKUEN GARDEN** Once owned by a former Mayor of Kobe, this lovely garden has a small grove of 200-year old cycads and camphor trees and a pond. Decked with azalea blooms in spring and chrysanthemums in autumn, the garden also contains typical Western-style buildings, including a brick stable, from the Meiji period. 10 min. by bus from Sannomiya.

● **SUWAYAMA PARK** This wooded hill is a pleasant park to stroll around and lovers have traditionally stood on Venus Bridge to view the city below at night. 3 min. by bus from Sannomiya.

● **KANTEIBYO TEMPLE** This is a Chinese temple revered by Kobe's many Chinese residents. 5 min. by subway from Sannomiya.

● **PORT ISLAND** Accessible by train from Sannomiya Station in 10 min., it was on this man-made island that the Portopia '81 festival was held. On the island are a hotel, gymnasium and science museum, and the Portopia Land amusement park.

SUBURBS OF KOBE

WHAT TO SEE

● **MT. ROKKO** A cable car, 30 min. by bus from Hankyū Rokkō Station, will take visitors from the foot to the summit of this highest peak in the Rokkō Mountains. Mt. Rokkō offers great views of Kobe and its environs.

● **ARIMA SPA** Located on the northern slope of Mt. Rokkō to which it is connected by a 5,000 m. - long ropeway, Arima Spa is one of Japan's most notable hot spring resorts. It serves as a cool mountain retreat in summer, and in autumn its trees are a blaze of red. Arima Spa can

also be reached in 40 min. by bus from Sannomiya Station.

● **MT. MAYA** Also accessible by cable car, this is the second highest peak in the Rokkō Mountains. It offers the visitor a spectacular view of the city at night.

● **NADA GOGO** With an abundance of natural spring water from the Rokkō Mountains, excellent rice, wood for casks and skilled workers, it is hardly surprising that this region is the source of some of Japan's finest sake. The three former brewery villages of Higashigō, Nakagō and Nishigō and their surrounding districts abound in sake breweries, both modern and old. Sawanotsuru Shiryōkan is a museum exhibiting many of the tools traditionally used in sake brewing. To get to it, take the train for 6 min. from Sannomiya to Oishi Station, from which it is only a 7 min. walk. Hakutsuru Sake Brewery Museum, once a

Mt. Rokkō Ropeway

brewery itself, is now a museum also, and here you can get a realistic picture of the *sake* brewing process.

● **TAKARAZUKA** Here the main attraction is Family Land comprising a zoo, botanical gardens, a health center with a large public bathhouse, a science museum, cinema and doll house, monorail and the Takarazuka Grand Theater. The latter is a 3-story structure capable of seating 3,000 people. It presents a variety of shows such as musical adaptations of foreign and Japanese stories, reviews and operas performed by all-girl groups trained at the Takarazuka School which is attached to the theater. Similar perfomances are presented at the Tokyo Takarazuka Theater at Hibiya. Takarazuka Spa, with both Japanese style inns and modern hotels, is also in the area. 35 min. by bus from Arima Spa.

● **SUMA BEACH** This beautiful white sandy beach, lined with pine trees, is safe for swimming and boating. Near Suma Beach Park can be found the Suma Aquarium, containing 10,000 fish of 300 different varieties, and Kobe Tropical Botanic Park. 15 min. by JR from Sannomiya.

WHAT TO EAT

Kobe is renowned for its high-quality beef, which can be eaten in a variety of ways, both cooked and raw. Kitano-chō has many international restaurants, but if you like Chinese food, Nankin-machi can offer you anything you like. For French cuisine try the Oriental Hotel. Kobe is also the birthplace of some famous Japanese confectionery companies, which began as small stores owned by foreigners selling homemade cookies and candies.

WHERE TO STAY

In Kobe itself there are some traditional first-class hotels, such as the Oriental Hotel, and many Japanese-style inns. However, visitors who have already seen the city are recommended to stay at one of the hotels or inns in the nearby beauty spots such as Suma or Arima Spa. If you want a room with a truly wonderful night view, you should stay at the Rokkōsan Hotel.

133

Tor Road

山陽・山陰
SAN-YO & SAN-IN

The Chūgoku district forms the western edge of Honshū and is divided by the Chūgoku mountain range into two distinct sections, the San-in in the north, facing the Sea of Japan, and the San-yō in the south, lying along the coast of the Inland Sea. Both areas have their own atmosphere and special attractions.

OKAYAMA & HIROSHIMA

An area that is growing in popularity with visitors, it offers the charm of quiet traditional cities like Kurashiki and Onomichi, and the scenic beauty of the Inland Sea as well as the bustle of modern cities like Hiroshima and Okayama.

TRANSPORTATION

● *BY AIR* Tokyo to Okayama: I hr. 55 min.; to Hiroshima: I hr. 30 min.

● *BY RAIL* San-yō Shinkansen *Hikari* and *Kodama* stop at Okayama and Hiroshima. Only *Kodama* stops at Shin-Kurashiki and other stations.

Tokyo to Okayama: 4 hrs.; to Hiroshima: 5 hrs.

The San-yō Line runs parallel to the Shinkansen Line, providing convenient access to all parts of the area.

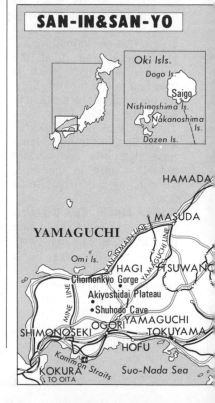

TOUR HINTS

There are many fascinating towns in the area, so an ideal course would be centered around a few that take your interest. For a little variety, try taking ferries to towns in Shikoku, for example from Uno (35min. by JR from Okayama Station) to Takamatsu (*See* p. 146): 25 min. by hovercrafts, or from Hiroshima and Iwakuni to Matsuyama (*See* p. 148).

HIMEJI & OKAYAMA

WHAT TO SEE

● *HIMEJI CASTLE,* in the center of the city, consists of a 5-story donjon, 3-story keeps and interconnecting passages all built in 1609. Many of the turrets, gates and stone walls are also well-preserved. Considered the best of Japanese feudal castles, it is also called *Shirasagi* (Egret) *jō*, since its white-plastered walls from

a distance give viewers the impression of a silhouette of one of the white egrets that often alight in nearby rice fields. It takes around 2 hrs. to see the castle.

● **OKAYAMA CASTLE** The ruins are called *Ujō* (Crow Castle) as it is painted black. *Hirajiro* (a castle constructed on flat land) was built in 1573, and the donjon's top floor is now set aside as an observation room, giving views over the city. It is located in the east of downtown Okayama, formerly a flourishing castle town and now a popular restaurant and shopping district. 10 min. by streetcar from Okayama Station.

● **KORAKUEN GARDEN**, fronting onto the south side of the castle, is regarded as one of the 3 finest gardens in Japan, along with Kairakuen Garden in Mito and Kenrokuen Garden in Kanazawa. It has tea ceremony houses, ponds and graceful contours.

● **BIZEN CITY** 45 min. by JR from Okayama, the city gives its name to the famous pottery it produces. There are around 100 kilns in the Imbe section of the city where visitors can watch potters at work or buy some of this pottery at its cheapest.

Kurashiki

● **KURASHIKI** 20 min. by JR from Okayama, offers visitors an authentic glimpse of old Japan. Along its willow-lined canal banks stand many white-walled and black-roofed warehouses, reminders of the city's position as a rice port in feudal days. Try seeing the city from a *jinrikisha*, rickshaws that have revived here.

Kurashiki Folkcraft Museum comprises 4 former warehouses, in which some 10,000 examples of pottery, textiles, dyed goods, wood craft and bamboo ware are displayed.

Ohara Art Gallery, built in 1930 by the late *Magosaburō Ohara*, is modeled after a Greek temple and houses his collection of western art, including works by Renoir, Matisse, Rodin, Cézanne, Picasso and Corot. The gallery's 3 annexes display Oriental art and Japanese paintings, woodblock prints and pottery.

WHAT TO BUY

Traditional folkcrafts still thrive in this region, such as Okayama's handbags and purses woven from rushes, and Bizen pottery. In Kurashiki, glass is a specialty and craftsmen produce a variety of hand-made items, including cups and dinnerware.

HIROSHIMA

WHAT TO SEE

● *HIROSHIMA* Hiroshima was completely razed by the atomic bomb explosion in August 1945 but has since been rebuilt into the cultural, economic and political heart of western Honshū.

Peace Memorial Park is situated on a delta between the Motoyasu and Hon Rivers. The Flame of Peace burns perpetually in the park which contains monuments and a museum related to the atomic bomb explosion in the last days of World War II. They include the Memorial Cenotaph, Children's Peace Monument, Fountain of Prayers and the Peace Memorial Museum. Near the park are the ruins of the former Municipal Industrial Promotion Hall topped by its skeletal dome. This building was at the epicenter of the blast and has been left untouched as a stark reminder of the atomic holocaust.

Shukkeien Garden A 5 min. bus ride takes you to a pond-centered landscape garden modeled after West Lake in China. Laid out in 1620, the garden is covered with cherry blossoms and a little later, azaleas blossom in spring.

● *MIYAJIMA ISLAND* 25 min. by JR to the ferry port from Hiroshima, is one of Japan's "Scenic Trio". With the steep Mt. Misen at its center, the whole island is covered in thick forest and, especially in Momijidani Park, boasts beautiful autumn colors. A 20 min. ropeway plus a 20 min. walk will bring you to the top of Mt. Misen. Visitors to Miyajima will soon see the 16 m. red wooden *torii* gate of Itsukushima Shrine, surrounded by water at high tide. The shrine itself consists of the Main Hall and several subsidiary shrines, all con-

Itsukushima Shrine Torii Gate

nected by bright vermilion corridors or galleries. At high tide the sea comes up to the level of these walkways, and the entire shrine appears to be floating on the water.

● **IWAKUNI** 45 min. by JR from Hiroshima, this industrial city produces synthetic fibers and pulp. Not far from the city is **Kintai Bridge** commonly called *Soroban Bashi* (Abacus Bridge) because of its shape. A 5-span structure, 193 m. - long, it was built in 1673, destroyed by floods in 1950 and rebuilt 3 years later — entirely without nails.

Fishing for *ayu* (sweet fish) using cormorants can be seen from the bridge in summer. **Iwakuni Castle** is a mountain fortress originally built in 1608 and restored in 1962.

● *GEIYO ISLANDS* These quiet Inland Sea islands can be reached by hydrofoil, express launch, or ferry. The main attraction on **Ikuchi Island** is **Kōsanji Temple**, which was built in styles imitating over 20 representative temples from the Asuka to Edo periods (6th~19th centuries). 30 min. by Express Launch from Onomichi.

WHAT TO EAT

Oysters are the most famous Hiroshima specialty, available at any restaurant in the city. The season is from November to March, and oyster lovers might like to try the "Oyster Boat" restaurant moored near the Heiwa Ohashi Bridge.

TOTTORI & SHIMANE

This region lacks a convenient transportation network and has always been "off the beaten track" for tourists. However, it is worth a visit as it offers visitors some of the quiet and simplicity of rural Japan.

TRANSPORTATION

● *BY AIR* Tokyo to Tottori: 2 hrs.; to Izumo: 1 hr. 30 min.

● *BY RAIL* Transfer from the San-yō Shinkansen to Limited Express.

Okayama to Yonago: 2 hrs. 20 min.; to Matsue: 2 hrs 55 min.; to Izumo: 3 hrs. 20 min.

An alternative is the Limited Express with sleeping cars from Tokyo. Limited Express and Express trains run quite frequently from Kyoto and Osaka. In the San-in district, the JR San-in Main Line is most convenient, running from east to west, and allows diversions to the coastline. There are good bus services to all sightseeing spots.

TOUR HINTS

The region has a lot of hot spring resorts, and a relaxed stay at **Misasa** or **Kaike Hot Springs,** indulging in fresh seafood from the Sea of Japan, would make an enjoyable trip. For viewing the coastline, the various excursion cruises available are recommended.

TOTTORI

WHAT TO SEE

● **TOTTORI,** one of the main cities in the San-in district, thrives as a spa resort. Though now a busy commercial center, Tottori's symmetrical city blocks show its former position as a castle town.

Tottori Sand Dunes, 20 min. by bus from Tottori, extend for 16 km. and are 1 to 2 km. wide. The dunes are easily accessible and the beautiful sunsets over them attract many visitors. **San-in Coast** is very scenic and full of variety. Excursion boats are available from Kasumi (50 min. by JR from Tottori),

Cape Hinomisaki near Izumo

Hamasaka, and Iwamoto.

● **MISASA SPA** 20 min. by bus from JR's Kurayoshi Station.

The largest radium spa in Japan, it is among the 3 major resorts in San-in along with Kaike and Tamatsukuri Spas.

MATSUE & IZUMO

WHAT TO SEE

139

● **MT. DAISEN,** at 1,711 m., the highest peak in the Chūgoku Mountains, is an extinct volcano resembling Mt. Fuji when viewed from the west. A 50 min. bus ride from JR's Yonago Station takes visitors halfway up the mountain to Daisenji Temple. The mountain is especially beautiful in autumn, while in winter extensive ski slopes are opened.

● **KAIKE SPA** 20 min. by bus from JR's Yonago Station, this is a pretty hot springs resort, with a row of pine trees along the beach and Mt. Daisen rising in the distance. It lies along Miho Bay and at night, the fires of night-fishing boats can be seen out to sea.

● **MATSUE** This city is the capital of Shimane Prefecture. Since it lies at the point where Nakanoumi Lagoon and Lake Shinji meet, Matsue is regarded as the "City of Water". Matsue Castle is a hill castle built in 1611 by the *Horio* clan. Its 5-story donjon gives good views of the surrounding area, and part of the castle grounds forms Shiroyama Park, bordered with many cherry trees.

Yakumo Memorial House, 10 min. by bus from Matsue Station, was built in 1933 in memory of *Yakumo Koizumi* (Lafcadio Hearn), a scholar and writer who taught English in the area for 15 months from 1890. The house displays a collection of manuscripts and other articles associated with him. It is next to Hearn's old home, a former *samurai* house which has remained unchanged since he left Matsue.

● **TAMATSUKURI SPA,** the most popular and time-honored spa in the San-in district, lies along the Tamatsukuri River. The resort now has many modern inns, but it still retains all the atmosphere of an historical hot springs town. 35 min. by bus from Matsue Station.

● **IZUMO TAISHA SHRINE** The oldest shrine in Japan, its buildings are fine specimens of *Shintō* shrine architecture with their dignified and imposing appearance. Izumo itself is a quiet town with many old white-walled houses standing along the Takase River.

● **THE OKI ISLANDS** North of Shimane Peninsula are a cluster of about 180 islands divided into 2 groups, Dōzen and Dōgo. The coast along the peninsula features spectacular sea-eroded cliffs over 100 m.-high.

WHAT TO EAT

Matsuba Crab is the favorite winter dish in the San-in district and is served at most inns and restaurants. August to October is the time for trying large juicy Nijusseiki Pears. In Daisen, wild vegetable dishes are popular. Daisen's specialty is Daisenji Soba—noodles with yam. It is served in the restaurants lining the approach to Daisenji Temple. Likewise in Izumo, Izumo Soba deserves attention.

In Matsue, your thoughts

will turn immediately to **sea-food**: white-bait, pond smelt, eels from Lake Shinji and Tai-meshi—rice topped with powdered fish.

WHAT TO BUY

The numerous folkcrafts produced in this area are the most popular souvenirs. They include clay bells in the shape of *tengu,* the supposed guardian of Mt. Daisen, papier-mache tigers bought as good luck charms, blue dyed tapestries, and Nagashi-bina, the area's traditional dolls.

YAMAGUCHI & HAGI

This area, with Yamaguchi Prefecture at its center, forms the western edge of Honshū. It contains a variety of sightseeing spots such as Hagi, an historic castle town, and fine scenery in the Akiyoshidai Quasi-National Park.

TRANSPORTATION

● **BY AIR** Tokyo to Ube (Yamaguchi Prefecture): I hr. 40 min.

● **BY RAIL** ＊Ogōri on the Shinkansen Line is the usual starting point for seeing the district. Tokyo to Ogōri: 5 hrs. 40 min.

＊To Tsuwano in Yamaguchi, take the Yamaguchi Line north. To Hagi and Akiyoshidai, take the bus from Yamaguchi city. To Omi Island, take the San-in Line from Hagi to Nagato-shi Station. On Sundays and holidays from spring to autumn, steam locomotives run on the JR Yamaguchi Line.

TOUR HINTS

Rental bicycles are an ideal way of getting around quiet old towns like Hagi, Tsuwano and Yamaguchi at a leisurely pace. A recommended side trip is a visit to the Akiyoshidai Quasi-National Park with its large limestone tableland and numerous caves.

YAMAGUCHI & TSUWANO

WHAT TO SEE

● *YAMAGUCHI* The capital of Yamaguchi Prefecture, its history dates back to the 14th century when it passed into the hands of the feudal lord, *Ouchi*. His family increased its prosperity by building numerous temples in imitation of Kyoto and introducing Kyoto's culture.

141

Xavier Memorial Park features a Roman Catholic cathedral built in 1952 in the Romanesque style. The cathedral honors the memory of Francisco de Xavier, the jesuit missionary who, in 1551, began evangelical work in Yamaguchi. Jōeiji Garden is a pond-centered garden laid out by Sesshū, a famous sumi-e painter, in the 15th century.

● **CHOMONKYO GORGE** This scenic valley, on the upper reaches of the Abu River, has beautiful autumn tints, ice-covered trees in winter, and cascades and pools along the river. 1 hr. 10 min. by JR from Ogōri.

● **TSUWANO** is a small castle town with many white-walled storehouses and old houses with lattice windows. Half a day is long enough to walk around it. Yōrōkan used to be a school building for the area's feudal clan but is now the Museum of Folk Materials, exhibiting various folk arts and materials related to the local history.

The Yasaka Shrine is best known for its Sagi-Mai (Heron Dance) performed on July 20 and 27. Dolls clad in the costume worn in this dance are displayed along with folk crafts, weapons and armor at the Jingasa Folk Crafts House.

142

WHAT TO BUY

Ouchi Lacquerware, noted for its elegance, has been made in the town for over 600 years and makes a beautiful souvenir of Yamaguchi. The same lacquering techniques are used in making Ouchi Dolls. Tsuwano abounds with folk crafts, the most notable being high quality Sekishū Paper. The process of making this paper can be seen at the Sekishū Japanese Paper Hall.

HAGI & SHIMONOSEKI

WHAT TO SEE

● **HAGI** This is an old, well-preserved castle town .and now a port and fishing center for this district. From 1600 it prospered as the castle town of the Mōri clan for 263 years. A whole day is needed to see its major attractions which include the Mōri Clan's Tenement House for their servant soldiers, the remains of Hagi Castle and the former houses of noted statesmen who served the shogunate before the Meiji Restoration (1868). The Shōkasonjuku School, where these noted figures

Shōkasonjuku School

used to study, has also been preserved.

● *AKIYOSHIDAI* Akiyoshidai Plateau is the largest limestone tableland in Japan, with Akiyoshidō (Akiyoshi Cave) located along its southern slopes. The cave stretches 10 km. in length, with its entrance measuring 24 m. high and 8 m. wide. Tourists are restricted to the first 1.5 km., and must be accompanied by a local guide. In the caves are rivers, waterfalls, and deep pools as well as stalactites, stalagmites and pillars.

● *OMI ISLAND* This can be visited by taking excursion boats which cruise around its rocky, eroded shoreline beneath steep cliffs.

● *SHIMONOSEKI* On the western edge of Honshū, this city faces Kyūshū across the Kammon Channel. It is a vital land and sea traffic link as well as a base for deep-sea fishing.

It has been the stage of numerous dramatic historical events, the most notable being the extermination of the *Taira* clan by the *Minamoto* clan in a battle on the city's beach in 1185.

WHAT TO EAT

In Shimonoseki, October to March is the season for tempting fate by indulging in fugu (blowfish) dishes. The innards of this fish are poisonous, and it can be prepared only by specially licensed cooks. This has reduced the number of fatalities but has made blowfish dishes more expensive. However, as far as taste goes, it's well worth it. A popular dish is fuku-sashi (raw)—the blowfish is sliced extremely thin, making it semi-transparent and allowing you to see the design on the blue platter.

143

WHAT TO BUY

In Hagi, numerous kilns and pottery shops sell the city's best souvenir — Hagi pottery. In the world of the tea ceremony it is said that Raku pottery is the best, then Hagi followed by Karatsu. For something completely different, lanterns made of real blowfish can be purchased in Shimonoseki.

四 国
SHIKOKU

Shikoku is the fourth largest Japanese island and is divided into 4 prefectures. Nicknamed "Blue Country" because of its magnificent coastal waters, it is a peaceful island and is famous for the Ohenrosan, pilgrims dressed in white who travel around the 88 temples of Kōbō-Daishi.

TRANSPORTATION

● **BY AIR** Tokyo to Tokushima: 1 hr. 5 min.; to Takamatsu: 2 hrs.; to Kōchi: 1 hr 10 min.; to Matsuyama: 1 hr. 20 min. It is convenient to transfer at Osaka.

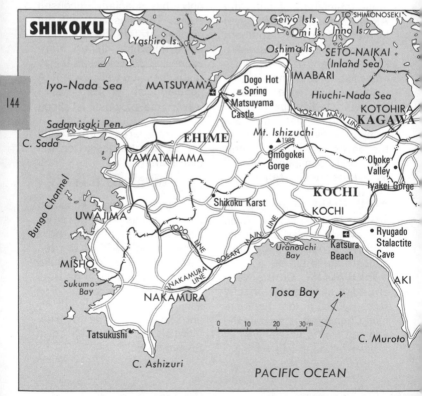

● **BY RAIL** Take the Shinkansen and transfer to one of several ferry terminals (often far from the train stations).

* To Takamatsu: take the Uno Line from Okayama to Uno or go by Limited Express from Tokyo to Uno (sleepers available). At Uno, transfer to the hovercraft: 25 min.

* To Matsuyama: from Hiroshima: 1 hr.; from Mihara: 1 hr. 20 min. by ferry.

TOUR HINTS

The *Awa* Dance Festival at Tokushima is a famous major attraction in August. Due to the festival's great popularity, travel and accommodation arrangements should be made well in advance.

EASTERN SHIKOKU

The most popular tourist attractions here are Tokushima, the major gateway to Shikoku, the beautiful city of Takamatsu, the great whirlpools of the Naruto Straits and the rich scenery in the south of the island. There are also lots of quiet spots off the beaten track.

145

TRANSPORTATION

In this part of the island, Takamatsu is the major railway terminal. However, by using Tokushima as a starting point, it is quicker to go direct to Tokushima by ferry from Osaka, Kobe or Wakayama than to go to Tokushima via Takamatsu by JR train.

Also, between the southern part of Anan, Muroto Point and Kōchi, only buses are available.

KAGAWA

WHAT TO SEE

● **TAKAMATSU** Formerly a castle town in the feudal 16th century, Takamatsu is now a thriving tourist resort. On the busy east side of Chūō-dōri Street, running south from the station, there are large department stores such as *Mitsukoshi*.

● **YASHIMA PLATEAU** From this tableland which juts out into the Inland Sea, you can take in some lovely views and see the relics of a 12th century battle. 35 min. by bus from Takamatsu Pier.

● **KOTOHIRA SHRINE** Dedicated to the God of Prosperity, this is popularly known as *Kompira-san*. The shrine precincts are set at the top of a flight of 785 steps and feature a 27 m.-high lantern erected in 1865 to light the path of millions of annual pilgrims and tourists. 1 hr. by Kotohira Electric Railway from Takamatsu.

WHAT TO EAT

Kagawa boasts the best noodles in Japan, named *Sanuki-Udon*, with over 2,000 *udon* restaurants in Takamatsu alone. Judge it for yourself!

WHAT TO BUY

Takamatsu's favorite toy is the *Hōkōsan* (papier-mache doll), which was important for girls at the time of their marriage, and it is a popular souvenir of the district. Elegant Sanuki lacquerware is also a famous product of this part of Japan.

TOKUSHIMA

WHAT TO SEE

● **TOKUSHIMA** The fourth largest city in Shikoku, Tokushima is associated with Wenceslao de Moraes, a Portugese consular officer who wrote many books about Japan. The city is also the location for the annual Awa Dance Festival in August.

The Residence of Awa Jūrobei At the ruins of this residence, named after the leading character in both *Kabuki* and *Jōruri*, large numbers of visitors are sometimes treated to impromptu performances in the indoor *Jōruri* theater. 20 min. by bus from Tokushima Station.

● **NARUTO STRAITS** The great whirlpools of these straits between Shikoku and Awaji Island can be observed by boat out of Okazaki Port in Naruto, which is 40 min. by train from Tokushima.

● *OBOKE / KOBOKE GORGE*
Situated at the upper end of
Yoshino River, these valleys,
with steep cliffs and jagged
rocks, form a very scenic
landscape. A 30 min. sightseeing boat trip is available.
20 min. walk from Oboke Station.

WHAT TO BUY

The area is noted for its
Awa Blue Dyeing Works. At
the Furushō Dyeing works you
can even try your own hand at
the skill. Otani Pottery
used in the dyeing process
can be purchased and makes
a good souvenir of your visit.

AWA DANCE FESTIVAL

Held every year from
August 12 to 15, this is the
biggest festival in Shikoku.
The dancing starts officially
from 6:00 p.m. and con-
tinues until 10:30 p.m. It
takes place on many stages
specially erected in the city
for the occasion and can
be watched from both pay-
ing and non-paying gal-
leries. The lyrics of the
dance music imply that "the
dancers are Stupid and also
the onlookers stupid. Then,
why don't you dance ? ".

WESTERN SHIKOKU

147

The major points of interest
in the western part of Shikoku
include the city of Matsuyama, which like Takamatsu
is a popular tourist resort,
and Cape Ashizuri at the
southern tip of the island.

TRANSPORTATION

● *BY RAIL* Takamatsu or
Tokushima to Kōchi: 3 hrs. by
JR express.
● *BY BUS* Nakamura Station
to Ashizuri point: 2 hrs.; or
from Kōchi (summer season
only) : 4 hrs. 35 min.

KOCHI

WHAT TO SEE

● *KOCHI* Kōchi is the birthplace of *Ryōma Sakamoto*,
the hero of the Meiji Revolu-
tion, about whom many works
have been written. With a
castle as its focal point, Kōchi
has many attractions for the
visitor.
● *ASHIZURI POINT* This is
notable for its steep cliffs,
which are continuously battered by the *Kuroshio* currents.

You can enjoy strolling along the promenade around the lighthouse overlooking the Pacific Ocean.

● **MUROTO POINT** Similar to Ashizuri Point, which it faces, Muroto Point also has a lighthouse standing above wild seas far below. 3 hrs. 10 min. by JR from Kōchi.

● **RYUGADO CAVE** Along with Akiyoshidō in Yamaguchi and Ryūsendō in Iwate, this is one of Japan's largest limestone caves.

WHAT TO EAT

The specialities of Kōchi are Sawachi and Sugata-zushi. *Sawachi* is raw porgy and bonito served on an Arita pottery dish. Make sure the porgy doesn't jump back into the water! *Sugata-zushi* is a pickled whole fish stuffed with rice. No soup for the fish head —eat the lot! You can wash these down with a cup of local *sake*.

WHAT TO BUY

One of the symbols of Kōchi is the Tosa dog, a renowned breed in the ever-popular world of dog fighting. Little wooden carvings of the Tosa dog make good souvenirs of the region.

EHIME

WHAT TO SEE

● **MATSUYAMA** The setting for *Sōseki Natsume*'s famous novel "*Botchan*", Matsuyama possesses one of Japan's best preserved castles. And here and there in the modern city can be found historical remains of long ago.

● **DOGO SPA** Considered the oldest spa in Japan, this has hot springs of clear, alkaline water. The 3-story wooden public bathhouse, part of which is reserved for the Imperial Family, has several interesting rooms, including a *tatami* parlor and tearoom.

● **UWAJIMA** This is a charming little castle city full of folklore and good homecooking. It is a center for all-year-round bullfighting without matadors and is the location for the Warei Shrine Festival on July 23 and 24.

Ashizuri Point

九 州

KYUSHU

Because of its proximity to the Eurasian continent, Kyushu, the southernmost of Japan's 4 main islands, came under Asian and European influence from early times. The numerous points of interest here include Nagasaki, a former gateway to the world and the active volcano of Mt. Aso.

TRANSPORTATION

● **BY AIR** From Tokyo it takes 1 hr. 40 min. to any one of Fukuoka, Nagasaki, Kumamoto, Oita, Miyazaki and Kagoshima. From Osaka the equivalent trip takes about 1 hr.

● **BY RAIL** Tokyo to Kokura: 6 hrs.; to Hakata (Fukuoka) : 6 hrs. 30 min. on the Shinkansen bullet train.

From Tokyo, Nagoya and Osaka, Limited Express trains with sleepers are available. However those with less time might consider flying to the major sightseeing spots.

TOUR HINTS

Kyushu can roughly be divided into 3 districts for sightseeing purposes: Northwest Kyushu with all its history, traditional crafts and beautiful coastline; Central Kyushu with its mountains, hot springs and Buddhist art; and Southern Kyushu with sunlit coastlines, spas and mountains. A tour taking in all the major attractions of Kyushu would take between 7 and 10 days.

NORTHWEST KYUSHU

Kita-Kyushu, a major industrial city and Fukuoka with important communication and transportation links are the main entrances of this area.

This region is famous for its potteries and for its early Christian inhabitants.

It celebrates several lively festivals which the visitor would enjoy.

TRANSPORTATION

● **BY RAIL** Hakata to Nagasaki: 2 hrs. 40 min. by the Limited Express "Kamome"; to

149

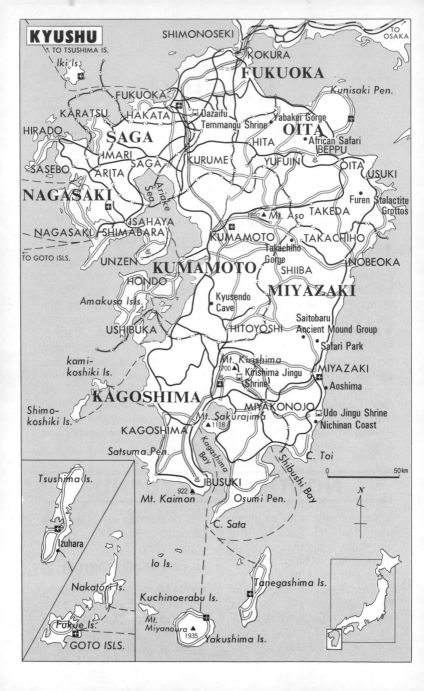

KYUSHU

SHIMONOSEKI
TO OSAKA
TO TSUSHIMA IS.
Iki Is.
KOKURA
FUKUOKA
Kunisaki Pen.
FUKUOKA
KARATSU
HAKATA
Dazaifu
Temmangu Shrine
Yabakei Gorge
SAGA
OITA
HIRADO
HITA
African Safari
BEPPU
SASEBO
IMARI
SAGA
KURUME
YUFUIN
OITA
ARITA
USUKI
NAGASAKI
Furen Stalactite
Grottos
Ariake
Sea
1592 ▲ Mt. Aso
TAKEDA
ISAHAYA
KUMAMOTO
TAKACHIHO
NAGASAKI
SHIMABARA
Takachiho
Gorge
NOBEOKA
UNZEN
KUMAMOTO
SHIIBA
HONDO
MIYAZAKI
Amakusa Isls.
Kyusendo
Cave
USHIBUKA
HITOYOSHI
Saitobaru
Ancient Mound Group
kami-
koshiki Is.
Safari Park
Mt. Kirishima
1700 ▲
MIYAZAKI
Shimo-
koshiki Is.
KAGOSHIMA
Kirishima Jingu
Shrine
Aoshima
MIYAKONOJO
Mt. Sakurajima
▲1118
Udo Jingu Shrine
Nichinan Coast
KAGOSHIMA
Satsuma Pen.
Kagoshima
Bay
C. Toi
Shibushi Bay
0   50 km
N
IBUSUKI
922 ▲
Mt. Kaimon
Osumi Pen.
C. Sata

Tsushima Is.
Izuhara
Nakatori Is.
Fukue Is.
GOTO ISLS.
Io Is.
Kuchinoerabu Is.
Mt.
Miyanoura ▲
1935
Yakushima Is.
Tanegashima Is.

Sasebo: 2 hrs. 20 min. by the Limited Express "Midori".

● **BY BUS** Many buses travel between the cities and the sightseeing spots in their surrounding areas.

FUKUOKA & HIRADO

WHAT TO SEE

● **FUKUOKA** During the Nara and Heian Periods, Fukuoka was the main port through which trade from the Asian continent entered Japan. East part of this city had once called "Hakata". It remains in the names of Station, Festivals and toys. The city's, ancient past lives on in the castle remains, and nearby Ohori Park completes the beautiful setting.

● **DAZAIFU** Just 40 min. by Nishitetsu Line from Fukuoka, this is the site of several historical relics, including the office of the former Governor General of Kyushu, the Kanzeonji Temple and Dazaifu Temmangū Shrine. The latter was built in 1591 in memory of Michizane Sugawara, a leading Chinese Literature scholar.

● **KARATSU** Karatsu is the home of traditional potteries and the location for the Karatsu Kunchi Festival, the Hikiyama (festival cars) of which can be seen in the Hikiyama Pavilion. Nearby is Niji-no-Matsubara, one of Japan's most famous pine groves which extends for 5 km. along the white sands of Matsuuragata Beach. I hr. 40 min. by express bus from Fukuoka.

● **ARITA** This is another center of the porcelain trade and visitors can see here some of the works of Arita masters of feudal times. I hr. 40 min. by JR Limited Express from Hakata.

● **IMARI** It is here that you will find skilled craftsmen using traditional methods to produce beautiful pieces of fine porcelain, called Imariyaki. 20 min. by JR from Arita.

● **SASEBO** Visitors to Sasebo should set aside some time to go to Saikai National Park, with Kujūku-shima scattered over its clear blue waters. 2 hrs. by JR Limited Express from Hakata.

● **HIRADO** Hirado was the first city to be opened to Portuguese trade in 1550. Many relics of ancient days can still be seen in this island city. One such relic is the 3-story Hirado Castle, built on the hill overlooking Kameoka Park and Hirado Straits. I hr. 30 min. by JR

151

Express from Sasebo.

WHAT TO EAT

Fukuoka's large entertainment districts, Nakasu and Tenjin, have streets crammed with bars, restaurants and clubs. Here you can try Mizu-taki, a chicken and vegetable soup, or sample Karashi Mentaiko — cod roe preserved in red pepper—at Fukuya or Itoya. What other way can you think of to round off a day's sightseeing than to try Odori-gui — whitebait eaten live with vinegar?

WHAT TO BUY

In Hakata there are many department stores and underground arcades clustered around Tenjin Station. Hakata-ori Textiles are beautiful silk fabrics woven with a fine wool and a thick warp. Aritayaki is brilliantly colored pottery featuring bright blue or orange drawings on a white background. Most pottery works in Arita display their products for visitors and a large market is held from May 1 to 5. Karatsuyaki pottery specializes in high-quality pots, cups and other tea ware.

NAGASAKI

WHAT TO SEE

● **NAGASAKI** Opened to foreign trade in 1571 the city flourished as the sole gateway through which western culture filtered into Japan during the period of isolation. The city is also associated with Christianity, which was introduced by Francis Xavier (1506-1552), a Spanish missionary, and hence the city has many historic places related to Christianity and the West.

● **SITE OF THE MARTYRDOM OF THE 26 SAINTS** It was here that Pedro Bautista, 5 other foreign and 20 Japanese Christians were crucified on Feb 5, 1597, as a result of the decree prohibiting Christianity issued by *Hideyoshi Toyotomi*, the military ruler at that time. In 1962, the centenary of their canonization as saints, a monument to the martyrs was built, along with a museum and a memorial sanctuary. 5 min. on foot from Nagasaki Station.

● **MEGANEBASHI BRIDGE** This is the oldest foreign-style stone bridge in Japan. Its double arches spanning the Nakajima River resemble large spectacles, giving the bridge its name—"Glasses

Harbor View from Glover Park

152

Bridge".

● **SOFUKUJI TEMPLE** Built in 1629, it is known as *Nankin-dera* (Chinese Temple) as it contains some excellent examples of Chinese architecture from the later period of the Ming Dynasty.

● **OURA CATHOLIC CHURCH** This is the oldest wooden church of Gothic architecture in Japan. It was built in 1864 under the supervision of Petit Jean, a French missionary, in memory of the 26 Christian martyrs who were crucified in Nagasaki.

● **GLOVER MANSION** Situated near Oura Catholic Church, the mansion is known as the alleged setting of the opera "Madame Butterfly". Standing on a hill overlooking the city, it is over a century old and is the former residence of a British merchant, Thomas Glover. Glover Park also contains other western style houses built in the Meiji Period, as well as the Nagasaki Traditional Entertainment House.

● **PEACE PARK** The park was laid out to commemorate the site of the atomic bomb explosion on August 9, 1945. In the park stand the International Cultural Hall and the bronze Statue of Peace. 10 min. by streetcar from Nagasaki.

FESTIVALS IN KYUSHU

● **HAKATA DONTAKU FESTIVAL** May 3 and 4. A popular fete with fancy dress processions as the main attractions. The Dontaku band plays folk music with *shamisen* parades.

● **HAKATA GION YAMAGASA FESTIVAL** July 1 to 15. Hakata's biggest festival, over 700 years old. On the last day, sumptuously decorated floats called *yamagasa* are carried by young men in *happi*-coats to Kushida Shrine.

● **NAGASAKI PERON TOURNAMENT** 4th Sunday in July. A boat tournament where youngsters row large boats to the accompaniment of drums and gongs.

● **NAGASAKI KUNCHI FESTIVAL** October 7 to 9. A variety of dances are performed, such as Dragon Dances, Sporting Whale Dances, and Ryūgū Ship Dances.

Kunch Festival

153

WHAT TO EAT

Shippoku is the representative local dish of Nagasaki. Vegetarian dishes introduced by Chinese priests were changed to suit the Japanese taste and *Shippoku* is one of these. It can be tried at first-class restaurants and inns in Maruyama. Nagasaki Champon is noodles in chicken soup with a variety of fried and flavored toppings.

WHAT TO BUY

A popular shopping area is Harusame Street from Nishihama-chō Streetcar Station to Shiambashi Bridge. Hamaichi Arcade at the northern end of the street is the largest arcade in Nagasaki. Bekkō Crafts are various items made from turtle shells. Nagasaki Biidoro is the city's glass craft, produced in a variety of colors. Tsuki-machi Market sells seafood, while Nagasaki's Chinatown, in Shinchi, has lots of restaurants and shops.

UNZEN & SHIMABARA

WHAT TO SEE

● *UNZEN SPA* This is the joint name for 3 quiet resorts: Furuyu, Shin-yu and Ko-

jigoku. Situated in the mountains, the surrounding trees in winter are coated with "silver thaw" ice, forming a majestic crystaline forest. The spa also features numerous sulphurous fumeroles and bubbling hot springs. 2 hrs. 10 min. by bus from Nagasaki Station.

● *SHIMABARA* A small photogenic port town, visitors can find here relics of *samurai* houses and small temples left over from Shimabara's days as a castle town. Shimabara Castle, built in 1625, has a 5-story donjon, restored in 1960. On display in the castle are records and documents concerning the 38,000 or so Japanese Christians who made their last stand in 1638 against the *Shōgun*'s army, only to be finally annihilated. There still remain old battlefields, tombs of the martyrs and other relics scattered throughout the islands. 1 hr. by Shimabara Railways from Isahaya.

Shimabara Castle

CENTRAL KYUSHU

This region is rich in magnificent scenery such as the awe-inspiring Mt. Aso, the world's largest caldera, and the beautiful Yabakei valley with its lush countryside, unusual rock formations and numerous spas.

TRANSPORTATION

● **BY RAIL** Shinkansen Hakata Station to Kumamoto: I hr. 40 min. by the Limited Express "Ariake"; Shinkansen Kokura Station to Beppu: I hr. 30 min. by the Limited Express "Nichirin".

● **BY BUS** On the Yamanami Highway from Kumamoto to Aso and Beppu, Limited Express buses and regular sightseeing buses are available.

AMAKUSA & KUMAMOTO

WHAT TO SEE

● **AMAKUSA ISLANDS** These comprise over 70 islands, the most attractive of which are now linked by 5 bridges. The very scenic trip across the islands and all 5 bridges is called the Pearl Line. The beauty of the undersea world around here can be seen by taking the glass boat cruises operating from Ushibuka in Shimojima Island.

Also, in Hondo there is the **Amakusa Ocean Floor Natural Aquarium**. The ruins of **Hondo Castle** are where early Japanese Christians were besieged by the Shōgun's army. 2 hrs. 20 min. by bus from Kumamoto to Hondo.

● **KUMAMOTO** Once noted as a castle town, this city is now the district's commercial and cultural center.

Kumamoto Castle is a hill castle built in 1607 by *Kiyomasa Katō*, a warlord of that period. The donjon was restored in 1960 and a number of turrets, stone walls and gates still remain to remind us of its former grandeur.

Suizenji Park (Jōjuen Garden) is a magnificent Japanese landscape garden laid out over 350 years ago. It includes representations, in garden form, of Mt. Fuji, lake Biwa and other well-known scenic attractions in Japan.

Tatsuta Natural Park is a tranquil park, containing an old teahouse and some old cedar trees, with a moss garden forming the center.

● **MT. ASO** The basin marking

155

the original crater of this active volcano is 24 km. from north to south and 18 km. from east to west, making it the world's greatest crater basin. 1 hr. 35 min. by bus from Kumamoto.

● **ASO NATIONAL PARK** This park includes volcanic Mt. Aso and Mt. Kujū as well as a group of mountains surrounding Beppu Spa. Mt. Aso itself contains 5 peaks with Mt. Nakadake at its center, constantly emitting high-temperature gas and sulphurous fumes, presenting an awe-inspiring sight. There are numerous hot spring resorts in the park, as well as picturesque towns and villages.

● **HITOYOSHI** A former castle town, this tourist city features a pleasant spa. The Kuma River which runs through the city is one of the fastest flowing in Japan where you can enjoy the thrills of shooting an 18 km. stretch of rapids. Near the end of the rapids is **Kyūsendō Cave**, a 2 km. long limestone cave open to the public.

WHAT TO EAT

Amakusa abounds in year-round fresh seafood. Shrimp and crabs are the local favorites, and shrimp are eaten raw or cooked in a variety of ways. The center for shopping in Kumamoto is the large arcade in **Kami-dōri** and **Shimo-dōri Streets**. There are numerous restaurants providing the local cuisine between **Shimo-dōri** and **Densha-dōri Streets**. A Kumamoto specialty is **Karashi Renkon**, deep fried lotus root stuffed with mustard and *miso*. If you've tried almost everything, you might like to consider **Basashi** — raw, high-grade horse meat. **Higo Dengaku** is grilled *tōfu* covered with *miso*. In Hitoyoshi, **Kuma Shōchū** is the area's liquor made from the best rice.

BEPPU & OITA

WHAT TO SEE

● **BEPPU** The largest hot springs resort in Kyushu with an enormous volume of hot water rushing from its many springs, Beppu is especially well-known for its **Sand**

Amakusa Pearl Line

Bath. As the name implies this means half-burying yourself in the sand on the beach warmed by hot water. Beppu also has several *jigoku* (literally: hell) boiling pools. The largest is *Umijigoku* — a hell, the color of the sea, and others include the vermilion colored *Chinoike-jigoku*.

● **TAKASAKIYAMA HILL** Wild but friendly monkeys, numbering over 1,600, are the main attraction here. 15 min. by bus from Beppu.

● **AFRICAN SAFARI PARK** Here, a variety of animals roam freely. Buses and rental cars are available at the park. 1 hr. by bus from Beppu.

● **YUFUIN** This quiet spa town is located in a scenic valley along the Yufu River. It is noted for the quintessential Japanese scenery presented by Mt. Yufu, which gradually appears as the thick mist rises at the break of an autumn day, and for the *Genjibotaru*, a species of firefly found along the river banks in summer. 1 hr. 10 min. by JR Express from Beppu.

● **USUKI** Near this town at the former site of Mangetsuji Temple are around 60 stone images of Buddha, standing in the open. These 1,000 year-old statues are regarded as the most artistic of their kind

Usuki stone images of Buddha

in Japan.

● **FUREN STALACTITE GROTTOS** These consist of 2 grottos. The older one is over 420 m. long and contains many beautiful stalactites, including those in the magnificent Ryūgū Castle cavern. The new grotto, situated above the older one is about 82 m. long.

● **YABAKEI GORGE** Situated along the upper reaches of the Yamakuni River, this gorge features fantastically shaped peaks and rocks, narrow ravines, meandering streams, and lush vegetation.

157

WHAT TO EAT

Beppu's specialty is *fugu* (blowfish) dishes, *sashimi* (raw) being the most popular along with *fuguchiri-nabe*, *fugu* boiled with vegetables. Hijimachi in northern Beppu is the place to try *Shiroshita garei* Flatfish *sashimi*.

SOUTHERN KYUSHU

This region, rich in scenery and with a sunlit coastline and lush subtropical foliage, is a popular destination for Japanese honeymooners.

TRANSPORTATION

● **BY RAIL** * Shinkansen Kokura Station to Miyazaki: 5 hrs. 30 min. on the Limited Express "Nichirin". * Shinkansen Hakata Station to Nishi-Kagoshima: 4 hrs. 30 min.; Miyazaki to Nishi-Kagoshima: 2 hrs. 10 min. on the Limited Express "Nichirin". To nearby attractions, buses and sightseeing cars are available for hire.

MIYAZAKI

WHAT TO SEE

● **TAKACHIHO** This area is noted for its extensive forests of hemlock-spruces and Japanese red pines, as well as its protected fauna. Also associated with the area is the *Iwato Kagura*, an ancient sacred dance performed at the Takachiho Shrine every night of the year. 1 hr. 50 min. by JR from Nobeoka.

● **TAKACHIHO GORGE** Walled in by 80 m.-high cliffs for several miles, the gorge lies along the upper reaches of the Gokase River. As well as its unusual rock formations, the gorge is known for its association with various myths concerning the origin of the country. The gorge and its vicinity are said to be the cradle of Japan. 30 min. on foot from Takachiho Station.

● **SAITOBARU MOUNDS** Saitobaru has a group of around 329 mounds, most of which were constructed in the 5th and 6th centuries. A well-known model ship excavated here is now kept in the National Museum in Tokyo.

● **MIYAZAKI** The political and economic center of Miyazaki Prefecture, the city boasts clean air and tidy streets and generally exudes the bright, fresh atmosphere characteristic of southern Kyushu.

Heiwadai Park, located on a hill overlooking the city, contains the garden of over 400 reproductions of figures excavated from burial mounds around Japan.

10 min. walk after a 25 min. bus ride from Miyazaki Station.

Miyazaki Shrine, built in 1907 entirely of cedar, is dedicated to Emperor *Jimmu*, the Legendary first Emperor of Japan. The prefectural Museum in the shrine grounds contains a valuable collection of ancient *haniwa* (clay figures) and other items of archeological interest. 20 min. by bus from Miyazaki Station.

● *MIYAZAKI SAFARI PARK* Here a total of 2,300 wild animals of 64 species roam freely. Buses and cars are available for the 6 km. drive through the park. 50 min. by bus from Miyazaki Station.

● *NICHINAN COAST QUASI NATIONAL PARK* This park extends for about 100 km. along Kyushu's southeastern coast, facing the Pacific Ocean. Scenically very pretty, it boasts a mild climate and lush tropical foliage.

Aoshima Island is one of the main attractions in the coastal park. It is covered with some 230 varieties of subtropical trees and shrubs, including *birō*. Another natural feature is a rock formation called "Goblin's Washboard" along the shore.

The Prefectural Subtropical Plant Garden, in the vicinity of Aoshima has over 400 varieties of subtropical plants and its large hothouse filled with luxuriant growth adds to the garden's lush subtropical atmosphere.

Nichinan Coast

Kodomo-no-kuni (Children's Land) is a large amusement park facing the Hyūga Sea and was laid out following the natural contours of the area.

Among its attractions are camels which can be ridden along the sand dunes.

WHAT TO EAT

The restaurant district in Miyazaki is centered around Tachibana-dōri Street going north of the Oyodo River. The bright lights of the entertainment quarter are around Nishi-Tachibana-dōri Street, a block west of Tachibana-dōri Street. Hiyajiru is a cold soup of fish and *miso*, garnished with delicious beefsteak plant and cucumber. Along the Nichinan Coast you can try cactus dishes — shoots of the fan cactus are pickled and eaten with salt, *sake* or sugar. You can wash this down with some ruby-colored hibiscus tea.

KAGOSHIMA

WHAT TO SEE

● **KIRISHIMA-YAKU NATIONAL PARK** Extending over Miyazaki and Kagoshima Prefectures, this park contains all the features of volcanic mountain scenery: 23 volcanos, 15 craters and 10 crater lakes as well as large forests, waterfalls, and rare plants. The Kirishima Volcanic Range extends nearly 16 km. between two outstanding peaks, Mt. Takachiho-no-mine and Mt. Karakunidake.

The park attracts visitors year round, and in spring, *Miyama-Kirishima*, a species of azalea and *nokaidō* (wild aronias), can be seen in full bloom.

● **KIRISHIMA SPA** With more than a dozen hot springs and a variety of lodging from luxury hotels to traditional inns, this is a popular tourist resort.

● **MIYAKONOJO** This city is in the center of the foggy Kirishima Basin, surrounded by the Kirishima mountains. An agricultural center, the city is known for its production of green tea. 55 min. by JR Limited Express from Miyazaki.

● **KAGOSHIMA** The cultural and economic hub of southern Kyushu, the city and vicinity offers numerous scenic spots, hot spring resorts and historical sites.

St. Xavier's Memorial Park, contains as well as a church, a bust commemorating St. Francis de Xavier, a Jesuit missionary who landed here in 1549. 5 min. by Streetcar from Nishi-Kagoshima Station.

Iso Park contains a stroll garden laid out by the *Shimazu* clan in 1661, as well as their former villa. Part of the garden features bamboo groves, originally transplanted from the south-sea islands. 25 min. by bus from Nishi-Kagoshima.

Shōkō-shūseikan building in Iso Park houses various materials showing the history of the *Shimazu* family. It includes a large house built in the *Shoin* style.

Shiroyama Park situated

The Sightseeing Carriage in Sakurajima

160

on Shiroyama Hill in the center of the city is where *Takamori Saigō*, a famous statesman, committed *harakiri* with his followers when the Kagoshima Rebellion of 1877 collapsed.

Yojirōgahama Beach features an International Jungle Park with a tropical garden and Kamoike Marine Park.

● *SAKURAJIMA* This active volcano used to be an island but has been connected with the Osumi Peninsula since an eruption in 1914. The volcano regularly covers the surrounding area with a layer of volcanic dust. 15 min. by ferry from Kagoshima Port.

● *IBUSUKI SPA* This year-round resort includes hot sand baths like those at Beppu. Most of its hot springs lie along the 10 km. beach.

WHAT TO EAT

The popular dining and entertainment area in Kagoshima is Tenmonkan. You can try the local cuisine and enjoy shopping in and around the arcade on the Shiroyama side of Denshadōri Street. On the other side of the street is the entertainment area, with lots of bars, restaurants and movie theaters. A Kagoshima specialty is Pork Ribs,

barbecued and then boiled with *miso* and muscovado added for flavor.

Satsuma-jiru is *miso* soup with chicken or pork and vegetables.

Sake-zushi, a rice dish with toppings of wild vegetables or seasonal seafoods, is soaked in *sake* and left overnight before eating. Strong flavors and lots of pork are Kagoshima's trademark and Kagoshima Ramen is the local Chinese noodle dish with a characteristic pork bone soup.

Kibinago are small fish around 8 cm.-long from the seas around Kyushu. They are eaten raw with vinegar and *miso*. Sakurajima Oranges are very small but extremely sweet and well worth trying.

161

WHAT TO BUY

Satsuma yaki Pottery: Originally introduced from Korea, there are two main types. The black pottery features articles designed for everyday use such as *Kurojoka*, a kind of liquor bottle, whereas the white pottery is represented mainly by elegantly shaped vases.

Satsuma yaki can be bought at department stores and folkcrafts shops in Kagoshima city.

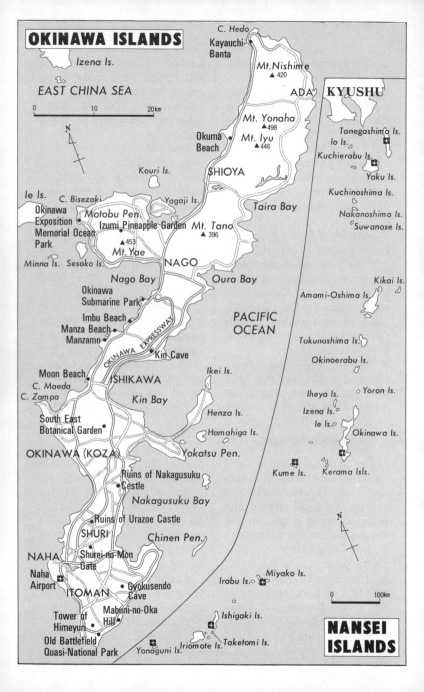

南西諸島
THE SOUTHWEST ISLANDS

With their white sand beaches, coral reefs beneath an emerald sea, bright tropical flowers and lush countryside, these islands are a colorful paradise for vacationers. The music, dances, crafts and cuisine of the local people reflect their original island culture as well as a heritage of Chinese and Japanese influences. The local dialect, often confusing to mainland Japanese, also reflects this exotic mixture.

TRANSPORTATION

These islands can be reached by ship, but for those with limited time, traveling by air is more convenient. Naha Airport in Okinawa is the terminal of direct flights from 11 cities. The Amami Islands can be reached by air from Osaka or Kagoshima Airports.

＊Tokyo to Naha: 2 hrs. 40 min. Osaka to Naha: 2 hrs 10 min.

TOUR HINTS

The region enjoys a warm subtropical climate all year round and is a perfect place to relax, so a leisurely stay is recommended. Besides at the major sightseeing spots on the Okinawa Main Island, there are large hotels on Kume, Miyako, Ishigaki, Kohama and Yoron Islands, as well as on Amami-Oshima in the Amami Islands.

163

OKINAWA MAIN ISLAND

The main island of the Okinawa Island chain abounds in places of historical interest, while its beautiful seascapes, beaches and variety of subtropical vegetation attracts visitors throughout the year. You can also enjoy large city's amenities.

TRANSPORTATION

Since there is no rail service in Okinawa, buses and taxis are used. The regular route bus service is well developed and regular sightseeing buses or taxis will take you to most attractions. Scenic flights are also available.

SOUTHERN OKINAWA

WHAT TO SEE

● **NAHA** The capital of Okinawa prefecture, Naha is the economic and commercial center of the islands.

Kokusai-dōri Street, the most fashionable shopping area in Naha, is lined with department stores, souvenir shops, restaurants and various places of entertainment.

Heiwa-dōri Avenue contains a market called *Machiguwa*, selling mainly food and daily supplies to the local people. There are also numerous restaurants providing large meals of the local cuisine very cheaply.

Naminoue Shrine is the site of the former castle oí the Ryūkyū Dynasty and is known as the guardian shrine of Okinawa. 10 min. by bus from the city center.

Sōgenji Ishimon (Stone Gates) Sōgenji Temple was a sacred place for the spirits of successive kings of Ryūkyū (the old name of Okinawa). The temple was destroyed during World War II, but its stone gates were later restored. 15 min. by bus from the city center.

Shurei-no-mon Gate (Gate of Courtesy) leads to the remains of Shuri Castle. Restored in 1958 to its original design, it symbolizes the time-honored courtesy of the Okinawan people.

● **NAMBU (SOUTHERN DISTRICT)** This area, centering around Itoman City, was the site of fierce battles during World War II and many of the fallen are buried here. There is a large underground trench network here.

● **GYOKUSENDO CAVE** Spectacular limestone formations make this the most outstanding grotto in Japan. About 800 m. of its total length of 5 km. is open to the public and the cave contains over 460,000 stalactites as well as stone pillars and giant stone bamboo shoots.

WHAT TO EAT

Okinawa has its own distinct cuisine featuring many dishes not found on mainland Japan and its restaurants are noted for being cheaper and serving larger portions. The Okinawan dishes show a Chinese influence. You can enjoy them while watching a local dance show at some restaurants in Naha.

Okinawa Noodles are flavored with a rich pork

stock. Mutton, uncommon in Japan, is eaten in a variety of ways including *sashimi* (raw) and in soup.

WHAT TO BUY

Bingata is an Okinawan fabric dyed in bright colors with characteristic designs of flowers, birds, mountains and water. The process of making *Bingata* can be seen in factories in Shuri. Tsuboya-yaki is the simple, colorful local pottery which can be purchased at the many potteries in Naha. Another specialty is dolls which are costumed in the garments worn in the Ryūkyū Dance.

CENTRAL & NORTHERN OKINAWA

WHAT TO SEE

● **OKINAWA CITY (OLD KOZA CITY)** This city developed around the large U.S. military base there and caters to its needs. The city's bullring features regular bullfights — between the bulls only. I hr. by bus from Naha.

● **OKINAWA SUBMARINE PARK** This park contains an underwater observatory where visitors can see some of the beauty of the surrounding seas. 2 hrs. by bus from Naha.

● **EXPO MEMORIAL OCEAN PARK** This park was the site

Local Dance Show in Naha

of Okinawa Expo '75, and includes gardens, an excellent aquarium, a man-made beach and Aquapolis. 2 hrs. 30 min. by bus from Naha.

RESORTS IN OKINAWA

● **MOON BEACH** Visitors can enjoy a variety of marine sports and excursions in glass-bottomed boats at this lovely beach which is popular for its cobalt blue water and white sand. I hr. 20 min. by bus from Naha.

● **MANZA BEACH RESORT** This is one of the main resorts of the islands and offers complete facilities for recreation and amusement. Its coral reef can be seen from the cliffs above the beach. I hr. 30 min. by bus from Naha.

● **OKUMA BEACH** This is a beautiful shoaling beach with white sand and is surrounded by reefs. Comprehensive sports and recreation facilities are offered here. I hr. 10 min. by bus from Nago.

OKINAWA & AMAMI ISLANDS

With Okinawa Main Island at the center, there are a large number of islands spread along a 1,000 km. arc. Many of these smaller islands have beautiful beaches and good facilities and it is popular to visit these outlying islands in addition to the Main Island.

OKINAWA ISLANDS

● **KUME ISLAND** 35 min. by air from Naha, Kume has abundant leisure facilities and accommodation.

● **KERAMA ISLANDS** There are around 20 islands in this group and most are uninhabited. The sea here is particularly beautiful and the numerous coral reefs surrounding the islands make them excellent places for diving.

● **MIYAKO ISLAND** Fields of sugar cane cover this peaceful island. It features many good swimming beaches and resort hotels and is a good place for leisurely bicycle rides.

● **ISHIGAKI ISLAND** The island is dominated by the highest mountain in the Okinawa region and has an indented coastline with bluffs and numerous inlets. There are also many old houses and other places of historical interest.

AMAMI ISLANDS

● **AMAMI OSHIMA ISLAND** The largest of the Amami group, the island is covered with lush subtropical vegetation. It has lively towns and numerous resort hotels.

● **TOKUNOSHIMA ISLAND** A very quiet island with an indented coastline, bullfighting is the local entertainment here. It is also renowned for the longevity of the lives of its inhabitants.

● **YORON ISLAND** This is one of the most popular islands, located not far from Okinawa, and offers excellent swimming, diving and fishing.

Taketomi Island

TRAVEL HINTS

❖

GENERAL INFORMATION

ENTERING THE COUNTRY

TRAVEL DOCUMENTS
You'll need a passport of course. When you arrive at immigration, present the passport and the entry card you filled out on the plane or boat you arrived on. Make sure you don't lose your copy until you leave the country.

VISAS
Unless you have an exemption, a valid passport containing a visa from a Japanese Embassy or Consulate is required for entry into Japan.

Tourist Visa: If you visit Japan to sightsee, visit relatives, participate in meetings, short study courses, or sports, or similar activities not involving remuneration, you can apply for a tourist visa. The term you can stay in Japan depends upon your nationality and purpose.

Documents Required to Apply For a Tourist Visa: The applicant must usually submit to a Japanese Embassy or Consulate the following: 1) A valid passport; 2) Two copies of the completed visa application forms (a passport-sized photograph must be affixed in most cases); 3) An air or sea passage ticket to and from Japan or evidence of possession thereof.

INOCULATION
No vaccinations are required to enter Japan from any country except for coming via infected areas.

ANIMAL AND PLANT QUARANTINE
Any animals and plants to be imported are subject to quarantine inspection upon arrival at Japanese ports.

CUSTOMS
Customs declaration: An oral declaration of one's belongings will suffice except when: 1) arriving by ship; 2) having unaccompanied baggage arriving on a later flight; or 3) having articles in excess of the duty free allowance (see next page). In these cases one must make a written declaration to the customs officer. (A written declaration must be made at the time and place of entry. Otherwise a claim for duty free import of

unaccompanied baggage will not be accepted.)

Free Import: Personal effects and professional equipment can be brought into Japan duty free as long as their contents and quantities are deemed reasonable by the customs officer. The articles listed below can also be imported duty free within the quantities indicated.

1) 400 cigarettes or 500 grams of tobacco or 100 cigars (no allowance for persons aged 19 years or younger.)

2) 3 bottles (760c.c. each) of alcoholic beverages. (No allowance for persons aged 19 years or younger).

3) 2 oz. of perfume

4) Gifts and souvenirs whose total market price is less than ¥200,000 or its equivalent value.

Import and Export of Currency: Import of foreign currencies is unlimited; Japanese currency up to ¥5 million. Export of foreign currencies is unlimited; Japanese currency up to ¥5 million.

DEPARTING THE COUNTRY

Departure tax:

It's not exactly a tax but all departing passengers on international flights leaving from Narita Airport will be charged a Passenger Service Facility Charge of ¥2,000 (¥1,000 for children aged 2 to 12 years).Transit passengers continuing their travels by the same or first connecting flights on the same day are not taxed; nor are infants aged 2 years or younger; or state guests and other official guests. There is no charge at Osaka or at other international airports.

Free export: (Not for commercial purposes). Reasonable quantities of tobacco products, alcoholic beverages, perfume, gifts, and other articles.

Articles purchased tax-free in Japan must be shown to the Customs officer at the airport/port of departure from Japan.

LANGUAGE

The official language is Japanese. However, English is understood in most first class hotels and tourist oriented facilities.

TIME ZONES

All Japan is in the same time zone, 9 hours ahead of G.M.T.

Daylight saving time is not in effect here.

CURRENCY

The unit of Japanese currency is yen (indicated by ¥). Coin denominations are 1, 5, 10, 50, 100 and 500 yen. The most commonly used coins are ¥10, ¥50, ¥100, and ¥500. Bank notes (bills) are ¥1,000, ¥5,000, and ¥10,000.

Yen can be bought at foreign exchange banks and other authorized money changers (found in department stores, hotels, etc.) on showing your passport. Travelers checks can also be cashed into yen. It is advisable for the visitor to carry U.S. dollars or pound sterling travelers checks whenever possible.

TRAVELERS CHECKS

These can be used at 1st class hotels, department stores, duty free shops, and similar places. They cannot be used at regular shops and restaurants because those places are not authorized to convert currency, so you will need cash in yen.

CREDIT CARDS

The following credit cards are accepted at most hotels, department stores, restaurants, etc.: *American Express, Visa International, Carte Blanche, Diners Club, and Master Card.*

TIPPING

Tipping is not a common practice in Japan. To obviate the need for individual tipping, a 10 to 15 percent service charge will be added to your bill in some hotels and restaurants. But for the most part, no gratuity is required.

ELECTRICITY

The electric current for home use is uniformly 100 volts AC throughout Japan but there are two different frequencies in use — 50 in eastern Japan, which includes Tokyo, and 60 in western Japan, which includes Nagoya, Kyoto, and Osaka.

DRINKING WATER

Japan has abundant clean water in its mountain streams. The tap water is germ-free and can be drunk without precautions.

WEIGHTS AND MEASURES

I kilometer(km.)=0.621 miles;	I mile = 1.609km.
I meter (m.) = 1.094 yards;	I yard = 0.914 m.
I meter (m.) = 3.280 feet;	I foot = 0.305 m.
I centimeter (cm.) = 0.39 inch;	I inch = 2.54 cm.
I kilogram (kg) = 2.205 lbs;	I lb = 0.454 kg
I liter (ℓ) = 0.264 U.S. gal;	I U.S. gal. = 3.785 liters
I liter (ℓ) = 0.22 Imp. gal;	I Imp.gal. = 4.546 liters

POSTAL SERVICES

The simple way to mail your letters and packages is to get assistance from the front desk in your hotel. Postal rates within Japan are ¥60 up to 25 grams, and ¥70 up to 50 grams, if the envelope is between 9×14 cm and 12×23.5 cm. Mail that does not fit within the above measurements costs ¥120 up to 50 grams, and ¥170 up to 100 grams. Postcards cost ¥40.

Air Mail Rates

	Asia, Oceania	North & Central Americas	Europe, Africa, South America Near & Middle East
Postcards	¥ 70	¥ 70	¥ 70
Aerograms	¥ 80	¥ 80	¥ 80
Letters:(Up to 10 grams)	¥ 80	¥100	¥120
(Each extra 10 grams)	¥ 60	¥ 70	¥100

171

TELEPHONE

PUBLIC TELEPHONE

Public telephones of various colors are found on almost every street corner in Japan. All of them accept ¥10 coins, but yellow and green (and recently some red ones) accept ¥100,

Area Codes

Sapporo	011	Hakone	0460	Hiroshima	082
Sendai	022	Nagoya	052	Fukuoka	092
Tokyo	03	Osaka	06	Beppu	0977
Yokohama	045	Kyoto	075	Nagasaki	0958
Nikko	0288	Nara	0742	Kagoshima	0992
Kamakura	0467	Kobe	078	Naha	0988

convenient for calling long distance. A local call costs ¥10 for 3 minutes and all unused coins will be returned, but no change is given for ¥100 coins. You can make direct inter-city calls from these phones. Green phones accept a magnetic pre-paid card, *Telephone Card*, available at local phone companies.

INTERNATIONAL CALLS

There are two ways to place international calls from Japan. One is to make direct (ISD=International Subscriber Dialing) calls from telephones which have been registered for ISD with KDD. Make sure that this service is available because it is not wide-spread in Japan. To call, dial 001+country code+area code+desired number. Another is to place your call through the KDD operator. Simply dial 0051 and you'll get the KDD operator. If you're calling from a hotel, ask the desk to place a call.

International Telephone Charges (Unit—Yen) as of Apr. 12, 1988

Area	Country Code	ISD Calls (Per 6 Seconds)			Station-to-Station Calls	Person-to-Person Calls	Each Additional Minute
		Standard Rate	Economy Rate	Discount Rate	Initial 3 Minutes		
U.S.A (Mainland)	1	50	40	30	1,890	3,150	520
United Kingdom	44	60	48	36	2,250	3,750	560
Australia	61	50	40	30	1,890	3,150	580
Korea	82	46	37	28	1,740	2,900	520
Hong Kong	852	48	38	29	1,830	3,050	580
Singapore	65	48	38	29	1,830	3,050	580

	0	5	8	19	23 24	
Mon.-Sat.						Standard Rate
Sun.						Economy Rate (Evenings and Sun.)
						Discount Rate (Late night)

The above times refer to Japan time, not the time in the country called.

Telegrams: The following KDD offices are open 24 hours a day throughout the year and handle telegrams, facsimiles and phototelegrams, and have booth's for ISD calls and telex.

Tokyo Telegraph Office — Tel.(03)275-4343
Nagoya Telegraph Office — Tel.(052)203-3311
Osaka Telegraph Office — Tel.(06)228-2151

BUSINESS HOURS

Banks: 9:00 a.m. — 3:00 p.m., Monday through Friday and 9:00 a.m. — noon on Saturdays. Closed on Sundays, the 2nd Saturday of each month, and national holidays.

Government and Business Offices: Most are open from 8:30 or 9:30 a.m. to 5 or 6 p.m. Monday through Friday and until noon on Saturdays, although more and more business offices are closed on Saturdays, Sundays and national holidays.

Post Offices: 9 a.m. to 5 p.m. Monday through Friday and Saturday from 9 a.m. to 12:30 p.m. Closed on Sunday, 2nd Saturday and national holidays. Main post offices also conduct postal transactions (excluding postal savings, etc.) on Sunday mornings.

Restaurants: Hours vary from place to place but most are open for lunch and dinner every day.

Shops: Department stores are open 10:00 a.m. to 6:00 p.m., even on Sundays and national holidays. Department stores have a regular holiday once a week, the day varying between each store.

REST ROOM

Department stores and hotel lobbies contain toilet facilities without rest room attendants. Most of the time these are Japanese squat toilets but you can find Western-style stool toilets in large office buildings and similar places.

LOST AND FOUND

If you leave your bag on a station bench or somewhere, you don't have to assume it's lost forever. You can go back to where you left it and it will probably still be there. If not, go to the Station Master's Office or to the nearest police station.

INFORMATION OFFICE

TIC's (Tourist Information Centers), staffed by multilingual personnel, offer various information services for visitors from abroad. They prepare free maps and booklets. Sightseeing, shopping and dining information and all other TIC services are free of charge. For more information see P186.

PACKAGE TOURS IN JAPAN

Package tours are convenient when you are unfamiliar with your destination.
Here we would like to introduce some of the many JTB Tours in English.

JTB PACKAGE TOURS (SUNRISE TOURS)

DYNAMIC TOKYO (FULL DAY TOUR)

Departure: Daily except Dec. 30—Jan. 4
8:50 a.m.—around 5:30 p.m.
Tour Fare: **¥11,000** (Child: **¥9,000**)(lunch incl.)
Tour Highlights ● Tokyo Tower (ascend) ● Imperial East Garden ● Asakusa Kannon Temple ● Barbecue lunch at Chinzanso Garden Restaurant ● Demonstrations of making cultured pearls ● Meiji Shrine

DAY TOUR TO TOKYO DISNEYLAND

Departure: Daily 8:50a.m.—around 6:30p.m.(Not operated when Tokyo Disneyland is closed)
Tour Fare: **¥8,500** (Child: **¥5,000**)(without lunch)
Tour Highlights ● Approx. 7-hour free time at Tokyo Disneyland (Park admission and "Big 10" attraction tickets are included.)

TOKYO KABUKI NIGHT

Departure: Daily (Not operated when no Kabuki performance)
6:00 p.m. (7:20 p.m.without dinner)—around 11:00 p.m.
Tour Fare: **¥13,000** (with dinner) **¥10,000** (without dinner)
Tour Highlights ● Sukiyaki dinner at Suehiro Restaurant (optional) ● Traditional Japanese theater–Kabuki ● Traditional Orian (elite Geisha) show with songs and dances at Matsubaya Restaurant

ART-AROUND-TOWN

■*Departure:* Every Mon. except Dec. 15—Jan. 20 & national holidays 9:00 a.m.—around 6:00 p.m.
Tour Fare: **¥11,000** (Child: **¥9,000**)(lunch incl.)
■*Tour Highlights* ● Process of traditional yūzen dyeing ● Lunch with demonstration of tea ceremony ● Demonstration of wearing the Kimono ● Exhibition of flower arranging and

making cultured pearls

VILLAGE LIFE & CRAFTS

Departure: Every Wed. (Apr. thru Oct. except Aug. 17)
8:50 a.m.—around 6:00 p.m.
Tour Fare: **¥10,000** (Child: **¥9,000**)(lunch incl.)
■*Tour Highlights* ● Garden Plants shop ● Lunch at Mansei Restaurant ● Making of Daruma (paper wish-making dolls) ● An agricultural association ● Bonsai garden ● Making of traditional bamboo fishing rods ● Making of traditional dolls ● Doll shop

INDUSTRIAL TOKYO

Departure: Every Tue. & Thu. except Dec. 21— Jan. 11, Apr. 28 — May 5, Aug. 12—15, Sep. 15 & Nov. 3
8:50 a.m.—around 5:30 p.m.
■*Tour Fare:* **¥10,000** (Child: **¥9,000**)(lunch incl.)
■*Tour Highlights Tuesday:* ● Ride on monorail ● JAL Maintenance Base ● Lunch at a local restaurant ● Isuzu Motors factory
Thursday: ● Drive via Tōmei Expressway ● Fujitsū Computer Laboratories ● Lunch at a local restaurant ● Isuzu Motors factory ● Note: The places to be visited are subject to change with or without notice.

175

MT.FUJI & HAKONE FULL DAY TOUR

■*Departure:* Daily (Mar. thru Nov.) 7:00 a.m.—around 7:30 p.m.
Tour Fare: **¥17,500** (Child: **¥13,200**)(Lunch incl.)
■*Itinerary* ● Drive along the expressway to Mt. Fuji and Hakone to see and enjoy eye-pleasing countryside ● Drive halfway up Mt. Fuji (see the note below) ● Lunch at Fuji View Hotel ● Cruise on Lake Hakone. Drive to Odawara to board the "Bullet" train for Tokyo.

NIKKO FULL DAY TOUR

Departure: Daily 7:00 a.m.—around 6:30 p.m.
Tour Fare: **¥17,500** (Child: **¥13,200**)(Lunch incl.)
Itinerary ● Train to Nikko ● Fabulous Tōshōgū Shrine ● Lunch at Nikko Kanaya Hotel ● Drive through the scenic Nikko Mountains ● A sacred dance at Futarasan Shrine ● Lake Chūzenji, Kegon Waterfall and Tachiki Kannon Temple ● Early evening train to Tokyo

SUNRISE EXPRESS 3 DAYS

■*Departure:* Daily
■*Tour Fare:* Standard **¥75,500** (Child: **¥56,700**) (2 lunches incl.)
■*Itinerary* ● *1st Day* Tokyo—Kyoto ● *2nd Day* Kyoto ● *3rd Day* Kyoto —Nara—Kyoto—Tokyo

TOHOKU 3 DAYS

Sendai ● *Matsushima* ● *Mt. Zao* ● *Yonezawa*
■*Departure:* Daily (May 6 thru Oct. 20)
■*Tour Fare:* Standard **¥210,000** (Child: **¥150,000**) (1 dinner & 1 breakfast incl.)
■*Itinerary* ● *1st Day* Tokyo—Sendai—Matsushima—Sendai
● *2nd Day* Sendai—Togatta—Mt.Zaō—Kaminoyama Spa
● *3rd Day* Kaminoyama—Yonezawa—Fukushima—Tokyo

TAKAYAMA & KANAZAWA 5 DAYS

Matsumoto ● *Takayama* ● *Kanazawa* ● *Awara Spa*
■*Departure:* Every Tue. (Apr., May, Sep., Oct.)
■*Tour Fare:* **¥180,000** (Child: **¥130,000**)(4 breakfasts & 2 Dinners incl. The tour ends in Kyoto.)
■*Itinerary:* ● *1st Day* Tokyo—Lake Shirakaba—Matsumoto
● *2nd Day* Matsumoto—Tsumago—Takayama ● *3rd Day* Taka-yama—Ogimachi—Kanazawa ● *4th Day* Kanazawa—Awara Spa
● *5th Day* Awara Spa—Eiheiji Temple—Kyoto

HOKKAIDO 4 DAYS

Sapporo ● *Lake Toya* ● *Noboribetsu Spa*
■*Departure:* Daily (Apr. 15 thru Oct. 31)
■*Tour Fare:* **¥190,000** (Child: **¥140,000**)(3 breakfasts, 1 lunch & 2 dinners incl.)
Note: The tour starts and ends at Chitose Airport.
■*Itinerary:* ● *1st Day* Arrive Sapporo ● *2nd Day* Sapporo—Na-kayama Pass—Lake Tōya ● *3rd Day* Lake Tōya—Noboribetsu Spa ● *4th Day* Noboribetsu Spa—Shiraoi—Chitose Airport

SUNRISE EASTBOUND TOUR 1 DAY

■*Departure:* Daily except Dec.3—Mar.2
■*Tour Fare:* Standard **¥36,800** (Child:**¥27,600**) (lunch incl.)
■*Itinerary:* ● Kyoto／Osaka—Toba—Nagoya—Tokyo

NORTHERN KYUSHU 5 DAYS

Fukuoka ●Beppu ●Mt. Aso ●Kumamoto ●Nagasaki

■**Departure:** Every Tue. and Sat. (Mar. 1 thru Nov. 26)

■**Tour Fare:** Standard **¥208,000** (Child: **¥156,500**) (3 lunches incl.)

■**Itinerary:** ● **1st Day** Kyoto／Osaka—Dazaifu—Fukuoka ● **2nd DAY** Fukuoka—Beppu ● **3rd Day** Beppu—Mt. Aso— Kumamoto ● **4th Day** Komamoto—Amakusa—Unzen—Nagasaki ● **5th Day** Nagasaki—Fukuoka—Osaka／Kyoto

＊JTB also offers private guided tours by car. The price varies depending on the number of people and destination. This is a luxurious way to travel.

●QUESTIONS AND RESERVATIONS

You can call any of the companies listed below directly or go to any major hotels in the city.

Japan Travel Bureau Sunrise Tour Center
        (Tokyo) ☎03-276-7777 (☎03-432-1111 at night)
                                 (Kyoto)☎075-361-7241

Fujita Travel Service (FTS)	☎03-573-1011
Hankyū Express International	☎03-508-0129
Hato Bus	☎03-435-6081
Japan Gray Line	☎03-436-6881
Tōbu Travel Service (tours of Nikko only)	☎03-272-1806

＊A special bus stops in front of most major hotels. Each includes a veteran guide who is very familiar with the area. Special Package Tours which include local holidays and festivals like the Sapporo Snow festival are also available.

＊Departure time refers to the time at the Prince Hotel in Tokyo, the New Miyako in Kyoto, and the Hakata Miyako Hotel in Hakata.

For pick-up service or further information contact the JTB office.

177

ANNUAL EVENTS

JANUARY

1:New Year's Day—In Japan, New Year's Day continues for at least 3 days. The doorways of the houses are decorated with pine branches and people flock to the shrines to pray for happiness.

15:Adults' Day (Seijin-no-hi)—Custom dictates that adulthood is reached at 20 and this day celebrates the new status of those who turned 20 in the last year.

FEBRUARY

3:Bean Throwing Ceremony (Setsubun)—On the last day of winter, beans are thrown to drive away evil sprits and welcome spring.

MARCH

3:Girls' Day (Hina Matsuri)—A special festival for girls in which a set of dolls representing the court are displayed.

May

5:Children's day (Kodomo-no-hi)—Originally Boys' Day, this holiday is marked by flying paper or cloth carp which symbolize strength and perseverance.

JULY

7:Tanabata—This is the one day of the year on which, according to ancient Chinese legend, the Weaver Princess (Vega) and the Cowherd (Altair) can cross the Milky Way that separates them and renew their love for each other.

13-16 (Luner calender): Bon Festival—According to Buddhist belief, this is the period when the spirits of the family ancestors return to visit.

Mid-Summer Moon Viewing (Tsukimi)—Tsukimi, or "moon-viewing" takes place at full moon in autumn. A spot is chosen from which to admire the moon, and decorations of tsukimidango (rice dumplings), susuki (pampas grass) and autumn fruit are displayed.

NOVEMBER

15:7-5-3 Festival—Girls who are 7 and 3 and boys who are 5 are dressed in kimono and taken to a Shintō shrine to pay homage.

DECEMBER

31:New Year's Eve—to close out the old year and greet the new. Rice is pounded for mochi, special soba is eaten, and temple bells ring in the new year at midnight.

FESTIVALS OF JAPAN

■HOKKAIDO
Sapporo Yuki Matsuri／Feb. 1—5／**Sapporo-shi**／Odori Park becomes a wonderland of intricately carved snow figures during this popular festival.

■AOMORI
Aomori Nebuta／**Aug. 2—7**／**Aomori-shi**／This festival began as a way to ward off the sleepiness that would interfere with the coming harvest. It features a parade of giant papier-mache floats.

Osorezan Taisai／**Jul.20—24**／**Entsū-ji Temple: Mutsu-shi**／The dismal peaks of Mt. Osore are believed to be the home of the spirits of the dead so the purpose of this festival is to allow people to contact their loved ones.

■IWATE
Chagu-chagu Umako／**Jun.15**　／**Takizawa-mura, Morioka-shi**／Homage given to the god of horses to promote prosperity for the horses and their owners. There is a picturesque parade of gaily decorated riders and mounts.

■AKITA
Kamakura／**Feb.15-17**／**Yokoté-shi**／An igloo is made out of snow and outfitted with a small shrine dedicated to the god of water.

Namahage／**Dec.31**／**Oga-shi**／Men dressed as demons enter houses to warn the children against laziness. The festival is to promote a bountiful harvest.

■MIYAGI
Tanabata Matsuri／**Aug.6-8**／**Sendai-shi**／This festival celebrates the meeting of the Weaver girl (Vega) and the Cowherd (Altair). Legend has it that these stars were ill-fated lovers who are only allowed to meet at one time every year.

■YAMAGATA
Hanagasa Odori／**Aug.6-8**／**Yamagata-shi**／One of the largest festivals in Tōhoku, thousands of dancers parade through the city with their hanagasa (paper hats).

■FUKUSHIMA
Yanaizu Hadaka Matsuri／**Jun.7**／**Enzō-ji Temple: Yanaizu-chō**／Young men clad only in loin cloths scramble to be the first to climb a rope hanging from the temple

179

ceiling and so receive good luck.

■IBARAKI

Hitachi Fūryūmono/May3-5/Hitachi-shi/The parade floats contain puppets, and performances with elaborate moving stages are held.

■TOCHIGI

Tōshōgū Haru no Reitaisai/May 17-18/Tōshōgū Shrine:Nikko-shi/This festival is held in honor of the first shōgun, Tokugawa Ieyasu. Tōshōgū shrine contains his remains. There is a costume parade.

■SAITAMA

Chichibu-no-Yomatsuri/Dec. 2-3/Chichibu Shrine: Chichibu-shi/Yomatsuri means night festival and the floats in the twilight are covered with beautiful paper lanterns.

■TOKYO

Sanja Matsuri/mid-May/Asakusa Shrine: Taitō-ku The 3 largest festivals in Tokyo are the Sanja Matsuri, the Sannō Matsuri, and the Kanda Matsuri. Bright mikoshi (portable shrines) are paraded through the streets surrounding the temple.

Tori-no-ichi/Tori-no-hi in Nov./Otori Shrine: Taitō-ku/Elaborately decorated ornamental rakes are sold to 'rake in' good fortune during the coming year.

Hagoita-ichi/Dec.17—19/Sensō-ji Temple: Taitō-ku/Gaily decorated traditional battledores are sold at this annual festival.

Hōzuki-ichi/Jul.9-10/Sensōji Temple: Taitō-ku/Lantern plants (hōzuki) are sold to repel summer insects. It is believed that visiting the shrine on July 10th will reap blessings on the visitor.

■KANAGAWA

Yokohama Minato Matsuri/May3—Jul.20/Yokohama-shi/Held to commemorate the opening of the port of Yokohama. The highlight of this festival is the International Parade on May 3.

Tsurugaoka Hachimangū Reitaisai/Sep. 14—16/Tsurugaoka-Hachimangū Shrine: Kamakura-shi/This festival features a parade and Yabusame, an event in which 3 mounted archers dressed in 12th century hunting costume shoot at targets.

■TOYAMA

Mikurumayama Matsuri/May 1/Kanno Shrine:

Takaoka-shi/The parades during this festival feature special floats with elaborately decorated wheels.

■**FUKUI**

Mikuni Matsuri/**May 19-21**/**Mikuni Shrine: Mikuni-shi**/The large festival floats mounted with huge carved warriors are known throughout Japan.

■**GIFU**

Takayama Matsuri/**Apr.14—15**/**Hie Shrine: Takayama-shi**/**Oct. 9—10**/**Sakuragaoka-Hachimangū Shrine**/The lavish festival floats are masterpieces of folk art. Tōkeigaku, a type of folk music, is also a major attraction.

■**MIE**

Ueno Tenjin Matsuri/**Oct.23—25**/**Sugawara Shrine**/During this festival you can see a parade of devils.This custom is said to have originated to frighten away a plague.

■**KYOTO**

Jidai Matsuri/**Oct.22**/**Heian-jingū Shrine: Kyoto-shi**/Held in commemoration of the founding of Kyoto in 794. The costumes in the historical pageant represent all modes of dress from that time through the present.

Gion Matsuri/**Jul.1—29**/**Yasaka Shrine: Kyoto-shi**/One of the most significant festivals in Japan. The floats are massive and are often decorated with cedar trees.

Kurama no Himatsuri/**Oct. 22**/**Yuki Shrine: Kyoto-shi**/The street leading to Yuki Shrine on Mr. Kurama is lined with torches. These are lit to signify the start of festivities.

Daimonji Yaki/**Aug. 16**/**Kyoto-shi**/A large bonfire in the shape of the Chinese character 'dai' is lit to guide the souls of the dead back to this world.

■**OSAKA**

Tōka Ebisu/**Jan.9—11**/**Imamiya Ebisu Shrine: Osaka-shi**/Held to supplicate Ebisu, the god of commerce. Thousands come to pray for financial success.

Tenjin Matsuri/**Jul.24—25**/**Osaka-Tenmangū Shrine: Osaka-shi**/The regular parade is complimented by a flotilla carrying the portable shrines used in the parade down the Dōjima River.

■**NARA**

Wakakusayama-yaki/**Jan.15**/**Wakakusayama: Nara-shi**/Every year priests from Tōdaiji Temple and Kōfuku-ji

181

Temple light the dry grass on Wakakusa Mountain and turn it into a brilliant beacon of flames.

Omizutori/**Mar.1—14**/**Tōdaiji Temple: Nara-shi**/The first water of spring is drawn from a well in Todaiji Temple and presented to the gods.

Kasuga Matsuri/**Mar.13**/**Kasuga-taisha Shrine: Nara-shi**/This festival celebrates customs of the 8th century.

SHIMANE

Izumo-taisha Jinzaisai/**Oct.11—17 by the luner calender**/**Izumo-taisha Shrine: Taisha-machi**/It is believed that all the gods assemble at Izumo-taisha shrine at this time so a wide range of activities are held for their benefit.

HIROSHIMA

Kangensai/**Jun.17 Lunar calendar**/**Itsukushima Shrine: Miyajima-chō**/This ancient ·festival includes a procession of gaily decorated ships and performances of gagaku, or court music.

■**TOKUSHIMA**

Awa Odori/**Aug.12—15**/**Tokushima-shi**/The focus of this festival is a simple dance which everyone joins in.

■**FUKUOKA**

Kokura Gion-daiko/**Jul.10—12**/**Yasaka Shrine:Kita-Kyūshū-shi**/The Gion festivals began as a way to ward off sickness, but the special event at this one is the drum performance.

Hakata Gion Yamagasa/**Jul.1—15**/**Kushida Shrine: Fukuoka-shi**/This festival includes a race between teams of 28 carrying 1 ton floats, and a purification rite in the sand on the beach.

Hakata Dontaku/**May2—4**/**Fukuoka-shi**/Dontaku is a corruption of Zontag, the Dutch word for Sunday. The festival started as a New Year's parade of merchants to the lord's manor.

NAGASAKI

Nagasaki Kunchi/**Oct.7—9**/**Suwa Shrine: Nagasaki-shi**/During this festival most of the houses in Nagasaki are decorated and a cosmopolitan array of performances, like the Chinese dragon dance, occur.

OKINAWA

Naha Tsunahiki/**Oct.8—10**/**Naha-shi**/Thousands of people participate in this gigantic tug-of-war with a massive rope that is 1 m. in diameter.

USEFUL TELEPHONE NUMBERS

AIRLINES

TOKYO(03),OSAKA(06)

Airport Information	
(Narita)	☎0476-32-2800
(Osaka)	☎06-856-6781
Aeroflot Soviet Airlines(SU)	
	☎03-434-9681
Air Canada(AC)	☎03-586-3891
	☎06-227-1180
Air France(AF)	☎03-475-2355
	☎06-201-5161
Air Nauru(ON)	☎03-581-9271
Kagoshima	☎0992-22-7575
Air-India(AI)	☎03-214-1981
	☎06-264-1781
Air New Zealand(TE)	☎03-287-1641
	☎06-241-1756
Alitalia Airlines(AZ)	☎03-580-2242
	☎06-341-3951
All Nippon Airways(NH)	
	☎03-552-6311
	☎06-372-1212
American Airlines(AA)	☎03-214-2111
British Airways(BA)	☎03-214-4161
	☎06-345-2761
Cathay Pacific Airways(CX)	
	☎03-504-1531
	☎06-245-6731
Canadian Pacific Airlines(CP)	
	☎03-281-7426
	☎06-346-5591
China Airlines(CP)	☎03-436-1661
Continental Airlines(CO)	
	☎03-592-1631
Delta Air Lines(DL)	☎03-213-8781
Egypt Air(MS)	☎03-211-4521
	☎06-341-1575
Finnair(AY)	☎03-423-0423
	☎06-363-0270
Garuda Indonesian	☎03-593-1181
Airways(GA)	☎06-445-6985
General Administration of Civil Aviation	
of China(CA)	☎03-404-3711
	☎06-946-1702
Iran Air(IR)	☎03-586-2101
	☎06-266-0341
Iraqi Airways(IA)	☎03-586-5801
Japan Air Lines(JL)	☎03-457-1111
	☎06-203-1212
Japan Asia Airways(EG)	
	☎03-455-7511
	☎06-223-2222
KLM Royal Dutch	☎03-216-0771
Airlines(KL)	☎06-345-6691

Korean Air Lines(KE)	☎03-211-3311
	☎06-264-3311
Lufthansa German Airlines(LH)	
	☎03-580-2111
	☎06-345-0231
Malaysian Airline	☎03-503-5961
System(MH)	☎06-245-7123
Northwest Orient Airlines(NW)	
	☎03-432-6000
	☎06-228-0747
Pakistan International(PK)	
Airlines	☎03-216-6511
	☎06-341-3106
Pan American World(PA)	
Airways	☎03-508-2211
	☎06-271-5951
Philippine Air Lines(PR)	
	☎03-593-2421
	☎06-444-2541
Qantas Airways(QF)	☎03-212-1351
	☎06-262-1341
Sabena Belgian World(SN)	
Airlines	☎03-585-6151
	☎06-341-8081
Scandinavian Airlines(SK)	
System	☎03-503-8101
	☎06-348-0211
Singapore Airlines(SQ)	☎03-213-3431
	☎06-364-0881
Swissair(SR)	☎03-212-1016
	☎06-345-7851
Thai Airways International(TG)	
	☎03-503-3311
	☎06-202-5161
Japan Air System (JD)	
	☎03-747-8111
	☎06-345-8111
Trans World Airlines(TW)	
	☎03-212-1477
	☎06-341-7131
United Air Lines(UA)	☎03-817-4411
	☎06-217-5951
UTA French Airlines(UT)	
	☎03-593-0773
	☎06-345-0610
Varig Brazilian Airlines(RG)	
	☎03-211-6751
	☎06-341-3571

FOREIGN BANKS

TOKYO(03)

Algemene Bank Nederland	
(General Bank of the Netherlands)	
	☎211-1761
American Express Bank	☎504-3341

183

Banca Commerciale Italiana
☎242-3521
Bangkok Bank ☎503-3333
Bank Indonesia ☎271-3415
Bank of America ☎587-3111
Deutsche Bank Ag. ☎588-1971
Bank of New Zealand ☎291-5651
Banque Nationale de Paris
☎214-2882
Canadian Imperial Bank
of Commerce ☎595-1531
Chase Manhattan Bank ☎287-4000
Citibank ☎279-5411
Development Bank of Singapore
☎213-4411
Hong Kong & Shanghai Banking Corp.
☎216-0110
Korea Exchange Bank ☎216-3561
National Australia Bank
☎241-8781
Swiss Bank Corporation ☎214-1731
Union Bank of Switzerland
☎214-7471
Credit Suisse ☎214-0035

OSAKA(06)

Algeneme Bank Nederland☎261-3251
Bank of America ☎231-8891
Korea Exchange Bank ☎263-2111
Citibank ☎227-5611
Hong Kong & Shanghai Banking
☎231-8701

CREDIT CARDS

TOKYO(03)

American Express Int.Inc. ☎220-6100
Diners Club of Japan ☎499-1311
Visa International ☎354-0161

RAILWAYS

TOKYO(03)

Japan Railways (JR) ☎212-4441

LOST AND FOUND

TOKYO(03)

Taxi: Tokyo Taxi Kindaika Center
☎648-0300
JR Trains: Lost & Found Section in
the JR Tokyo Stn. ☎231-1880
Subways: Lost & Found Center in the
Subway Ueno Stn. ☎834-5577
All Items: Central Lost & Found Office
of the Metropolitan Police Board
☎814-4151

RENT A CAR

TOKYO(03) OSAKA(06)

Hertz Japan Ltd. ☎03-499-3621
Japan Rent A Car System
☎03-354-5531
☎06-632-4881

Nippon Rent A Car Service
☎03-496-0919
☎06-371-9354
Nissan Motorist Service Co.,Ltd.
☎03-587-4123
☎06-371-4123
Tokyo Nissan Rent-A-Car
☎03-407-4431
Osaka Nissan Rent-A-Car
☎06-372-0289
Toyota Rent-A-Car- Service
☎03-264-2834
☎06-452-0100

CHURCHES

TOKYO(03)

Tokyo Bahã'i Center ☎209-7521
Tokyo Baptist Church ☎461-8425
St.Ignatius Church ☎263-4584
Franciscan Chapel Center
☎401-2141
St.Alban's Church ☎431-8534
Tokyo Union Church ☎400-0047
International Christian University
Church ☎0422-33-3323
Jewish Community of Japan
☎400-2559
Ginza Church ☎561-0236
International Azabu Church
☎464-4512
St. Paul's International Lutheran
Church ☎261-3740

KYOTO(075)

Japan Baptist Church ☎231-1351
St. Xavier's Kawaramachi Francisco
Church ☎231-4785
St.Mary's Church ☎771-2581
Heian Church ☎721-2589
Rakuyo Church ☎231-1276

OSAKA(06)

Christ Church Cathedral Anglican
☎581-5061
Osaka Christian Center ☎762-7701

HOSPITALS

TOKYO(03)

National Medical Center of Hospital
☎202-7181
2nd Tokyo National Hospital
☎411-0111
Japan Red Cross Medical Center
☎400-1311
St. Luke's International Hospital
☎541-5151
Toranomon Hospital ☎588-1111
University of Tokyo Hospital
☎815-5411
Keio University Hospital ☎353-1211

KYOTO(075)

Central City Hospital ☎311-5311

Japan Baptist Hospital ☎781-5191
Kyoto University Hospital ☎751-3111
Kyoto Prelectual University of Medicine
Attached Hospital ☎251-5111
OSAKA(06)
Osaka National Hospital ☎942-1331
Yodogawa Christian Hospital
☎322-2250
Osaka Prefectural Hospital
☎692-1201

SOCIAL ORGANIZATIONS

TOKYO(03)
Tokyo American Club ☎583-8381
America-Japan Society ☎201-0780
American Chamber of Commerce in
Japan ☎433-5381
British Council ☎264-3721
Deutsche Gesellschaft feur Natur-und
Vóélkerkunde Óstasiens"O.A.G"
☎582-7743
International House of Japan
☎470-4611
Japan-British Society ☎211-8027
Foreign Correspondents Club
☎211-3161
Lions Club ☎263-2920
Rotary Club ☎201-3888

SHOWROOMS

TOKYO(03)
NEC C&C Plaza ☎595-0511
Canon Showroom ☎455-9870
Ginza Nikon Salon ☎562-5756
Nissan Gallery ☎573-1261
Noritake House ☎591-3241
Olympus Photo Plaza ☎209-4821
Sony Showroom Tokyo ☎573-2371

EMBASSIES

TOKYO(03)
Algerian ☎711-2661
Apostolic Nunciature (Vatican)
☎263-6851
Argentina ☎592-0321
Australian ☎453-0251
Austrian ☎451-8281
Belgian ☎262-0191
Bolivian ☎499-5441
Brazilian ☎404-5211
Bulgarian ☎465-1021
Burmese ☎441-9291
Canadian ☎408-2101
Central African Republic ☎707-5061
Chilean ☎452-7561
Chinese ☎403-3380
Colombian ☎440-6451
Côte d'Ivoire ☎499-7021
Cuban ☎449-7511
Czechoslovakian ☎400-8122

Danish ☎496-3001
Dominican ☎499-6020
Ecuadorian ☎499-2800
Egyptian ☎770-8021
El Salvador ☎499-4461
Ethiopian ☎585-3151
Fiji ☎587-2038
Finnish ☎442-2231
French ☎473-0171
German Democratic Republic
☎585-5401
Federal Republic of Germany
☎473-0151
Ghana ☎409-3861
Greek ☎403-0871
Guatemala ☎400-1830
Guinea ☎499-3281
Haiti ☎486-7070
Honduras ☎409-1150
Hungarian ☎476-6061
Indian ☎262-2391
Indonesian ☎441-4201
Iranian ☎446-8011
Iraqi ☎423-1727
Ireland ☎263-0695
Israeli ☎264-0911
Italian ☎453-5291
Jordan ☎580-5856
Kenya ☎479-4008
Korean ☎452-7611
Kuwait ☎455-0361
Laos ☎408-1166
Liberia ☎499-2451
Libya ☎477-0701
Madagasy ☎446-7252
Malaysian ☎770-9331
Mexican ☎581-1131
Mongolia ☎469-2088
Morocco ☎478-3271
Nepalese ☎706-5558
Netherlands ☎431-5126
New Zealand ☎467-2271
Nicaragua ☎499-0400
Nigeria ☎468-5531
Norwegian ☎440-2611
Pakistan ☎454-4861
Peru ☎406-4240
Poland ☎711-5224
Portugal ☎400-7907
Romania ☎479-0311
Saudi Arabia ☎589-5241
Singapore ☎586-9111
Spain ☎583-8531
Sudanese ☎406-0811
Sultanate of Oman ☎402-0877
Sweden ☎582-6981
Switzerland ☎473-0121
Syria ☎586-8977
Thai ☎441-7352
Turkey ☎470-5131

185

Union of Soviet Socialist Rep.
☎583-4224
United Kingdom ☎265-5511
United States of America☎583-7141
Yugoslavia ☎447-3571

INFORMATION

Operator assisted Calls Dial 0051
(4 digits number from anywhere in Japan)
Teletourist Service(taped information Service of current events)
    (Tokyo 03:English) ☎503-2911
    (Tokyo 03:French) ☎503-2926
    (Kyoto 075:English) ☎361-2911
Asahi Evening News ☎546-7111
Japan Times ☎453-5311
Yokohama Municipal Tourist
 Association ☎045-641-5824
Tokyo Tourist Information Center
☎03-502-1461
Tourist Information New Tokyo International Airport Center
☎0476-32-8711
Kyoto Tourist Information Center
☎075-371-5649
Sapporo City Tourism Department
☎011-211-2376
Sendai Tourist Information Office
☎022-222-3269
Kanagawa Prefectural Tourist Association
☎045-681-0007
Yokohama Municipal Tourist Association(Silk Center)
☎045-641-0841
(Shin-Yokohama Station)
☎045-473-2895
City Tourist Information (Nagoya)
☎052-541-4301
Nagoya International Center
☎052-581-5678
Nara City Tourist Center
☎0742-22-3900
Osaka Municipal Tourist Information Office ☎06-345-2189
Osaka Tourist Information Center
☎06-305-3311
Tourist Information Service
☎06-941-9200
Kobe International Tourist Association
☎078-303-1010
Hiroshima City Tourist Association
☎082-249-9329
Fukuoka City Tourist Association
☎092-411-0068
Nagasaki City Tourist Information
☎0958-23-3631
Nagasaki Prefecture Tourist Federation
☎0958-26-9407
Kagoshima Prefectural Tourist Federa-

tion ☎0992-23-9171
Kagoshima City Tourist Service
☎0992-53-2500

PRINCIPAL JTB OFFICE

Sapporo Office	☎011-241-6201
Morioka Office	☎0196-51-3331
Sendai Office	☎022-222-5243
Akita Office	☎0188-63-6616
Yamagata Office	☎0236-23-6633
Fukushima Office	☎0245-23-2851
Utsunomiya Office	☎0286-22-1801
Omiya Office	☎0486-44-4161
Chiba Office	☎0472-27-9221
Akasaka Office	☎03-580-4251
Ginza Office	☎03-563-4091
Hamamatsuchō Office	☎03-435-5391
Ikebukuro Office	☎03-981-6753
In Ginza Dai-ichi Hotel	☎03-543-2945
In Hotel Century Hyatt Tokyo(Closed on Thursdays)	☎03-345-0889
In Hotel Grand Palace	☎03-261-5818
In Hotel New Otani	☎03-261-4015
In Hotel Okura	☎03-583-6007
In Imperial Hotel	☎03-501-2606
In Keio Plaza Inter-Continental Hotel	☎03-344-0573
In Marunouchi Bldg.	☎03-213-9181
In Palace Hotel	☎03-211-7016
In Takanawa Prince Hotel	☎03-445-5879
In Tokyo Central Station, Yaesu-North Exit(Open daily)	☎03-201-8161
In Tokyo Hilton Hotel	☎03-343-2573
In Tokyo Prince Hotel	☎03-434-8577
Shibuya Office	☎03-770-0021
Shimbashi Office	☎03-504-3521
Shinjuku Office	☎03-356-1211
Yokohama Office	☎045-641-4111
Yokosuka Office	☎0468-24-4211
Niigata Office	☎025-222-4141
Kanazawa Office	☎0762-61-6171
Nagano Office	☎0262-26-0267
Gifu Office	☎0582-64-7401
Shizuoka Office	☎0542-53-4131
Nagoya Office	☎052-951-8515
Kyoto Office	☎075-371-6131
Osaka Umeda Office	☎06-341-8291
Nara Office	☎0742-23-2525
Kobe Sannomiya Office	☎078-231-4701
Hiroshima Office	☎082-247-4511
Yamaguchi Office	☎0839-22-3322
Takamatsu Office	☎0878-51-2111
Matsuyama Office	☎0899-31-2281
Fukuoka Office	☎092-712-0111
Nagasaki Office	☎0958-23-1261
Kumamoto Office	☎096-322-4111
Kagoshima Office	☎0992-22-8135
Okinawa Office	☎0988-64-1321

TRAVEL LIFE

❖

LODGING

Japan offers tourists two very different types of accommodation facilities—Western style hotels and Ryokan, traditional Japanese hotels. Lower priced accommodation is available in Youth Hostels, "Pensions", Kokumin Shukusha (People's Lodges), Kokumin Kyūka Mura (National Vacation Villages), and Minshuku (Family Inns).

WESTERN STYLE HOTELS

● DELUXE AND FIRST CLASS HOTELS

Practically all of these hotels are registered with the government and belong to the Japan Hotel Association. Service and facilities are of a uniformly high standard and include excellent restaurants, shopping arcades (including duty-free), travel information counters, and direct airport connections. Some hotels offer "executive salons" for businessmen which allow guests to utilize various secretarial services.

● BUSINESS HOTELS

Developed as budget hotels for traveling businessmen, these offer clean, reasonably priced and conveniently located lodging. Room service and other similar services are not offered but there are usually restaurants and vending machines on the premises.

● PENSIONS

These are a more recent type of western style accommodations. The name is borrowed from the French and pensions feature a homely atmosphere and hearty meals. They are often located near ski resorts or lakes and hence are very popular with sports enthusiasts. Pensions are usually built in a rustic lodge style and are owned and managed by young couples. They are excellent places for a relaxing stay amid natural surroundings. The average price is ¥6,000 per person, including 2 meals.

● YOUTH HOSTELS

Japan has more than 500 youth hostels around the country catering for the budget traveler. 75 of them are publicly run and are open to anyone, the others are privately managed and membership is required in the Japan Youth Hostels, Inc. or the International Youth Hostel Federation. The average charge is from ¥1,100 — ¥1,900 without meals. Some privately run hostels are Japanese style.

● CAPSULE HOTELS

A uniquely Japanese style of lodging, the rooms in these hotels are literally capsules, like train berths, and contain a TV and telephone along with a bed. Toilets and bathing facilities are usually communal. They average about ¥4,000 a night.

● HOTEL HINTS

1. Room charges cover lodging and service only.
2. Check-in: 11:00 a.m. or noon. (4:00 p.m. for business hotels).
3. Check-out: 11:00 a.m. or noon. (10:00 a.m. for business hotels).
4. A service charge of 10% to 15% is added to your check.
5. Yukata (light cotton kimono) are provided to wear when sleeping or relaxing in your room.

JAPANESE STYLE LODGING

● RYOKAN

Staying at a ryokan provides the visitor with an opportunity to enjoy the atmosphere of traditional Japanese accommodation. The rooms are laid with tatami (reed matting) and guests sleep on the floor. Bathrooms are usually communal (but separated by sex).

Room rates range from ¥5,000 to ¥60,000 per person and are usually quoted on a basis of 2 or more per room. This includes breakfast and dinner. The meals, which are usually elaborate affairs featuring local or seasonal specialties, will often be brought to your room. There are approximately 90,000 ryokans in Japan and over 2,000 belong to the Japan Ryokan Association.

● ECCONOMY INNS

These are low-priced ryokans with room rates averaging ¥4,000, excluding meals.

● RYOKAN HINTS

1. Check-in: around 4:00 p.m. Check-out: around 10:00 a.m.
2. Guests leave their shoes at the entrance and change into the slippers provided which are used for walking inside the ryokan but never on tatami floors.
3. A maid will serve tea, bring meals to your room, and lay out your futon (bedding) at night.
4. You will be provided with a yukata (light cotton kimono) or a padded dotera, depending on the season. These are worn anywhere inside the ryokan but are not

usually worn on the street.

5. Except in some modern *ryokans*, bathing is communal (but separated by sex). Baskets are provided for your clothes. Washing takes place outside the hot bath, which is reserved for sitting and soaking in. Hence, soap and shampoo are never used in the bath itself.

6. Most rooms do not have keys so valuables should be left at the front desk or in the safe provided in your room.

● MINSHUKU

Minshuku are something like guest houses and can be found in every city and town. They are operated by families, and the atmosphere is homely and relaxed. The rates are usually around ¥4,500 which includes 2 meals. Toilet articles and other amenities usually available at hotels and *ryokans* are not provided.

● KOKUMIN SHUKUSHA (PEOPLE'S LODGES)

These are generally located in national parks to offer people a chance to enjoy recreational activities at a reasonable price. Reservations can be made through travel agencies or directly with the lodge. Detailed information about public lodges is available from the People's Lodges Association; for private lodges, contact the National Park Association. Neither of these associations takes reservations, however.

● KOKUMIN KYUKA MURA (NATIONAL VACATION VILLAGES)

These Villages consist of lodging and recreational facilities, usually including sites for camping and boating and sports grounds. At present there are 31 Villages located in national park areas. Reservations can be made through travel agencies, directly with the Village, or through the reservation offices.

HOME VISITS

Over 60 Japanese families are registered with the Tokyo Municipal Government and open their homes to visitors interested in seeing something of Japanese daily life. Visits usually take place in the evening when all of the family are at home. No charge is required but, in accordance with Japanese custom, it is a good idea to take a small gift when visiting. Interested parties should apply at the Tourist Information Center, Tokyo Office.

RESERVATIONS

For all types of accommodation, it is best to make reservations as early as possible, especially for lodging in the peak travel seasons of summer and New Year.

SERVICE CHARGES AND TAXES

A 10% tax is added when total room and meal charges exceed ¥5,000 per person per night. At first class and deluxe hotels, a 10% service charge is added and hence no tipping is necessary. At *ryokans*, where each room has a maid, a 15% service charge is usu-

ally added. There are no service charges at business hotels, youth hostels, pensions, economy inns or *minshuku*.

● Room Charge: in hundreds of yen.
● Prices for hotels show twin room charges only.
● Prices for business hotels show single room charges only.
● Prices for Ryokans show the charge for one person to stay in a twin room including 2 meals.
● Location lined North to South.
● H = Hotel, R = Ryokan.
● (H) = member of Japan Hotel Association
　(R) = member of Japan Ryokan Association
　(B) = member of Japan Business Hotel Association

Name	R.C.	address	Tel.
〈HOKKAIDO〉			
● **Sapporo** ☎011			
Keiō Plaza H. Sapporo(H)	144-197	2-1 N5 W7, Chūō-ku, Sapporo	☎271-0111
H. New Otani Sapporo (H)	158-205	N2 W1,Chūō-ku, Sapporo	☎222-1111
Sapporo Grand H. (H)	126-233	N1 W4, Chūō-ku, Sapporo	☎261-3311
Sapporo Prince H. (H)	160-185	S2 W11, Chūō-ku, Sapporo	☎241-1111
Sapporo Tōkyu H. (H)	138-191	N4 W4, Chūō-ku, Sapporo	☎231-5611
Sapporo Tōkyu Inn	126-127	S4 W5, Chūō-ku, Sapporo	☎531-0109
● **Jōzankei Spa** ☎011			
Jōzankei Park H. (R)	100-160	W4, Jōzankei, Minami-ku, Sapporo	☎598-2345
Jōzankei H. (R)	100-200	W4-340, Jōzankei, Minami-ku, Sapporo	☎598-2111
Jōzankei Grand H. (R)	100-230	E4-328, Jōzankeionsen, Minami-ku, Sapporo	☎598-2214
H. Shikanoyu (R)	105-170	W3, Jōzankei, Minami-ku, Sapporo	☎598-2311
● **Noboribetsu Hot Springs** ☎01438			
Daiichi Takimotokan (R)	145-220	55 Noboribetsuonsenmachi, Noboribetsu	☎4-2111
H. Manseikaku (R)	130-350	Noboribetsuonsenmachi, Noboribetsu	☎4-2266
Noboribetsu Grand H. (R)	140-300	154 Noboribetsuonsenmachi, Noboribetsu	☎4-2101
〈AKITA〉			
● **Akita** ☎0188			
Akita Castle H. (H)	130-144	1-3-5 Naka-dōri, Akita	☎34-1141
Akita New Grand H. (H)	110-1000	5-2-1 Naka-dōri, Akita	☎34-5211
R. Eitarō (R)	120-150	6-15 Senshūyadomemachi, Akita	☎33-4151
〈YAMAGATA〉			
● **Zaō Hot Springs** ☎0236			
Miyamasou Takamiya (R)	90-150	Zaōonsen, Yamagata	☎94-9333
Zaō Astoria H. (R)	100-120	Yokokuragerende, Zaōonsen, Yamagata	☎94-9603

191

⟨MIYAGI⟩

● Sendai ☎022

H. Rich Sendai (H)	125-500	2-2-2 Kokubuchō, Sendai	☎262-8811
H. Sendai Plaza (H)	155-950	2-20-1 Honchō, Sendai	☎262-7111
Sendai Tōkyū H. (H)	150-950	2-9-25 Ichibanchō, Sendai	☎262-2411

⟨NIKKO⟩ ☎0288

● Nikko City

Konishi R. Bekkan (R)	100-140	1115 Kamihatsuishimachi, Nikko-shi	☎54-1105
Nikkō Kanaya H. (H)	70-300	1300 Kamihatsuishimachi, Nikko-shi	☎54-0001
Tamozawa Kaikan (R)	60-180	2010 Hanaishimachi, Nikko-shi	☎54-1152

● Chūzenji Spa

Chūzenji Kanaya H. (H)	120-160	2482 Chūgūshi, Nikko-shi	☎55-0356
Nikkō Lake Side H. (H)	170-600	2482 Chūgūshi, Nikko-shi	☎55-0321
Nikkō Prince H. (H)	190-520	2485 Shōbugahama, Chūgūshi, Nikko-shi	☎55-0661

● Kinugawa Spa

Iwaburo Suimeikan (R)	100-200	1-17 Fujiwaramachi, Shioya-gun	☎77-2211
Kinugama Onsen H. (R)	150-300	545 Taki, Fujiwaramachi, Shioya-gun	☎77-0025

⟨NAGANO⟩

● Karuizawa ☎0267

H. Kajimanomori	160-600	Hanareyama, Karuizawamachi, Kitasaku-gun	☎42-3535
Karuizawa Mampei H. (H)	190-290	925 Sakuranosawa, Karuizawamachi, Kitasaku-gun	☎42-2771
Karuizawa Prince H. (H) (R)	220	1016-75, Karuizawa, Karuizawamachi, Kitasaku-gun	☎42-8111
Oiwake Aburaya R. (R)	70-100	607 Oiwake, Karuizawamachi, Kitasaku-gun	☎45-1111

⟨TOKYO⟩ ☎03

● Major Hotels

Akasaka Prince H. (H)	280-850	1-2 Kioichō, Chiyoda-ku	☎234-1111
Akasaka Tōkyū H. (H)	190-1350	2-14-3 Nagatachō, Chiyoda-ku	☎580-2311
Capitol Tōkyū H. (H)	270-2500	2-10-3 Nagatachō, Chiyoda-ku	☎581-4511
Ginza Dai-ichi H. (H)	155-600	8-13-1 Ginza, Chūō-ku	☎542-5311
Ginza Tōkyū H. (H)	240-1550	5-15-9 Ginza, Chūō-ku	☎541-2411
H. Century Hyatt (H)	215-3000	2-7-2 Nishi-Shinjuku, Shinjuku-ku	☎349-0111
H. Grand Palace	190-800	1-1-1 Iidabashi, Chiyoda-ku	☎264-1111
H. New Otani (H)	240-4500	4-1 Kioichō, Chiyoda-ku	☎265-1111
H. Okura (H)	215-3500	2-10-4 Toranomon, Minato-ku	☎582-0111
H. Pacific Tokyo (H)	200-2000	3-13-3 Takanawa, Minato-ku	☎445-6711
H. Sunroute Tokyo (H)	140-600	2-3-1 Yoyogi, Shibuya-ku	☎375-3211
Imperial H. (H)	265-6000	1-1-1 Uchisaiwaichō, Chiyoda-ku	☎504-1111
Keiō Plaza H. (H)	210-2000	2-2-1 Nishi-Shinjuku, Shinjuku-ku	☎344-0111
Marunouch H. (H)	200-600	1-6-3 Marunouchi, Chiyoda-ku	☎215-2151
Miyako H. Tokyo	180-1500	1-1-50 Shiroganedai, Minato-ku	☎447-3111
Palace H. (H)	235-2000	1-1-1 Marunouchi, Chiyoda-ku	☎211-5211
Shiba Park H. (H)	180-500	1-5-10 Shibakōen, Minato-ku	☎433-4141
Shimbashi Dai-ichi H. (H)	155-200	1-2-6 Shimbashi, Minato-ku	☎501-4411
Takanawa Prince H. (H)	210-3000	3-13-1 Takanawa, Minato-ku	☎447-1111

Tokyo Hilton International (H) 340-2400   6-6-2 Nishi-Shinjuku, Shinjuku-ku ☎344-5111

● Youth Hostel · YMCA · YWCA

Tokyo International Youth Hostel	33	21-1 Kagurakashi, Shinjuku-ku	☎235-1107
Tokyo Yoyogi Youth Hostel	17	3-1 Yoyogi-Kamisonochō, Shibuya-ku	☎467-9163
Tokyo YMCA H.	52	7 Kanda Mitoshirochō, Chiyoda-ku	☎293-1911
Tokyo YWCA H.	44	1-8-11 Kanda-Surugadai, Chiyoda-ku	☎293-5421
YMCA Asia Youth Center	55	2-5-5 Sarugakuchō, Chiyoda-ku	☎233-0611

● Japanese Inn Groupe

Inabasō R.	70-80	5-6-13 Shinjuku, Shinjuku-ku	☎341-9581
R. Mikawaya Bekkan	90	1-31-11 Asakusa, Taitōku	☎843-2345
R. Sansuisō	66-70	2-9-5 Higashi Gotanda, Shinagawa-ku	☎441-7475
Sawanoya R.	75	2-3-11 Yanaka, Taitō-ku	☎822-2251
Suigetsu H./Ogaisō	95-150	3-3-21 Ikenohata, Taitō-ku	☎822-4611

● Minshuku

Minsuku Center	45-60	Kōtsūkaikan, 2-10-1 Yūrakuchō, Chiyoda-ku ☎216-6556

The People's Lodges Association
        Nishi-Shimbashi Chūō Bldg. 3-5-8 Nishi-Shimbashi, Minato-ku ☎03-437-5361
The National Park Association
        Toranomon Denki Bldg. 2-8-1 Toranomon, Minato-ku ☎03-502-0488
National Vacation Villages
Sendai	Sendai Sta. 1-1-1 Chūō, Sendai-shi	☎022-227-4806
Tokyo	Kōtsū-Kaikan Bldg. 2-10-1 Yūrakuchō, Chiyoda-ku	☎03-216-2085
Osaka	Osaka Sta. 3-1-1 Umeda, Kita-ku, Osaka-shi	☎06-343-0131
Hiroshima	Fujii Bldg. 2-6-31 Otemachi, Naka-ku, Hiroshima-shi	☎082-247-1819
Fukuoka	Ohakata Bldg. 2-20-1 Hakata-ekimae, Hakata-ku, Fukuoka-shi	☎092-472-5501

〈YOKOHAMA〉 ☎045

H. New Grand (H)	120-280	10 Yamashitachō, Naka-ku, Yokohama-shi	☎681-1841
The H. Yokohama (H)	180-800	6-1 Yamashitachō, Naka-ku Yokohama-shi	☎662-1321
Yokohama Prince H. (H)	139-235	3-13-1, Isogo, Isogo-ku, Yokohama-shi	☎753-2211
Yokohama Tōkyū H.	185-350	1-1-12 Minami-Saiwai, Nishi-ku Yokohama-shi	☎311-16882

193

〈HAKONE〉 ☎0460

● Hakone Yumoto Hot Springs

Fujiya H. (H)	130-650	256 Yumoto, Hakonemachi, Ashigarashimo-gun	☎5-6111
Tenseien (R)	190-330	682 Hakonemachi, Ashigarashimo-gun	☎5-5521

〈IZU〉

● Atami ☎0557

Atami Fujiya H. (R)	130-320	13-8 Ginzamachi, Atami	☎81-7111
Hōrai (R)	310-700	750-6 Izusan, Atami	☎80-5151
New Fujiya H. (H)	180-500	1-16 Ginzamachi, Atami	☎81-0111
Tsuruya H. (R)	150-350	6-45 Higashikaiganmachi, Atami	☎82-1212

〈KANAZAWA〉 ☎0762

Araya R. (R)	85-95	76 Bakurōmachi, Kanazawa-shi	☎31-4188
Kanazawa New Grand H. (H)	128-235	1-50 Takaokamachi, Kanazawa-shi	☎33-1311
Holiday Inn Kanazawa	120-145	1-10 Horikawachō, Kanazawa-shi	☎23-1111
Tsubajin (R)	400-500	5-1-8 Teramachi, Kanazawa-shi	☎41-2181

⟨NAGOYA⟩ ☎052

H. Nagoya Castle (H)	180-1600	3-19 Hinokuchimachi, Nishi-ku Nagoya	☎521-2121
Meitetsu Grand H.	120-200	1-2-4 Meieki, Nakamura-ku, Nagoya	☎582-2211
Nagoya Kankō H. (H)	180-1600	1-19-30 Nishiki, Naka-ku, Nagoya	☎231-7711
Nagoya Kokusai H.	180-800	3-23-3 Nishiki, Naka-ku, Nagoya	☎961-3111
Nagoya Miyako H.	120-700	4-9-10 Meieki, Nakamura-ku, Nagoya	☎571-3211
Nagoya Terminal H.	110-300	1-1-2 Meieki, Nakamura-ku, Nagoya	☎561-3751

⟨TOBA⟩ ☎0599

Nemu-no-Sato (R)	160-410	Osaki Hamashimamachi, Shima-gun	☎52-1111
R. Kaigetu (R)	150-200	1-10-52 Toba, Toba-shi	☎26-2056
Toba Kokusai H. (H)	150-450	1-23-1 Toba, Toba-shi	☎25-3121

⟨KYOTO⟩ ☎075

Benkeirō (R)	130-250	Gojō-Agaru, Kiyamachidōri, Shimogyō-ku	☎351-8558
H. Ginmomd (H)	120-170	Takakuranishi-hairu, Oikedōri, Nakagyō-ku	☎221-4111
H. Keihan Kyoto	130-260	31 Higashikujō-Nishiannōchō, Minami-ku	☎661-0321
Hiiragiya R. (R)	300-700	Fuyachō-Oikekado, Nakagyō-ku	☎221-1136
Izutsuyasu R. (R)	100-150	Higashitōin-shōmen-kudaru, Shimogyō-ku	☎371-1574
Kyoto Grand H. (H)	130-700	Shiokōji, Horikawa, Shimogyō-ku	☎341-2311
Kyoto Kokusai H. (H)	100-1500	Nijō-kudaru, Aburanokōji, Nakagyō-ku	☎222-1111
Kyoto Royal H. (H)	135-350	Sanjō-agaru, Kawaramachi, Nakagyō-ku	☎223-1234
Kyoto Shin-Hankyū H.	130-300	Kyotoeki-Shomen, Shiokōjidōri, Shimogyō-ku	☎343-5300
Kyoto Tōkyū H. (H)	165-800	Gojō-kudaru, Horikawadōri, Shimogyō-ku	☎341-2411
Miyako H. (H)	120-1680	Sanjō-keage, Higashiyama-ku	☎771-7111
Nisshō Bessō (R)	90-250	Sanjō-Tominokōji, Nakagyō-ku	☎221-7878
Sumiya R. (R)	300-700	Sanjō-kudaru, Fuyamachi, Nakagyō-ku	☎221-2188
Tawaraya R. (R)	410-630	Anegakōji-agaru, Fuyamachi, Nakagyō-ku	☎211-5566

⟨NARA⟩ ☎0742

Edosan (R)	130-150	1167 Takahatamachi, Nara-shi	☎26-2662
H. Fujita Nara	120-300	47-1 Shimosanjōmachi, Nara-shi	☎23-8111
Kikusuirō (R)	340-500	1130 Takahatamachi, Nara-shi	☎23-2001
Nara H. (R)	159-231	1096 Takahatamachi, Nara-shi	☎26-3300
Shikitei (R)	300-550	Ichinotorii-yoko, Narakōen-nai, Nara-shi	☎22-5531

⟨OSAKA⟩ ☎06

H. Plaza (H)	180-2300	2-2-49 Oyodominami Oyodo-ku, Osaka-shi	☎453-1111
Holiday Inn Nankai Osaka (H)	185-1000	28-1 Kyūzaemonchō, Minami-ku, Osaka-shi	☎213-8281
Osaka Dai-ichi H. (H)	130-600	1-9-20 Umedachō, Kita-ku, Osaka-shi	☎341-4411
Osaka Grand H. (H)	160-750	2-3-18 Nakanoshima, Kita-ku, Osaka-shi	☎202-1212
Osaka Kokusai H.	130-800	58 Uchihonmachi-Hashizumechō, Higashi-ku	☎941-2661
Osaka Terminal H. (H)	160-700	3-1-1 Umeda, Kita-ku, Osaka-shi	☎344-1235
Osaka Tōkyū H. (H)	145-600	7-20 Chayamachi, Kita-ku, Osaka-shi	☎373-2411
Osaka Zennikkū Sheraton	200-2000	1-3-1 Dōzimahama, Kita-ku, Osaka-shi	☎347-1112
Royal H. (H)	240-3500	5-3-68 Nakanoshima, Kita-ku, Osaka-shi	☎448-1121
Shin-Hankyū H. (H)	130-210	1-1-35 Shibata, Kita-ku, Osaka-shi	☎372-5101
Tōyō H. (H)	130-350	3-16-19, Toyosaki, Oyodo-ku, Osaka-shi	☎372-8181

⟨KOBE⟩ ☎078

Kōbe Portpia H. (H)	180-2000	6-1-10 Minatoshima-Nakamachi, Kōbe-shi	☎302-1111
Oriental H. (H)	140-1000	25 Kyōmachi, Chūō-ku, Kōbe-shi	☎331-8111

Rokkōsan H. (H)   105-350   1034 Minamirokkō, Rokkōsanmachi, Nada -ku, Kōbe-shi   ☎891-0301

〈OKAYAMA〉 ☎0862

H. New Okayama (H)	160-800	1-1-25 Ekimaemachi, Okayama-shi	☎23-8211
Okayama Grand H. (H)	80-120	2-10 Funabashimachi, Okayama-shi	☎33-7777
Okayama Plaza H. (H)	100-350	2-3-12 Hama, Okayama-shi	☎72-1201
Yamasa Honjin (R)	120-200	8-23 Honchō, Okayama-shi	☎24-1241

〈HIROSHIMA〉 ☎082

Hiroshima Grand H. (H)	125-2000	4-4 Kamihacchōbori, Naka-ku, Hiroshima-shi	☎227-1313
Hiroshima Kokusai H. (H)	100-155	3-13 Tachimachi, NaKa-ku, Hiroshima-shi	☎248-2323
Hiroshima Zennikkū H. (H)	135-1600	7-20 Nakamachi, Naka-ku, Hiroshima-shi	☎241-1111

〈TAKAMATSU〉 ☎0878

H. Rich Takamatsu (H)	110-500	9-1 Furushinmachi, Takamatsu-shi	☎22-3555
Keio Plaza H. Takamatsu (H)	115-400	11-5 Chūōchō, Takamatsu-shi	☎34-5511
Takamatsu Grand H. (H)	100-180	1-5-10 Kotobukichō, Takamatsu-shi	☎51-5757
Takamatsu Kokusai H. (H)	145-700	2191-1 Kitachō, Takamatsu-shi	☎31-1511

〈MATSUYAMA〉 ☎0899

Matsuyama Zennikkū H. (H)   150-650   3-2-1 Ichibanchō, Matsuyama-shi   ☎33-5511

〈HAKATA〉 ☎092

H. New Otani Hakata (H)   180-1400   1-1-2 Watanabedōri, Chūō-ku, Fukuoka-shi   ☎714-1111

〈NAGASAKI〉 ☎0958

Nagasaki Kankō H. Shūmeikan (R)	100-500	3-11 Chikugomachi, Nagasaki-shi	☎22-5121
Nagasaki Kokusai H. Nisshōkan (R)	120-250	210-1 Nisizakamachi, Nagasaki-shi	☎24-2151
Nagasaki Tōkyū H. (H)	158-1000	1-18 Minamiyamatemachi, Nagasaki-shi	☎25-1501
Yataro (R)	110-200	2-1 Kazagashıramachı, Nagasakı-shı	☎22-8166

〈KUMAMOTO〉 ☎096

Chitose H. (R)	80-120	1-12-4 Kyōmachi, Kumamoto-shi	☎354-1851
Kumamoto H. Castle (H)	108-800	4-2 Jōtōmachi, Kumamoto-shi	☎326-3311
New Sky H. (H)	130-1200	2 Higashiamidateramachi, Kumamoto-shi	☎354-2111
R. Shin-Tokiwa (R)	80-150	1-6 Funabamachishita, Kumamoto-shi	☎325-4111

〈OITA〉

● Beppu ☎0977

Gasensō H. (R)	80-100	6-9 Motomachi, Beppu-shi	☎22-4101
Kamenoi H. (H)	85-180	5-17 Chūōcho, Beppu-shi	☎22-3301
Suginoi H. (H)	120-1200	2272 Oaza-Minamitateishi, Beppu-shi	☎24-1141

〈MIYAZAKI〉 ☎0985

H. Plaza Miyazaki (H)	80-510	1-1 Kawaramachi, Miyazaki-shi	☎27-1111
Miyazaki Grand H. (H)	70-120	2-2-42 Matsuyama, Miyazaki-shi	☎22-2121
Miyazaki Kankō H. (H)	120-1000	1-1-1 Matsuyama, Miyazaki-shi	☎27-1212
R. Bokusui (R)	60-120	1-8-14 Hiroshima, Miyazaki-shi	☎22-2007

〈OKINAWA〉

Manza Beach H. (H)	210-1000	2,260 Seralaki, Onnason, Kunigami-gun	☎09896-5-1211
Naha Tokyu H. (H)	145-800	1,002 Ameku, Naha-shi	☎0988-68-2151
Naha Grand H.	70-95	1-5-7 Matsuo, Naha-shi	☎0988-62-6161
Okinawa Harbor View H.	130-1400	2-46 Izumizaki, Naha-shi	☎0988-53-2111

DINING

Japan is a gourmet's paradise, offering an enormous variety of dishes including every kind of international cuisine in addition to traditional fare.

RESTAURANTS

● RYOTEI

Top-class restaurants in Japan serve the best of the country's dishes in elegant surroundings with quiet, discreet service. *Ryōtei* are traditional restaurants in this class and most require reservations. Some will only serve guests introduced through established customers.

● INEXPENSIVE RESTAURANTS

There is a limitless variety of friendly, inexpensive restaurants to be found on almost every street and alley in Japan. The plastic samples in the display cases, which are accurate replicas of what you are actually served, will help you decide what to order.

JAPANESE DELICACIES

● KAISEKI RYORI

Traditionally served after the tea ceremony, *Kaiseki* cuisine is now available in restaurants. A full course includes small portions of numerous dishes all beautifully presented. The focus is aesthetic, with emphasis placed on shape and color, so *Kaiseki* tends to be expensive but is a true feast for the eyes.

● TEMPURA

Introduced by the Portuguese in the 16th century, *tempura* has been refined over the years and the result is a feather-light batter deep-fried in the purest vegetable oil. Numerous ingredients are used, popular ones being shrimp, squid, eggplant, and sweet potato. The hot *tempura* is dipped into a special soy sauce before eating.

● SUSHI

One of the best-known Japanese dishes, *sushi* (raw fish on vinegared rice) is made to order in all but the cheapest shops, so you can point to the desired topping in the glass case in front of the counter when ordering.

● SUKIYAKI AND SHABU-SHABU

Sukiyaki consists of thin strips of beef, sliced green onion, *tōfu*, vegetables and *shirataki* (a gelatinous noodle), all cooked at your table.

When ready, take a portion with your chopsticks and dip it in your bowl of beaten raw egg.

For *shabu-shabu* you do the cooking! Thinly sliced beef is dipped in a pot of boiling water and vegetables.

● *TONKATSU*

This is deep-fried, crumbed pork cutlets. A *tonkatsu teishoku* (set meal) will probaly include *tonkatsu*, shredded cabbage, tomato, *miso* soup, and rice.

● *NOODLES*

Noodles were introduced into Japan from China, and there are 3 basic types: *soba* (buckwheat noodles), *udon* (wheat noodles), ramen or *chūka soba* (thin egg noodles). Noodles are an extremely popular and generally inexpensive dish.

● *YAKITORI*

Pieces of chicken, liver and spring onions are threaded on bamboo skewers and grilled over charcoal or gasfires. *Yakitori* is accompanied by a tangy sauce and is not so much a meal as a snack when drinking.

INTERNATIONAL CUISINE

In addition to specialty restaurants, the leading hotels in major cities offer almost every kind of Continental, American and Oriental cuisine.

ALCOHOL

Both domestic and imported liquor are available at hotels, restaurants and nightclubs among other places. Imported liquor is naturally more expensive. Whisky is very popular in Japan and the local distillations are quite good. Japanese beer, both lager and draught, is generally excellent. *Sake* is brewed from rice and is served warm or over ice. *Shōchū* is becoming increasingly popular, especially with the nation's young people. It is lighter than *sake* and is distilled from rice, wheat, or sweet potatos.

197

Name	address	Tel

⟨TOKYO⟩ ☎03

● Japanese

Botan (Chicken)	1-15 Kanda-Sudachō, Chiyoda-ku	☎251-0577
Chikuyōtei (Eel)	8-14-7 Ginza, Chūō-ku	☎542-0787
Daikokuya (Tempura)	1-38-10 Asakusa, Taitō-ku	☎844-1111
Edogyū (Sukiyaki)	2F Mitsuhide Bldg., 3-11-19 Akasaka, Minato-ku	☎585-9442
Hanagiri (Kyoto Cuisine)	ABC Kaikan, 2-6-3 Shibakōen, Minato-ku	☎436-6851
Hōraitei(Tonkatsu)	2-22-11 Shibuya, Shibuya-ku	☎409-8806

Ima-asa (Shabu-Shabu)	2F Imaasa Bldg, 1-1-21 Higashi-Shimbashi, Minato-ku	☎572-5286
Isegen (Anglen)	1-11-1 Kanda-Sudachō, Chiyoda-ku	☎251-1229
Kakiden (Kaiseki)	Yasuyo Bldg., 3-37-11 Shinjuku, Shinjuku-ku	☎352-5121
Kanda Yabusoba (Soba)	2-10 Kanda-Awajichō, Chiyoda-ku	☎251-0287
Komagata Dozeu (Loach)	1-7-12 Komagata, Taitō-ku	☎842-4001
Mimiu (Udon)	3-6-4 Kyōbashi, Chūō-ku	☎567-6571
Nakasei (Tempura)	1-39-13 Asakusa, Taitō-ku	☎841-4015
Nakata (Sushi)	5-6-9 Ginza, Chūō-ku	☎571-0063
Namiki Yabusoba (Soba)	2-11-9 Karinarimon, Taitō-ku	☎841-1340
Neboke (Tosa District)	3-11-17 Akasaka, Minato-ku	☎585-9640
Niigata Inakaya (Niigata District)	1-9-24 Minami-Ikebukuro, Toshima-ku	☎984-6437
Otakō (Oden)	5-4-16 Ginza, Chūō-ku	☎571-0057
Asakusa Rokku Sushihatsu (Sushi)	2-11-4 Asakusa, Taitō-ku	☎844-3293
Suehiro (Sukiyaki)	6-11-2 Ginza, Chūō-ku	☎571-9271
Ten-ichi (Tempura)	6-6-5 Ginza, Chūō-ku	☎571-1949
Tentake (Blowfish)	6-16-6 Tsukiji, Chūō-ku	☎541-3881
Torichō (Yakitori)	7-8-2 Roppongi, Minato-ku	☎401-1827
Tsukiji Edogin (Sushi)	4-5-1 Tsukiji, Chūō-ku	☎543-4401
Tsukiji Tamura (Kaiseki)	2-12-11 Tsukiji, Chūō-ku	☎541-1611
Tsunahachi (Tempura)	3-31-8 Shinjuku, Shinjuku-ku	☎352-1011
Zakuro (Shabu-shabu)	TBS Kaikan, 5-3-3 Akasaka, Minato-ku	☎582-6841

● International

Ajanta (Indian)	1-15-14 Kudan-kita, Chiyoda-ku	☎264-4255
Antonio (Italian)	7-3-6 Minami-Aoyama, Minato-ku	☎797-0388
Bodegon (Spanish)	Chiba Bldg., 3-10-9 Roppongi, Minato-ku	☎404-3430
Cafe Central (Philippine)	Central Apartment, 4-30-6 Jingū-mae, Shibuya-ku	☎403-6557
Chinzan-sō (Barbecue)	2-10-8 Sekiguchi, Bunkyō-ku	☎943-1111
Double AX (Greek)	3-10-4 Roppongi, Minato-ku	☎401-7384
Grill Chateau (Stew)	Akiyama Bldg., 2-3-22 Tranomon, Minato-ku	☎591-4530
Lohmeyer (German)	Igami Bldg., 5-3-14 Ginza, Chūō-ku	☎571-1142
Maxim's de Paris (French)	Sony Bldg., 5-3-1 Ginza, Chūō-ku	☎572-3621
Nair Restaurant (Indian)	4-10-7 Ginza, Chūō-ku	☎541-8246
Rogoski (Russian)	9F Tōkyū Plaza, 1-2-2 Dōgenzaka, Shibuya-ku	☎463-3665
Stockholm (Swedish)	Sweden Center, 6-11-9 Roppongi, Minato-ku	☎403-9046
Takano World Restaurant	Takano Bldg., 3-26-11 Shinjuku, Shinjuku-ku	☎354-0222
Wadamon (Steak)	Hanatsubaki Bldg., 3-15-23 Roppongi, Minato-ku	☎470-4431

● Chinese

Heichinrō (Canton)	Fukoku Seimei Bldg., 2-2-2 Uchi-Saiwaichō, Chiyoda-ku	☎508-0555
Jade Garden (Canton)	4-1-8 Shimbashi, Minato-ku	☎431-6701
Reikyō (Taiwan)	2-25-18 Dōgenzaka, Shibuya-ku	☎461-4220
Rōgairo Hanten (Shanghai)	2-12-8 Akasaka, Minato-ku	☎585-1231
Setsuen (South Tonchin)	3-8-9 Shinjuku, Shinjuku-ku	☎354-4028
Shin-a Hanten (Shanghai)	2-3-2 Shiba-Daimon, Minato-ku	☎434-0005
Shisen Hanten (Szechwan)	Fujiya Bldg., 7-2-17 Ginza, Chūō-ku	☎573-4010
Shōdōten (Canton)	1-2-17 Nihombashi, Chūō-ku	☎272-1071
Shōryū	6-10-14 Ueno, Taitō-ku	☎832-0847

⟨NIKKO, YOKOHAMA, KAMAKURA, HAKONE⟩

N (Nikko) ☎0288, Y (Yokohama) ☎045, K (Kamakura) ☎0467, H (Hakone) ☎0460

Ebiya (Yuba)	948 Shimo-Hatsuishi, Nikko-shi	N.53-1177

Gyōshintei (Kaiseki)	2339-1 Sannai, Nikko-shi	N.53-3751
Hagehachi (Sushi)	594 Yumoto, Hakone-machi	H.5-5558
Hachinoki (Keiseki)	7 Yamanouchi, Kamakura-shi	K.22-8719
Hatsuhana (Soba)	635 Yumoto, Hakone-machi	H.5-8287
Junkaikaku (Chinese)	147 Yamashitachō, Naka-ku, Yokohama-shi	Y.681-1324
Komachi (Tonkatsu)	1-6-12 Komachi, Kamakura-shi	K.22-2025
Kōshō (Chinese)	185 Yamashitachō, Naka-ku, Yokohama-shi	Y.681-5181
Manchinrō (Chinese)	153 Yamashitachō, Naka-ku, Yokohama-shi	Y.681-4004
Meiji-no-Yakata (Steak)	2339-1 Sannai, Nikko-shi	N.53-3751
Märchenhütte (German)	4-8-16 Kamakurayama, Kamakura-shi	K.31-0428
Monte Costa (Italian)	1-5-7 Yukinoshita, Kamakura-shi	K.23-0808
Mutekirō (French)	2-96 Motomachi, Naka-ku, Yokohama-shi	Y.681-2926
Nakamura-an (Soba)	1-7-6 Komachi, Kamakura-shi	K.25-3500
Noge Oden (Oden)	2-6 Yoshida-machi, Naka-ku, Yokohama-shi	Y.251-3234
Roast Beef Kamakurayama (French)	3-11-1 Kamakurayama, Kamakura-shi	K.31-5454
Takaichi (Fish)	1-45 Noge-machi, Naka-ku, Yokohama-shi	Y.242-0458

⟨KYOTO⟩ ☎075

● Japanese

Ayujaya Hiranoya (Sweetfish)	Saga-toriimoto-Sennōchō, Ukyō-ku	☎861-0359
Chimoto (Kaiseki-ryōri)	Shijōōhashi-Nishizume-Minami-iru, Shimogyō-ku	☎351-1846
Chinchikurin (Zōsui, Rice Soup)		
	Nishikiyamachi-Shijōsagaru-Higashi, Shimogyō-ku	☎351-9205
Daitokuji Ikkyū (Shōjin-ryōri)	Murasakino-Daitokujimonzenchō, Kita-ku	☎493-0019
Gontaro Honten (Soba) Fuyamachi-Nishikikoji-sagaru-Masuya-chō, Nakagyō-ku		☎221-5810
Hiranoya Honten (Imobō)		
	Maruyamakōen-chionin-Minamimonmae, Higashiyama-ku	☎561-1603
Hyōtei (Kaiseki-ryōri)	35, Nanzenji-kusakawachō, Sakyō-ku	☎771-4116
Ichiryuan (Shabu-Shabu)	Shijō-Agaru-nishi, Pontochō, Nakagyō-ku	☎221-2405
Izuu (Mackerel Sushi)	Shijō-Agaru-higashigawa, Kiritōshi, Higashiyama-ku	☎561-0750
Izusen (Shōjin-ryōri)	Murasakino-Daitokujichō, Daijiin-nai, Kita-ku	☎491-6665
·Junsei (Kyō-ryōri)	60, Nanzenji-Kusakawachō, Sakyō-ku	☎761-2311
Kanidōraku (Crab)	Teramachi-Sanjō-kado, Nakagyō-ku	☎211-0671
Kawashige (Kyō-Bentō)		
1 Sujime-higashi-hairu-nishi, Sanjō-sagaru, Kawaramachi, Nakagyō-ku		☎221-5031
Kinsuitei (Bamboo shoot)	2-15-15, Tenjin, Nagaokakyō-shi	☎951-5151
Mankamerō (Kaiseki-ryōri)	Demizu-agaru-Nishi, Inokumadōri, Kamigyō-ku	☎441-5020
Matsuba (Nishin Soba)		
	Minamizatonari, Shijōōhashi-higashi-zume, Higashiyama-ku	☎561-1451
Minokichi (Kyō-ryōri)		
	Sanjōagaru, Dōbutsuenmaedōri, Amataguchitoriichō, Sakyō-ku	☎771-4185
Mishimatei (Sukiyaki)	Teramachi-Sanjō-sagaru, Nakagyō-ku	☎221-0003
Misokaan Kawamichiya (Soba)	Fuyachō-Sanjō-agaru, Nakagyō-ku	☎221-2525
Nishiki (Kyō-Bentō)	Nakanoshimakōennai, Arashiyama, Ukyō-ku	☎871-8888
Okutan (Yudōfu)	Nanzenjisannai, Sakyō-ku	☎771-8709
Sakahoko (Chanko-Nabe, Hot pot dish)	Kiyamachi-shijō-agaru, Nakagyō-ku	☎221-0845
Seizansōdō (Yudōfu)	63, Saga-tenryūji-Susukinobabachō, Ukyō-ku	☎861-1609
Shin-Miura (Chicken)	570-125 Gionmachi-Minamigawa, Higashiyama-ku	☎561-3175
Sōrin-an (Yuba)	45, Kamikatsura-Higashinokuchichō, Nishigyō-ku	☎381-7384
Warajiya (Eel)	Higashihairu-Kita, Nanajo-Hommachi, Higashiyama-ku	☎561-1290

199

Yamatomi (Skewered fried dish)　　　Shijôagaru, Pontochô, Nakagyô-ku　　　☎221-1364

● *International*

Chinmin (Chinese)　　　Shijô-Hanamikôji-kado, Higashiyama-ku　　　☎551-2671
Grill Tominaga (Steak)　　　Shimogamo-Shibamotochô, Sakyô-ku　　　☎791-2830
Java (Curry)　　　2-Sujime-Higashi-iru-Kita, Kawaramachi, Nakagyô-ku　　　☎221-7851
Man-yoken (French)　　　Shijô-Fuyachô-Higashi-iru-Kitagawa, Shimogyô-ku　　　☎221-1022
Restaurant Izutsu (Teppanyaki)　　　Yamatoôji-Sanjôsagaru, Higashiyama-ku　　　☎541-2121
Suehiro (Steak)　　　Kawaramachi-Shijôagaru-Higashi, Nakagyô-ku　　　☎221-7188
Tôkasaikan (Chinese)　　　Shijôôhashi-Nishizume, Shimogyô-ku　　　☎221-1147

‹OSAKA›　☎06

● *Japanese*

Ajikitchô (Japanese)
　　　8F Daimaru Dept. Store 1-118 Shinsaibashi-suji, Minami-ku　　　☎251-1436
Amano (Kishimen)　　　Umeda-chika-center 2-5 Kakutachô, Kita-ku　　　☎312-3470
Bonchi (Tonkatsu)　　　1-10-7 Dôtombori, Minami-ku　　　☎211-5594
Botejû Sôhonke (Okonomiyaki)　　　56, Soemonchô, Minami-ku　　　☎211-4478
Bubutei (Akashiyaki)　　　7F Navio Hankyû, 7-10 Kadota-chô, Kita-ku　　　☎316-0777
Gansô Marumasa (Sushi)　　　1-23 Edobori, Nishi-ku　　　☎441-4258
Hishitomi (Eel)　　　53 Soemonchô, Minami-ku　　　☎211-5329
Hon Miyake (Sukiyaki)　　　10F Asahi Bldg, 3-2-4 Nakanoshima, Kita-ku　　　☎231-3188
Itchô (Yakiniku)　　　9 Dôjima Chika Center, 1 Dojima, Kita-ku　　　☎344-9080
Izumo Soba (Soba)　　　2-10-18 Shima-no-uchi, Minami-ku　　　☎211-7252
Jôyatô (Oden)　　　2-5-14 Sonezaki, Kika-ku　　　☎361-7823
Kameyoshi (Sushi)　　　1F Hishitomi Bldg, 1-9-6 Sonezaki-Shinchi, Kita-ku　　　☎345-7697
Yotarô Honten (Porgy rice)　　　2-48, Kôraibashi, Higashi-ku　　　☎231-5561
Kushinobô Honten (Kushikatsu)　　　1-5-6, Namba, Minami-ku　　　☎211-1628
Rogetsu Bekkan (Kami-Nabe)　　　1-7-10 Sonezaki-Shinchi, Kita-ku　　　☎341-6351
Shabu-tei (Shabu-Shabu)　　　Kappa-Yokochô 1-7-2 Shibata-cho, Kita-ku　　　☎373-0739
Shiga (Chanko-Nabe)　　　B1, Dôjima Grand Bldg, 1-5-17 Dôjima, Kita-ku　　　☎345-1815
Shin-Akashi (Blowfish)　　　2-2-4 Dôtombori, Minami-ku　　　☎211-2523
Shiruyoshi (Tôfu-Nabe)　　　50, Higashi-shimizuchô, Minami-ku　　　☎251-8971
Shusenbô Robata Tome (Robatayaki)　　　2-10-24 Sonezaki, Kita-ku　　　☎311-9546
Suehiro Honten (Beef)　　　1-11-11 Sonezaki-Shinchi, Kita-ku　　　☎341-1638
Suisha-an (Japanese)　　　9 Dôjima Chika Center, 1 Dôjima, Kita-ku　　　☎346-5916
Tokuya (Whale)　　　1-8-2 Sennichimae, Mimami-ku　　　☎211-4448
Tori-ichi (Chicken)　　　3 Sennichimae, Namba, Minami-ku　　　☎649-6734
Yaetei (Yakitori)　　　2-9-9 Sonezaki, Kita-ku　　　☎311-7914
Yukiya (Kama-meshi)　　　8 Saemonchô, Minami-ku　　　☎213-2385

● *International*

Ashoka (Indian)　　　B2 Osaka-Maru Bldg 1 Umeda, Kita-ku　　　☎346-0333
Azuma (Taiwan)　　　4-4-8 Nishitemma, Kita-ku　　　☎363-1712
Cafe Brasserie Arema Arema (Italian)
　　　Honkan B1 Namba-City 5-1-60 Namba, Minami-ku　　　☎643-6714
Chico's & Charlie's (Mexican)　　　16F Acty-Osaka, 3-1-1 Umeda, Kita-ku　　　☎347-0303
Chinmin (Chinese)　　　1-3-18 Dôjimahama, Kita-ku　　　☎341-7001
Dorian (Indonesian)　　　2 Azuchimachi, Higashi-ku　　　☎261-0629
Joen (Chinese Peking)　　　1-15-30 Edobori, Nishi-ku　　　☎448-5263
Moscow (Russian)　　　Beer Cafe Winds, 2 Shinsaibashisuji, Minami-ku　　　☎211-9042
Rodhos Aege 27 (Greece)　　　27F Acty-Osaka 3-1-1 Umeda, Kita-ku　　　☎347-1527

SHOPPING

Whether you are buying products that reflect centuries of craftsmanship or the latest fruits of high technology, you're sure to find it in Japan.

WHERE TO SHOP

Although not always the cheapest places, department stores offer variety and dependable quality — all in one convenient location. They are also great places just to browse, and most hold regular art and handicraft exhibitions. Souvenir shops can be found in hotel shopping arcades and around tourist attractions and many offer duty-free shopping. Department stores and major shops also offer delivery and shipping services.

HOW TO BUY

● DUTY-FREE SHOPPING

Some items may be purchased duty-free (see the list below) at authorized shops upon presentation of your passport. When you make a duty-free purchase you are given a form called the "Record of Commodities Tax Exempt for Export". This should be kept to show customs officials when leaving the country. If you ship a duty-free item, you must show proof to customs. The exemption rate is 5% to 40%.

1. Precious stones.
2. Pearls, articles decorated with pearls.
3. Articles made or plated with precious metals.
4. Cloisonne and articles made of tortoise shell, coral and amber ivory.
5. Furs and household implements made of fiber.
6. Hunting guns and fishing tackle.
7. TV sets, projectors and screens, video recorders and players.
8. Radios, tape recorders, hi-fi equipment.
9. Cameras, motion picture cameras and projectors, including photometers, lenses, bodies and tripods.
10. Timepieces, including those with cases decorated with gold, platinum and other precious metals.
11. Smoking utensils.
12. Passenger vehicles.
13. Dolls, doll cases and toys.

● CREDIT CARDS

Credit cards are honored at

department stores and major shops. American Express, Visa International and Master Card are the most frequently accepted. Department stores and major souvenir shops are also authorized money changers.

WHAT TO BUY

Whatever you choose to buy, a generally high standard of workmanship and quality is assured. Some suggestions are:

● CHINAWARE

Ranging from purely utilitarian to extravagantly ornamental, Japanese pottery is world renowned. Kiyomizu Pottery (Kyoto), Mashiko Pottery (Tochigi), Kutani Pottery (Ishikawa), and Arita Pottery (Saga) are some of the more famous styles.

● PEARLS

Cultured pearls were developed in Japan by *Kōkichi Mikimoto* and Japanese pearl jewelry is crafted with the utmost care.

● FANS

Decorative folding fans (called *sensu* or *ōgi*) are used in dances, tea ceremonies and other aspects of traditional culture and make attractive souvenirs. The round fans (*uchiwa*) usually cost less and are basically to create a breeze on a hot day.

● PAPER LANTERNS

Once actually used to light rooms, these are now mostly used for decoration.

● DOLLS

There are many kinds including elaborate *kimono* clad dolls, wooden *kokeshi* dolls, clay dolls and paper dolls. Each kind has its own characteristic shape and features reflecting local styles.

● KIMONO

An art form in itself, the traditional *kimono* combines the superb skills of the maker with the finest fabrics. New, silk *kimonos* are very expensive, but reasonably priced *kimono* coats can be found in major tourist stores.

● WOVEN AND DYED FABRIC

The traditional art of fabric making and dyeing still thrives in many places throughout Japan. Silk, cotton and flax are commonly used materials and fabrics are dyed in a variety of patterns by using one of the several traditional processes. Buying a large length of *kimono* material is very expensive, however, smaller articles made from waste pieces are reasonable. Famous fabrics are Yūzen Dyeing and Nishijin Fabric (Kyoto), Edo Komom (Tokyo), Oshima Pongee (Kagoshima)

202

and Ryūkyū Kasuri, cloth with a splashed pattern (Okinawa).

● **CAMERAS AND OPTICAL GOODS**

Japanese cameras are world famous and can be purchased cheaply at discount stores in Shinjuku in Tokyo (Yodobashi Camera and Camera-no-Sakuraya). The best place for audio-visual goods is in duty-free stores such as those in Akihabara.

● **ELECTRICAL APPLIANCES**

Again, the best place is at duty-free stores, particularly in Akihabara. Make sure appliances can be used with the correct voltage.

● **TIMEPIECES**

There are numerous stores selling quality watches and clocks at a range of prices.

● **OTHER SUGGESTIONS**

Bambooware, cloisonne, cherry bark crafts, hand-made paper, folkcrafts, antiques, lacquerware and toys.

Name	address	Tel.

〈TOKYO〉 ☎03

● **Department Store · Tax Free**

International Arcade (Tax-Free)	1-7-23 Uchisaiwaichō, Chiyoda-ku	☎501-5726
Isetan	3-14-1 Shinjuku, Shinjuku-ku	☎352-1111
Japan Tax Free Center	5-8-6 Toranomon, Minato-ku	☎432-4351
Mitsukoshi Honten	1-4-1 Nihombashi-Muromachi, Chūō-ku	☎241-3311
Parco · Shibuya	15-1 Udagawachō, Shibuya-ku	☎464-5111
Printemps Ginza	3-2-1 Ginza, Chūō-ku	☎567-0077
Seibu · Yūrakuchō	2-5-1 Yūrakuchō, Chiyoda-ku	☎286-0111
Takashimaya	2-4-1 Nihombashi, Chūō-ku	☎211-4111

● **Fashion Building · Boutique · Shopping Center**

Hanae Mori Building (Haute Couture)	3-6-1 Kita-Aoyama, Minato-ku	☎400-6987
Issey Miyake Boutique		
	From First Bldg. 1F 5-3-10 Minami-Aoyama, Minato-ku	☎499-6476
Laforet Harajuku (Shopping Centem)	1-11-6 Jingūmae, Shibuya-ku	☎475-0411
Roi Roppongi (Fashion Bldg.)	5-5-1 Roppongi, Minato-ku	☎404-2357
The Ginza (Fashion Bldg.)	7-8-10 Ginza, Chuo-ku	☎572-2121

● **Japanese Goods**

Dōmyō (Cord)	2-11-1 Ueno, Taitō-ku	☎831-3773
Fujiya (Towel)	2-2-15 Asakusa, Taitō-ku	☎841-2283
Hiranoya (Accessories)	8-7-4 Ginza, Chūō-ku	☎571-4410
Jūsan-ya (Comb)	2-12-21 Ueno, Taitō-ku	☎831-3238
Kishiya (Kimono)	5-4-9 Ginza, Chūō-ku	☎572-5291
Matsuzakaya (Hair Ornament)	1-20-1 Asakusa, Taitō-ku	☎841-8520
Momosuke (Make-Up)	2-2-14 Asakusa, Taitō-ku	☎841-7058
Yonoya (Comb)	1-37-10 Asakusa, Taitō-ku	☎844-1755

● **Precious Metals · Cameras · Electrical Appliances**

Ishimaru Denki (Electricity)	1-9-14 Soto-Kanda, Chiyoda-ku	☎255-3111

203

Laox (Audio)	1-2-9 Soto-Kanda, Chiyoda-ku	☎253-7111
Mikimoto (Pearl)	4-5-5 Ginza, Chūō-ku	☎535-4611
Sakuraya (Camera)	3-17-2 Shinjuku, Shinjuku-ku	☎354-3636
Tasaki Shinju Pearl Gallery (Pearl)	1-3-3 Akasaka, Minato-ku	☎584-0904
Wakō (Precious Metals)	4-5-11 Ginza, Chūō-ku	☎562-2111
Wave (Record)	6-2-27 Roppongi, Minato-ku	☎408-0111
Nishi Ginza Electric Center	2-1-1 Yūrakuchō, Chiyoda-ku	☎501-5905
Yamagiwa (Electricity)	3-13-10 Soto-Kanda, Chiyoda-ku	☎253-4311
Yodobashi Camera (Camera)	1-11-1 Nishi-Shinjuku, Shinjuku-ku	☎346-1010

● Books · Records · Stationery

Hagurodō (Ukiyo-e)	Yushima High Town, 4-6-11 Yushima, Bunkyō-ku	☎815-0431
Haibara (Japanese Paper)	2-7-6 Nihombashi, Chūō-ku	☎272-3801
Itōya (Stationery)	2-7-15 Ginza, Chūō-ku	☎561-8311
Kinokuniya Book Store (Book)	Kinokuniya Bldg, 3-17-7 Shinjuku, Shinjuku-ku	☎354-0131
Kyūkyodō (Stationery)	5-7-4 Ginza, Chūō-ku	☎571-4429
Maruzen (Book)	2-3-10 Nihombashi, Chūō-ku	☎272-7211

● Unique Goods · etc.

Arai Bunsendō (Fan)	1-20-2 Asakusa, Taitō-ku	☎841-0088
Axis (Shopping Center)	5-17-1 Roppongi, Minato-ku	☎587-2781
Imaemon (Pottery)	2-6-18 Minami-Aoyama, Minato-ku	☎401-3441
Kanesō (Cutlery)	1-18-12 Asakusa, Taitō-ku	☎844-1379
Kiddy Land (Toy)	6-1-9 Jingūmae, Shibuya-ku	☎409-3431
Kiya (Cutlery)	1-8 Nihombashi-Muromachi, Chūō-ku	☎241-0110
Kyōya (Lacquerware)	2-12-10 Ueno, Taitō-ku	☎831-1905
Oriental Bazaar (Antique)	5-9-13 Jingūmae, Shibuya-ku	☎400-3933
Sony Plaza (General Goods)	B2 Sony Bldg, 5-3-1 Ginza, Chūō-ku	☎575-2525
Sukeroku (Toy)	2-3-1 Asakusa, Taitō-ku	☎844-0577
Tōkyū Hands (Material)	12-18 Udagawachō, Shibuya-ku	☎476-5461

⟨NIKKO · YOKOHAMA · KAMAKURA · HAKONE⟩

N (Nikko) ☎0288, Y (Yokohama) ☎045, K (Kamakura) ☎0467, H (Hakone) ☎0460

Ebiya (Yuba)	948 Shimohatsuishi, Nikko-shi	N.53-1177
Hatajuku Yosegi Kaikan (Parquetry Work)	103 Hatajuku, Hakone-machi	H.5-8170
Iinuma Chōchinten (Japanese lantern)	2-9 Sakaechō, Odawara-shi	☎0465-23-2625
Inoue Kamabokoten (Fish Cake)	1-4-4 Komachi, Kamakura-shi	K.23-3111
Kiyōken (Chinese Dumpling)	2-13-12 Takashima, Nishi-ku, Yokohama-shi	Y.441-8851
Mukai (Sculpture)	8-9 Yasukawachō, Nikko-shi	N.54-1540
Satō (Paper)	2-7-27 Komachi, Kamakura-shi	K.22-2601
Shinobu (Batik)	2-12-33 Komachi Kamakura-shi	K.22-4889
Tazawa Shōten (Iron ware)	5-183 Motomachi, Naka-ku, Yokohama-shi	Y.641-0556
Watanabe's (Souvenir)	1042 Kamihatsuishimachi, Nikko-shi	N.54-3038

⟨KYOTO⟩ ☎075

Ashidaya Nakayama Ningyo (Doll)		
	Dotemachidōri-shōmensagaru-nishigawa, Shimogyō-ku	☎361-6246
BAL Building (Fashion complex)		
	258 Yamazaki-chō Kawaramachi-sanjōsagaru-Higashi, Nakagyō-ku	☎223-0501
Erizen (Kimono)	Shijō-otabichō, Shimogyō-ku	☎221-1618
Fūgado (Antique)	Sannenzaka-shita, Kiyomizu, Higashiyama-ku	☎551-0713
Honda Miso Honten (Miso)	558 Ichijō, Muromachi-dōri, Kamigyō-ku	☎441-1121

SHOPPING

Ichihara Heibei Shōten (Chop Stick)
Shijōsagaru, Sakaimachi-dōri, Shimogyō-ku ☎341-3831
Ippōdō Chaho (Green tea) Nijōagaru-Higashigawa, Teramachi, Nakagyō-ku ☎211-3421
Itō Kumihimo-ten (Braid) Rokkaku-Hokuseikado, Teramachi, Nakagyō-ku ☎221-1320
Itotsune Shōten (Kyo-Fan) 6 Kiyomizu-Shinmichi, Higashiyama-ku ☎561-0141
Jūsanya (Tsuge-Comb) Teramachi-iru-Kitagawa, Shijō-dōri, Shimogyō-ku ☎211-0498
Kasagen (Paper umbrella) Gionmachi-Kitagawa, Shijō-dōri, Higashiyama-ku ☎561-2832
Kazurasei Shinise (Hair ornament)
285 Gionmachi-Kitagawa, Shijō-dōri, Higashiyama-ku ☎561-0672
Kyoto Craft Center (Craft) Shijō-Hanamikoji-iru, Gion, Higashiyama-ku ☎561-9660
Kyoto Handi Craft Center (Craft) Kumanojinja-Higashi, Sakyō-ku ☎761-5080
Kyoto Tōjiki Kaikan (Pottery) Higashiōji-Higashi-iru, Gojō-dōri, Higashiyama-ku ☎541-1102
Kyoto Yūzen Bunka Kaikan (Yūzen fabrics)
6 Mametachō, Nishi-Kyōgoku, Ukyō-ku ☎311-0025
Kyūkyodo (Stationery) Anekōji-kado, Teramachi, Nakagyō-ku ☎231-0509
Nishijin-ori Kaikan (Nishijin fabrics) Imadegawa-Horikawasagaru, Kamigyō-ku ☎451-9231
Semmaruya (Yuba) Sakaimachi-Shijōagaru Nakagyō-ku ☎221-0555
Shibakyu (Pickles) Shōrinmachi, Ohara, Sakyō-ku ☎744-2226
Shichimiya (Red pepper) Sannenzaka-kado, Kiyomizu Higashiyama-ku ☎541-0738
Shoeido (Incense) Karasuma-Nijōagaru-Higashigawa Nakagyō-ku ☎231-2307
Sugukiya Rokurōbē (Pickles) Kamigamojinja-toriimae, Kita-ku ☎791-7374
Vivre 21 (Fasion building) Takoyakushi-Nishi-iru, Kawaramachi, Nakagyō-ku ☎223-1331
Zouhiko (Lacquerware) 10 Okazaki-saishōjimachi, Sakyō-ku ☎761-0212

〈OSAKA〉 ☎06

Acty Osaka(Shopping complex) 3-2-18 Umeda, Kita-ku ☎346-1631
Daimaru Department Store 1-118 Shinsaibashi-suji, Minami-ku ☎271-1231
Fujii (Kimono) 1-23 Shinsaibashi-suji, Minami-ku ☎251-0025
Hankyu Department Store 8-7 Kakutacho, Kita-ku ☎361-1381
Hannari (Craft) B2 Hankyū Sambangai, 1-1-3 Shibata, Kika-ku ☎372-8702
Hanshin Department Store 1-13-13 Umeda, Kita-ku ☎345-1201
Japan Life Building (Interior) 2-20 Shinsaibashi-suji, Minami-ku ☎213-3473
Kintetsu Department Store 1-1-43 Abeno-suji, Abeno-ku ☎624-1111
Namba City (Shopping complex) 1-3-1 Namba, Minami-ku ☎644-2960
Nihon Tabacco Service Center B2 Minami-OS Bldg., Minami-ku ☎213-5555
Osama-no-Idea (Toy) 31F Hankyū Grand Bldg., Kakutachō, Kita-ku ☎315-7751
Shinsaibashi Parco (Fashion building) 1-45 Shinsaibashi-suji, Minami-ku ☎245-0101
Sogō Department Store 1-38 Shinsaibashi-suji, Minami-ku ☎281-3111
Sony Tower (Electrical Appliances) 1-47 Shinsaibashi-suji, Minami-ku ☎251-2391
Takashimaya Department Store 5-1-5 Namba, Minami-ku ☎631-1101
Wakō (Jewelry) 1-27 Shinsaibashi-suji, Minami-ku ☎245-0666

ENTERTAINMENT

Everyone has a favorite way of spending their free time and Japan offers entertainment to suit all tastes. Tickets to theater and other events can be obtained at "Playguides" in department stores, or at the venue itself.

CLASSICAL DRAMA

● KABUKI

A melodramatic form of drama enlivened by songs and dances, *Kabuki* employs bold, exaggerated make-up and costumes with brilliant colors. Although all the actors are now male, *Kabuki* was actually created in the 17th century by a woman named *Okuni* who was attached to Izumo Taisha Shrine. Women were banned from performing by the Shogunate, forcing the adoption of all-male casts and the infamous *onnagata* or *oyama* (the men playing women's roles). Throughout the Edo Period, *Kabuki* was entertainment for the common man. These days, though no longer very poular with young people, it still thrives as drama which displays the vitality of the Japanese spirit.

Kabuki plays are often up to 5 hours long, however, no one is obliged to watch the entire play. The "Earphone Guide" provides comments and explanations about the story and other features of *Kabuki* at Kabukiza Theater.

● NOH

A narrative in dance, *Noh* relies heavily on the abstract. The stage is almost bare of props and the main characters are masked. The word *Noh* simply means performance and *Noh* developed from an older dramatic form called *sarugaku.* It has kept its present form since the 15th century. In contrast to *Kabuki, Noh* was the entertainment of the aristocracy, so the dances are often stately and elegant. Like *Kabuki* (which was greatly influenced by *Noh*), performances are long but the serious dramas are interspersed with comical plays called *kyōgen.* Verging on slapstick, they are designed as relief from the serious themes dealt with in *Noh.*

● BUNRAKU

Bunraku is a unique style of puppet theater, employing elaborate and exquisitely dressed dolls. The dolls are about 50 cm tall and have built-in mechanisms to aid movement. They are skillfully manipulated to act out an entertaining narrative to the accompaniment of *shamisen* music. Usually, three puppeteers operate one puppet and the master puppeteer is often dressed in a brilliant *kimono* while the assistants wear black in order to act as a foil to their leader and the colorful puppets.

● *YOSE (VARIETY THEATER)*

Yose is Japan's traditional variety theater. A variety of popular entertainments are presented, the main one being *Rakugo* (comic storytelling), in addition to *Kōdan* (dramatic narration), *Kijutsu* (conjuling), and *Rōkyoku* (recital of ancient ballads).

MOVIES

Movie theaters abound in entertainment districts of the large cities, and include large, first-run theaters showing both domestic and foreign films. Admission fees range from ¥1,500 up to ¥2,500 for a reserved seat.

STAGE SHOWS

The most famous stage shows in Japan are performed by the Takarazuka troupe, which is headquartered in Takarazuka city near Osaka and performances are also held in Tokyo. Over 400 female dancers perform to large crowds on colorfully decorated stages.

THEATER

Japan has a range of both amateur and professional theater companies which offer everything from traditional entertainment to avant-garde drama.

CONCERTS

There is always a wide variety of concert performances to choose from in Japan with everything from symphony orchestras to rock groups, both domestic and foreign. The Japanese are a nation of music lovers and every kind of music has a following here. There is also a wide variety of venues, from large halls like Tokyo's *Budōkan* to live jazz and rock houses.

SPORTS

● *BASEBALL*

Baseball has a tremendous following in Japan. Like the U.S.A., Japan has 2 major leagues: the Central League and the Pacific League. There are 12 professional teams in Tokyo, Nagoya, Osaka, Hiro-

207

shima and the playing season is from April to October. Baseball is also a popular high school sport and the national high school tournament held every August is one of the sporting highlights of the year.

● SUMO

Ranking in popularity with baseball, *Sumō* is Japan's national sport and is always an exciting spectacle. The professional wrestlers are powerfully built, usually weighing between 130 and 150 kg. The sport is clothed in ancient ceremony but has reasonably basic rules. Two wrestlers wearing only heavy silk loincloths enter a sanded ring 4.55 m. in diameter.

After a series of false proceeds — the wrestlers squat and glare at each other — designed to intimidate the opponent, they grapple, and the first to touch the ground with any part of his body, or step out of the ring, is the loser. *Sumō* tournaments are held in Tokyo in January, May, and September at the Ryōgoku New Kokugikan Hall.

● AIKIDO

This martial art is strictly for self defense and uses no weapons. It was originated by *Morihei Ueshiba* around 1925 and the spiritual aspect of the sport is stressed, the central aim being self-realization through discipline as well as physical fitness. It employs the idea of using your adversary's strength against him.

● JUDO

Developed from *Jujutsu* during the Edo period, *Jūdō* is Japan's best-known sport and another system of fighting without weapons. Dr. *Jigorō Kanō* (1860-1938) introduced scientific training systems based on modern athletic principles and *Jūdō* has since developed into an Olympic sport.

The school organized by *Kanō* is called *Kōdōkan Jūdō*, displays of which can be seen at the Kōdōkan Hall.

● KARATE

This martial art was introduced from China and was further modified by the influence of indigenous martial arts. There are now many schools, each supporting a different theory on the art.

● KENDO

The oldest of the martial sports, *Kendō* is a style of fencing developed during the feudal era and is still a popular sport today. Two masked and padded opponents assail each other with bamboo swords with the aim of training mind and body.

Name	address	Tel.

⟨TOKYO⟩ ☎03

●Kabuki · Noh · Yose

Name	address	Tel.
Asakusa Engei Hall (Yose)	1-43-12 Asakusa, Taitō-ku	☎841-8126
Asakusa Mokubatei (Yose)	2-7-5 Asakusa, Taitō-ku	☎844-6293
Hōshō Nohgakudō (Noh)	1-5-9 Hongō, Bunkyō-ku	☎811-4843
Kabukiza Theater (Kabuki)	4-12-15 Ginza, Chūō-ku	☎541-3131
Meijiza (Kabuki)	2-31-1 Nihombashi-Hamachō, Chūō-ku	☎660-3939
Shimbashi Embujō (Kabuki)	6-18-2 Ginza, Chūō-ku	☎541-2211
Suehirotei (Yose)	3-6-12 Shinjuku, Shinjuku-ku	☎351-2974

●Modern Play · Concert · Movie

Name	address	Tel.
Ikebukuro Engeijō	Umeda Bldg. Nishi-Ikebukuro, Toshima-ku	☎988-8759
Kinokuniya Hall (Play)	4F Kinokuniya Bldg., 3-17-7 Shinjuku, Shinjuku-ku	☎354-0131
Kokuritsu Gekijō (National Theater)	4-1 Hayabusachō, Chiyoda-ku	☎265-7411
Shinjuku Koma Theater (Play)	1-19-1 Kabukichō, Shinjuku-ku	☎202 8111
Suntry Concert Hall (Concert)	1-13-1 Akasaka, Minato-ku	☎505-1001
Tokyo Takarazuka Gekijō (Play)	1-1-3 Yūrakuchō, Chiyoda-ku	☎591-1711

●Sports Facilities

Name	address	Tel.
Aiki Kai (Aikidō)	17-18 Wakamatsuchō, Shinjuku-ku	☎203-9236
Nippon Budōkan (Kendō)	2-3 Kitanomarukōen, Chiyoda-ku	☎216-0781
Japan Karate Association (Karate)	1-6-1 Ebisu-Nishi, Shibuya-ku	☎462-1415
Kōdōkan (Jūdō)	1-16-30 Kasuga, Bunkyō-ku	☎811-7152
New Kokugikan (Sumō)	1-3-28 Yokoami, Sumida-ku	☎623-5111

●Things Japanese

Name	address	Tel.
Daiichi Engei (Bonsai)	1-1-4 Shibuya, Shibuya-ku	☎409-6671
Omote Senke (Tea Celemony)	6 Nibanchō, Chioyda-ku	☎261-1352
Sōgetsu School (Flower Arrangement)	7-2-21 Akasaka, Minato-ku	☎408-1126
Ura Senke (Tea Celemony)	7 Nibanchō, Chiyoda-ku	☎264-7801

⟨KYOTO⟩ ☎075

Name	address	Tel.
Gion Corner (Japanese Show)	570-2 Gionmachi-Minamigawa, Higashiyama-ku	☎561-1115
Gion (Kōbu) Kaburenjō (Japanese Show)	570-2 Gionmachi-Minamigawa, Higashiyama-ku	☎561-1115
Kanze Kaikan (Noh)	44 Enshōjichō, Okazaki, Sakyō-ku	☎771-6114
Kyoto Municipal Museum of Traditional Industry	Seishōjichō Okazaki, Sakyō-ku	☎761-3421
Minamiza Theater (Kabuki)	Higashizume Shijō-ohashi, Higashiyama-ku	☎561-1155
Miyagawachō Kaburenjō Theater (Japanese Show)	4 Miyagawa-suji, Higashiyama-ku	☎561-1151
Nishijin Textile Center (Textile Exhibition)	Imadegawa-Minami, Horikawa-dori, Kamigyo-ku	☎451-9231
Yūzen Cultural Hall (Textile Exhibition)	6 Mametachō, Nishi-Kyōgoku, Ukyō-ku	☎311-0025
Pontochō Kaburenjō Theater (Kamogawa-odori Dance)	Sanjō-sagaru Pontochō, Nakagyō-ku	☎221-2025

⟨OSAKA⟩ ☎06

Name	address	Tel.
Umeda Koma Stadium (Play)	5-14 Kakutachō, Kita-ku	☎313-3251
National Bunraku Theater (Bunraku)	1-12-10 Nihombashi, Minami-ku	☎212-2531
Otsuki Seiinkai Nohgakudō (Noh)	2 Uemachi, Higashi-ku	☎761-8055
Shin-Kabukiza Theater (Kabuki)	4-3-25 Namba, Minami-ku	☎631-2121

NIGHTLIFE

Japan's large cities probably have more cabarets, nightclubs and bars than any other cities in the world and consequently there is also an enormous variety in quality and price.

CLUBS AND CABARETS

Clubs are usually the more expensive and have hostesses serving drinks and providing entertaining conversation. Cabarets are about ¥10,000 to ¥20,000 per person and feature live floor shows. More risque cabarets often employ energetic touts to lure you in. If you intend to be adventurous, be sure to check prices beforehand.

BARS

Inexpensive bars can be found in almost any section of the city. Traditional bars are usually small, friendly and lively and are good places to soak up the local atmosphere along with some *sake* or *shō-*

chū.

PUBS

Generally low-priced, pubs differ from bars only in the type of patron they attract and seem to be favored by the younger generation.

DISCOS

Discos flourish in entertainment areas. The cover charge averages between ¥3,000 and ¥5,000 per person.

CAFE-BARS

Cafe-Bars have become increasingly popular and a great variety of interesting places now exist. They serve cocktails, coffee and light meals.

Name	address	Tel.
〈TOKYO〉 ☎03		
Chakras Mandala (Disco)	Square Bldg., 3-10-3 Roppongi, Minato-ku	☎479-5600
Cleo Palazzi (Cafe-bar)	Shada Bldg., 3-18-2 Roppongi, Minato-ku	☎586-8494
Cordon Bleu (Supper Club)	6-6-4 Akasaka, Minato-ku	☎582-7800
Kuremutsu (Sake)	2-2-13 Asakusa, Taitō-ku	☎842-0906
Lexington Queen (Disco)	Daisan Gotō Bldg., 3-13-14 Roppongi, Minato-ku	☎401-1661
Lion (Beer Hall)	7-9-20 Ginza, Chūō-ku	☎571-2590
New Latin Quarter (Club)	2-13-8 Nagatachō, Chiyoda-ku	☎581-1326

Pit inn (Jazz)	YK Bldg., 3-16-4 Shinjuku, Shinjuku-ku	☎354-2024
Bagpipe (Pub)	3-16-5 Akasaka, Minato-ku	☎582-0048
Tsubaki House (Disco) Shinjuku Theater Bldg., 3-14-20 Shinjuku, Shinjuku-ku		☎354-3236
Véglia (Disco)	4-7-16 Akasaka, Minato-ku	☎583-3430
Wan-ya (Sake & Rakugo)	Kyōdō Bldg., 2-8-15 Ginza, Chūō-ku	☎564-3966
Yorozuya Matsukaze (Sake)	1-24-5 Nishi-Ikebukuro, Toshima-ku	☎986-1047
Yoshiwara Matsubaya (Geisha Show)	4-33-1 Senzoku, Taitō-ku	☎874-9401

〈KYOTO〉 ☎075

CBGB (Live House)

	Kyōya Bldg. Ginkakuji-kōsaten-agaru, Shirakawa-dōri, Sakyō-ku	☎721-2428
Club Hong Kong (Night Club)	Takoyakushi-agaru Kawaramachi, Nakagyō-ku	☎211-0710
Glass Moon (Café Bar)	Shokubutsuen-Kitamon-mae Kitayama-dōri, Kita-ku	☎791-0110
Maharaja (Disco)	Fujikankō Bldg. 574 Gionmachi-Minami, Higashiyama-ku	☎541-5421

〈OSAKA〉 ☎06

Cabaret Universe (Cabaret)	2-3-9 Sennichi-mae, Minami-ku	☎641-8731
Club Arrow (Night Club)	Dōyamachō, Kita-ku	☎361-0636
Hiiki-ya (Izaka-ya)	2 Sonezaki, Kita-ku	☎315-8558
Jōdan Sakaba (Theater Pub)	2 Sonezaki, Kita-ku	☎361-4540
Metropolitan (Cabaret)	6 Soemonchō, Minami-ku	☎211-9131
Samba Club (Disco)		
	B2 Hotel Nikkō Osaka, 7 Daihōjimachi-Nishichō, Minami-ku	☎244-1433
Tom Tom Club (Pub Restaurant)		
	Shinsaibashi Bldg. Shinsaibashi-suji, Minami-ku	☎244-9515
Water Stage 0180 (Bar)	2F Benten-Bldg. 4-15 Dōyamachō, Kita-ku	☎314-0180
Yoshida Bar (Bar)	2-4-6 Namba, Minami-ku	☎213-1385

SIGHTSEEING

211

213

N

O

P

R

S

215

TRAVEL GUIDE JAPAN
〈英文日本案内〉

1971年8月20日 初版発行
1988年10月1日 改訂13版
(Oct. 1, 1988 13th edition)
編集人 斉藤晃雄
発行人 木下幸雄
発行所 日本交通公社出版事業局
〒101 東京都千代田区神田鍛冶町3—3
大木ビル8階（Tel. 03-257-8391）

編集制作 ㈱アーバン・トランスレーション
地図制作 ㈱千秋社
写真協力 石井裕之
交通公社フォトライブラリー
表紙カバー・イラスト 東芳純
翻訳 LINC Japan Ltd.
Brian O'Flaherty

交通公社発行の図書のご注文は
JTB出版販売センター
〒101 東京都千代田区神田須田町1-28
タイムビル3階Tel. 03-257-8337
振替 東京7-99201 送料(実費共)275円
写真植字 株式会社電算プロセス
印刷所 凸版印刷株式会社

定価 1,800円

883216 711012
ISBN4-533-00303-6 C2026 ¥1800E

Meet Japan Through
Sunrise Tours!

The Japan Travel Bureau operates its famed Sunrise Tours to a wide variety of destinations, including Tokyo, Nikko, Hakone, Mt. Fuji, Kyoto, the Inland Sea, Kyushu, etc. Let JTB host you to the best of Japan. Pick-up service from major hotels.

Sights in Tokyo

- Tokyo Morning ¥3,000
- Tokyo Afternoon ¥3,000
- Dynamic Tokyo Full Day ¥11,000

Special interest tours

Adventures into Japanese arts and crafts, industrial technology, and rural life. ¥10,000

Night tours

- Tokyo Kabuki Night ¥13,000
- Tokyo Night Club ¥11,000
- Tokyo Bright Night ¥9,000

Short excursions from Tokyo

- Nikko ¥17,500
- Kamakura·Hakone ¥14,000 & ¥17,500
- Mt. Fuji·Hakone ¥14,000 & ¥17,500
- Kyoto trips From ¥45,000

The above are only part of JTB's huge assortment of Sunrise Tours.

Fares are effective as of September 1, 1988.

For information and reservations,
call *any day* Tokyo 276-7777 (*at night* till 11:00 p.m. 432-1111 ext. 483)

jtb Japan Travel Bureau, Inc.
LICENSED TRAVEL AGENT No. 64
Foreign Tourist Div., 1-13-1 Nihombashi, Tokyo 103, Japan